ISBN 0-8373-1082-2

C-1082 CAREER EXAMINATION SERIES

*This is your
PASSBOOK® for...*

Administrative Trainee

Test Preparation Study Guide

Questions & Answers

NLC

NATIONAL LEARNING CORPORATION

Copyright © 2015 by

National Learning Corporation

212 Michael Drive, Syosset, New York 11791

All rights reserved, including the right of reproduction in whole or in part, in any form or by any means, electronic or mechanical, including photocopying, recording, or by any information storage and retrieval system, without permission in writing from the Publisher.

(516) 921-8888
(800) 645-6337
FAX: (516) 921-8743
www.passbooks.com
sales @ passbooks.com
info @ passbooks.com

PRINTED IN THE UNITED STATES OF AMERICA

PASSBOOK®
NOTICE

This book is SOLELY intended for, is sold ONLY to, and its use is RESTRICTED to *individual*, bona fide applicants or candidates who qualify by virtue of having seriously filed applications for appropriate license, certificate, professional and/or promotional advancement, higher school matriculation, scholarship, or other legitimate requirements of educational and/or governmental authorities.

This book is NOT intended for use, class instruction, tutoring, training, duplication, copying, reprinting, excerption, or adaptation, etc., by:

(1) Other publishers

(2) Proprietors and/or Instructors of "Coaching" and/or Preparatory Courses

(3) Personnel and/or Training Divisions of commercial, industrial, and governmental organizations

(4) Schools, colleges, or universities and/or their departments and staffs, including teachers and other personnel

(5) Testing Agencies or Bureaus

(6) Study groups which seek by the purchase of a single volume to copy and/or duplicate and/or adapt this material for use by the group as a whole without having purchased individual volumes for each of the members of the group

(7) Et al.

Such persons would be in violation of appropriate Federal and State statutes.

PROVISION OF LICENSING AGREEMENTS. — Recognized educational commercial, industrial, and governmental institutions and organizations, and others legitimately engaged in educational pursuits, including training, testing, and measurement activities, may address a request for a licensing agreement to the copyright owners, who will determine whether, and under what conditions, including fees and charges, the materials in this book may be used by them. In other words, a licensing facility exists for the legitimate use of the material in this book on other than an individual basis. However, it is asseverated and affirmed here that the material in this book *CANNOT* be used without the receipt of the express permission of such a licensing agreement from the Publishers.

NATIONAL LEARNING CORPORATION
212 Michael Drive
Syosset, New York 11791

Inquiries re licensing agreements should be addressed to:
  The President
  National Learning Corporation
  212 Michael Drive
  Syosset, New York 11791

PASSBOOK® SERIES

THE *PASSBOOK® SERIES* has been created to prepare applicants and candidates for the ultimate academic battlefield – the examination room.

At some time in our lives, each and every one of us may be required to take an examination – for validation, matriculation, admission, qualification, registration, certification, or licensure.

Based on the assumption that every applicant or candidate has met the basic formal educational standards, has taken the required number of courses, and read the necessary texts, the *PASSBOOK® SERIES* furnishes the one special preparation which may assure passing with confidence, instead of failing with insecurity. Examination questions – together with answers – are furnished as the basic vehicle for study so that the mysteries of the examination and its compounding difficulties may be eliminated or diminished by a sure method.

This book is meant to help you pass your examination provided that you qualify and are serious in your objective.

The entire field is reviewed through the huge store of content information which is succinctly presented through a provocative and challenging approach – the question-and-answer method.

A climate of success is established by furnishing the correct answers at the end of each test.

You soon learn to recognize types of questions, forms of questions, and patterns of questioning. You may even begin to anticipate expected outcomes.

You perceive that many questions are repeated or adapted so that you can gain acute insights, which may enable you to score many sure points.

You learn how to confront new questions, or types of questions, and to attack them confidently and work out the correct answers.

You note objectives and emphases, and recognize pitfalls and dangers, so that you may make positive educational adjustments.

Moreover, you are kept fully informed in relation to new concepts, methods, practices, and directions in the field.

You discover that you are actually taking the examination all the time: you are preparing for the examination by "taking" an examination, not by reading extraneous and/or supererogatory textbooks.

In short, this PASSBOOK®, used directedly, should be an important factor in helping you to pass your test.

ADMINISTRATIVE TRAINEE

DUTIES
Performs beginning level staff work in the process of learning varied and special administrative assignments. Performs related duties as required.

SCOPE OF THE EXAMINATION
The written test will cover knowledge, skills and/or abilities in such areas as:

1. Arithmetic reasoning;
2. Evaluating conclusions in light of known facts;
3. Preparing written material;
4. Understanding and interpreting tabular material; and
5. Understanding and interpreting written material.

HOW TO TAKE A TEST

I. YOU MUST PASS AN EXAMINATION

A. *WHAT EVERY CANDIDATE SHOULD KNOW*

Examination applicants often ask us for help in preparing for the written test. What can I study in advance? What kinds of questions will be asked? How will the test be given? How will the papers be graded?

As an applicant for a civil service examination, you may be wondering about some of these things. Our purpose here is to suggest effective methods of advance study and to describe civil service examinations.

Your chances for success on this examination can be increased if you know how to prepare. Those "pre-examination jitters" can be reduced if you know what to expect. You can even experience an adventure in good citizenship if you know why civil service exams are given.

B. *WHY ARE CIVIL SERVICE EXAMINATIONS GIVEN?*

Civil service examinations are important to you in two ways. As a citizen, you want public jobs filled by employees who know how to do their work. As a job seeker, you want a fair chance to compete for that job on an equal footing with other candidates. The best-known means of accomplishing this two-fold goal is the competitive examination.

Exams are widely publicized throughout the nation. They may be administered for jobs in federal, state, city, municipal, town or village governments or agencies.

Any citizen may apply, with some limitations, such as the age or residence of applicants. Your experience and education may be reviewed to see whether you meet the requirements for the particular examination. When these requirements exist, they are reasonable and applied consistently to all applicants. Thus, a competitive examination may cause you some uneasiness now, but it is your privilege and safeguard.

C. *HOW ARE CIVIL SERVICE EXAMS DEVELOPED?*

Examinations are carefully written by trained technicians who are specialists in the field known as "psychological measurement," in consultation with recognized authorities in the field of work that the test will cover. These experts recommend the subject matter areas or skills to be tested; only those knowledges or skills important to your success on the job are included. The most reliable books and source materials available are used as references. Together, the experts and technicians judge the difficulty level of the questions.

Test technicians know how to phrase questions so that the problem is clearly stated. Their ethics do not permit "trick" or "catch" questions. Questions may have been tried out on sample groups, or subjected to statistical analysis, to determine their usefulness.

Written tests are often used in combination with performance tests, ratings of training and experience, and oral interviews. All of these measures combine to form the best-known means of finding the right person for the right job.

II. HOW TO PASS THE WRITTEN TEST

A. NATURE OF THE EXAMINATION

To prepare intelligently for civil service examinations, you should know how they differ from school examinations you have taken. In school you were assigned certain definite pages to read or subjects to cover. The examination questions were quite detailed and usually emphasized memory. Civil service exams, on the other hand, try to discover your present ability to perform the duties of a position, plus your potentiality to learn these duties. In other words, a civil service exam attempts to predict how successful you will be. Questions cover such a broad area that they cannot be as minute and detailed as school exam questions.

In the public service similar kinds of work, or positions, are grouped together in one "class." This process is known as *position-classification*. All the positions in a class are paid according to the salary range for that class. One class title covers all of these positions, and they are all tested by the same examination.

B. FOUR BASIC STEPS

1) Study the announcement

How, then, can you know what subjects to study? Our best answer is: "Learn as much as possible about the class of positions for which you've applied." The exam will test the knowledge, skills and abilities needed to do the work.

Your most valuable source of information about the position you want is the official exam announcement. This announcement lists the training and experience qualifications. Check these standards and apply only if you come reasonably close to meeting them.

The brief description of the position in the examination announcement offers some clues to the subjects which will be tested. Think about the job itself. Review the duties in your mind. Can you perform them, or are there some in which you are rusty? Fill in the blank spots in your preparation.

Many jurisdictions preview the written test in the exam announcement by including a section called "Knowledge and Abilities Required," "Scope of the Examination," or some similar heading. Here you will find out specifically what fields will be tested.

2) Review your own background

Once you learn in general what the position is all about, and what you need to know to do the work, ask yourself which subjects you already know fairly well and which need improvement. You may wonder whether to concentrate on improving your strong areas or on building some background in your fields of weakness. When the announcement has specified "some knowledge" or "considerable knowledge," or has used adjectives like "beginning principles of..." or "advanced ... methods," you can get a clue as to the number and difficulty of questions to be asked in any given field. More questions, and hence broader coverage, would be included for those subjects which are more important in the work. Now weigh your strengths and weaknesses against the job requirements and prepare accordingly.

3) Determine the level of the position

Another way to tell how intensively you should prepare is to understand the level of the job for which you are applying. Is it the entering level? In other words, is this the position in which beginners in a field of work are hired? Or is it an intermediate or advanced level? Sometimes this is indicated by such words as "Junior" or "Senior" in the class title. Other jurisdictions use Roman numerals to designate the level – Clerk I, Clerk II, for example. The word "Supervisor" sometimes appears in the title. If the level is not indicated by the title, check the description of duties. Will you be working under very close supervision, or will you have responsibility for independent decisions in this work?

4) Choose appropriate study materials

Now that you know the subjects to be examined and the relative amount of each subject to be covered, you can choose suitable study materials. For beginning level jobs, or even advanced ones, if you have a pronounced weakness in some aspect of your training, read a modern, standard textbook in that field. Be sure it is up to date and has general coverage. Such books are normally available at your library, and the librarian will be glad to help you locate one. For entry-level positions, questions of appropriate difficulty are chosen – neither highly advanced questions, nor those too simple. Such questions require careful thought but not advanced training.

If the position for which you are applying is technical or advanced, you will read more advanced, specialized material. If you are already familiar with the basic principles of your field, elementary textbooks would waste your time. Concentrate on advanced textbooks and technical periodicals. Think through the concepts and review difficult problems in your field.

These are all general sources. You can get more ideas on your own initiative, following these leads. For example, training manuals and publications of the government agency which employs workers in your field can be useful, particularly for technical and professional positions. A letter or visit to the government department involved may result in more specific study suggestions, and certainly will provide you with a more definite idea of the exact nature of the position you are seeking.

III. KINDS OF TESTS

Tests are used for purposes other than measuring knowledge and ability to perform specified duties. For some positions, it is equally important to test ability to make adjustments to new situations or to profit from training. In others, basic mental abilities not dependent on information are essential. Questions which test these things may not appear as pertinent to the duties of the position as those which test for knowledge and information. Yet they are often highly important parts of a fair examination. For very general questions, it is almost impossible to help you direct your study efforts. What we can do is to point out some of the more common of these general abilities needed in public service positions and describe some typical questions.

1) General information

Broad, general information has been found useful for predicting job success in some kinds of work. This is tested in a variety of ways, from vocabulary lists to questions about current events. Basic background in some field of work, such as sociology or economics, may be sampled in a group of questions. Often these are principles which have become familiar to most persons through exposure rather than through formal training. It is difficult to advise you how to study for these questions; being alert to the world around you is our best suggestion.

2) Verbal ability

An example of an ability needed in many positions is verbal or language ability. Verbal ability is, in brief, the ability to use and understand words. Vocabulary and grammar tests are typical measures of this ability. Reading comprehension or paragraph interpretation questions are common in many kinds of civil service tests. You are given a paragraph of written material and asked to find its central meaning.

3) Numerical ability

Number skills can be tested by the familiar arithmetic problem, by checking paired lists of numbers to see which are alike and which are different, or by interpreting charts and graphs. In the latter test, a graph may be printed in the test booklet which you are asked to use as the basis for answering questions.

4) Observation

A popular test for law-enforcement positions is the observation test. A picture is shown to you for several minutes, then taken away. Questions about the picture test your ability to observe both details and larger elements.

5) Following directions

In many positions in the public service, the employee must be able to carry out written instructions dependably and accurately. You may be given a chart with several columns, each column listing a variety of information. The questions require you to carry out directions involving the information given in the chart.

6) Skills and aptitudes

Performance tests effectively measure some manual skills and aptitudes. When the skill is one in which you are trained, such as typing or shorthand, you can practice. These tests are often very much like those given in business school or high school courses. For many of the other skills and aptitudes, however, no short-time preparation can be made. Skills and abilities natural to you or that you have developed throughout your lifetime are being tested.

Many of the general questions just described provide all the data needed to answer the questions and ask you to use your reasoning ability to find the answers. Your best preparation for these tests, as well as for tests of facts and ideas, is to be at your physical and mental best. You, no doubt, have your own methods of getting into an exam-taking mood and keeping "in shape." The next section lists some ideas on this subject.

IV. KINDS OF QUESTIONS

Only rarely is the "essay" question, which you answer in narrative form, used in civil service tests. Civil service tests are usually of the short-answer type. Full instructions for answering these questions will be given to you at the examination. But in case this is your first experience with short-answer questions and separate answer sheets, here is what you need to know:

1) Multiple-choice Questions

Most popular of the short-answer questions is the "multiple choice" or "best answer" question. It can be used, for example, to test for factual knowledge, ability to solve problems or judgment in meeting situations found at work.

A multiple-choice question is normally one of three types—
- It can begin with an incomplete statement followed by several possible endings. You are to find the one ending which *best* completes the statement, although some of the others may not be entirely wrong.
- It can also be a complete statement in the form of a question which is answered by choosing one of the statements listed.

- It can be in the form of a problem – again you select the best answer.

Here is an example of a multiple-choice question with a discussion which should give you some clues as to the method for choosing the right answer:

When an employee has a complaint about his assignment, the action which will *best* help him overcome his difficulty is to
  A. discuss his difficulty with his coworkers
  B. take the problem to the head of the organization
  C. take the problem to the person who gave him the assignment
  D. say nothing to anyone about his complaint

In answering this question, you should study each of the choices to find which is best. Consider choice "A" – Certainly an employee may discuss his complaint with fellow employees, but no change or improvement can result, and the complaint remains unresolved. Choice "B" is a poor choice since the head of the organization probably does not know what assignment you have been given, and taking your problem to him is known as "going over the head" of the supervisor. The supervisor, or person who made the assignment, is the person who can clarify it or correct any injustice. Choice "C" is, therefore, correct. To say nothing, as in choice "D," is unwise. Supervisors have and interest in knowing the problems employees are facing, and the employee is seeking a solution to his problem.

2) True/False Questions

The "true/false" or "right/wrong" form of question is sometimes used. Here a complete statement is given. Your job is to decide whether the statement is right or wrong.

SAMPLE: A roaming cell-phone call to a nearby city costs less than a non-roaming call to a distant city.

This statement is wrong, or false, since roaming calls are more expensive.

This is not a complete list of all possible question forms, although most of the others are variations of these common types. You will always get complete directions for answering questions. Be sure you understand *how* to mark your answers – ask questions until you do.

V. RECORDING YOUR ANSWERS

Computer terminals are used more and more today for many different kinds of exams.

For an examination with very few applicants, you may be told to record your answers in the test booklet itself. Separate answer sheets are much more common. If this separate answer sheet is to be scored by machine – and this is often the case – it is highly important that you mark your answers correctly in order to get credit.

An electronic scoring machine is often used in civil service offices because of the speed with which papers can be scored. Machine-scored answer sheets must be marked with a pencil, which will be given to you. This pencil has a high graphite content which responds to the electronic scoring machine. As a matter of fact, stray dots may register as answers, so do not let your pencil rest on the answer sheet while you are pondering the correct answer. Also, if your pencil lead breaks or is otherwise defective, ask for another.

Since the answer sheet will be dropped in a slot in the scoring machine, be careful not to bend the corners or get the paper crumpled.

The answer sheet normally has five vertical columns of numbers, with 30 numbers to a column. These numbers correspond to the question numbers in your test booklet. After each number, going across the page are four or five pairs of dotted lines. These short dotted lines have small letters or numbers above them. The first two pairs may also have a "T" or "F" above the letters. This indicates that the first two pairs only are to be used if the questions are of the true-false type. If the questions are multiple choice, disregard the "T" and "F" and pay attention only to the small letters or numbers.

Answer your questions in the manner of the sample that follows:

32. The largest city in the United States is
    A. Washington, D.C.
    B. New York City
    C. Chicago
    D. Detroit
    E. San Francisco

1) Choose the answer you think is best. (New York City is the largest, so "B" is correct.)
2) Find the row of dotted lines numbered the same as the question you are answering. (Find row number 32)
3) Find the pair of dotted lines corresponding to the answer. (Find the pair of lines under the mark "B.")
4) Make a solid black mark between the dotted lines.

VI. BEFORE THE TEST

Common sense will help you find procedures to follow to get ready for an examination. Too many of us, however, overlook these sensible measures. Indeed, nervousness and fatigue have been found to be the most serious reasons why applicants fail to do their best on civil service tests. Here is a list of reminders:

- Begin your preparation early – Don't wait until the last minute to go scurrying around for books and materials or to find out what the position is all about.
- Prepare continuously – An hour a night for a week is better than an all-night cram session. This has been definitely established. What is more, a night a week for a month will return better dividends than crowding your study into a shorter period of time.
- Locate the place of the exam – You have been sent a notice telling you when and where to report for the examination. If the location is in a different town or otherwise unfamiliar to you, it would be well to inquire the best route and learn something about the building.
- Relax the night before the test – Allow your mind to rest. Do not study at all that night. Plan some mild recreation or diversion; then go to bed early and get a good night's sleep.
- Get up early enough to make a leisurely trip to the place for the test – This way unforeseen events, traffic snarls, unfamiliar buildings, etc. will not upset you.
- Dress comfortably – A written test is not a fashion show. You will be known by number and not by name, so wear something comfortable.

- Leave excess paraphernalia at home – Shopping bags and odd bundles will get in your way. You need bring only the items mentioned in the official notice you received; usually everything you need is provided. Do not bring reference books to the exam. They will only confuse those last minutes and be taken away from you when in the test room.
- Arrive somewhat ahead of time – If because of transportation schedules you must get there very early, bring a newspaper or magazine to take your mind off yourself while waiting.
- Locate the examination room – When you have found the proper room, you will be directed to the seat or part of the room where you will sit. Sometimes you are given a sheet of instructions to read while you are waiting. Do not fill out any forms until you are told to do so; just read them and be prepared.
- Relax and prepare to listen to the instructions
- If you have any physical problem that may keep you from doing your best, be sure to tell the test administrator. If you are sick or in poor health, you really cannot do your best on the exam. You can come back and take the test some other time.

VII. AT THE TEST

The day of the test is here and you have the test booklet in your hand. The temptation to get going is very strong. Caution! There is more to success than knowing the right answers. You must know how to identify your papers and understand variations in the type of short-answer question used in this particular examination. Follow these suggestions for maximum results from your efforts:

1) Cooperate with the monitor

The test administrator has a duty to create a situation in which you can be as much at ease as possible. He will give instructions, tell you when to begin, check to see that you are marking your answer sheet correctly, and so on. He is not there to guard you, although he will see that your competitors do not take unfair advantage. He wants to help you do your best.

2) Listen to all instructions

Don't jump the gun! Wait until you understand all directions. In most civil service tests you get more time than you need to answer the questions. So don't be in a hurry. Read each word of instructions until you clearly understand the meaning. Study the examples, listen to all announcements and follow directions. Ask questions if you do not understand what to do.

3) Identify your papers

Civil service exams are usually identified by number only. You will be assigned a number; you must not put your name on your test papers. Be sure to copy your number correctly. Since more than one exam may be given, copy your exact examination title.

4) Plan your time

Unless you are told that a test is a "speed" or "rate of work" test, speed itself is usually not important. Time enough to answer all the questions will be provided, but this does not mean that you have all day. An overall time limit has been set. Divide the total time (in minutes) by the number of questions to determine the approximate time you have for each question.

5) Do not linger over difficult questions

If you come across a difficult question, mark it with a paper clip (useful to have along) and come back to it when you have been through the booklet. One caution if you do this – be sure to skip a number on your answer sheet as well. Check often to be sure that you have not lost your place and that you are marking in the row numbered the same as the question you are answering.

6) Read the questions

Be sure you know what the question asks! Many capable people are unsuccessful because they failed to *read* the questions correctly.

7) Answer all questions

Unless you have been instructed that a penalty will be deducted for incorrect answers, it is better to guess than to omit a question.

8) Speed tests

It is often better NOT to guess on speed tests. It has been found that on timed tests people are tempted to spend the last few seconds before time is called in marking answers at random – without even reading them – in the hope of picking up a few extra points. To discourage this practice, the instructions may warn you that your score will be "corrected" for guessing. That is, a penalty will be applied. The incorrect answers will be deducted from the correct ones, or some other penalty formula will be used.

9) Review your answers

If you finish before time is called, go back to the questions you guessed or omitted to give them further thought. Review other answers if you have time.

10) Return your test materials

If you are ready to leave before others have finished or time is called, take ALL your materials to the monitor and leave quietly. Never take any test material with you. The monitor can discover whose papers are not complete, and taking a test booklet may be grounds for disqualification.

VIII. EXAMINATION TECHNIQUES

1) Read the general instructions carefully. These are usually printed on the first page of the exam booklet. As a rule, these instructions refer to the timing of the examination; the fact that you should not start work until the signal and must stop work at a signal, etc. If there are any *special* instructions, such as a choice of questions to be answered, make sure that you note this instruction carefully.

2) When you are ready to start work on the examination, that is as soon as the signal has been given, read the instructions to each question booklet, underline any key words or phrases, such as *least, best, outline, describe* and the like. In this way you will tend to answer as requested rather than discover on reviewing your paper that you *listed without describing*, that you selected the *worst* choice rather than the *best* choice, etc.

3) If the examination is of the objective or multiple-choice type – that is, each question will also give a series of possible answers: A, B, C or D, and you are called upon to select the best answer and write the letter next to that answer on your answer paper – it is advisable to start answering each question in turn. There may be anywhere from 50 to 100 such questions in the three or four hours allotted and you can see how much time would be taken if you read through all the questions before beginning to answer any. Furthermore, if you come across a question or group of questions which you know would be difficult to answer, it would undoubtedly affect your handling of all the other questions.

4) If the examination is of the essay type and contains but a few questions, it is a moot point as to whether you should read all the questions before starting to answer any one. Of course, if you are given a choice – say five out of seven and the like – then it is essential to read all the questions so you can eliminate the two that are most difficult. If, however, you are asked to answer all the questions, there may be danger in trying to answer the easiest one first because you may find that you will spend too much time on it. The best technique is to answer the first question, then proceed to the second, etc.

5) Time your answers. Before the exam begins, write down the time it started, then add the time allowed for the examination and write down the time it must be completed, then divide the time available somewhat as follows:
    - If 3-1/2 hours are allowed, that would be 210 minutes. If you have 80 objective-type questions, that would be an average of 2-1/2 minutes per question. Allow yourself no more than 2 minutes per question, or a total of 160 minutes, which will permit about 50 minutes to review.
    - If for the time allotment of 210 minutes there are 7 essay questions to answer, that would average about 30 minutes a question. Give yourself only 25 minutes per question so that you have about 35 minutes to review.

6) The most important instruction is to *read each question* and make sure you know what is wanted. The second most important instruction is to *time yourself properly* so that you answer every question. The third most important instruction is to *answer every question*. Guess if you have to but include something for each question. Remember that you will receive no credit for a blank and will probably receive some credit if you write something in answer to an essay question. If you guess a letter – say "B" for a multiple-choice question – you may have guessed right. If you leave a blank as an answer to a multiple-choice question, the examiners may respect your feelings but it will not add a point to your score. Some exams may penalize you for wrong answers, so in such cases *only*, you may not want to guess unless you have some basis for your answer.

7) Suggestions
    a. Objective-type questions
        1. Examine the question booklet for proper sequence of pages and questions
        2. Read all instructions carefully
        3. Skip any question which seems too difficult; return to it after all other questions have been answered
        4. Apportion your time properly; do not spend too much time on any single question or group of questions

5. Note and underline key words – *all, most, fewest, least, best, worst, same, opposite,* etc.
6. Pay particular attention to negatives
7. Note unusual option, e.g., unduly long, short, complex, different or similar in content to the body of the question
8. Observe the use of "hedging" words – *probably, may, most likely,* etc.
9. Make sure that your answer is put next to the same number as the question
10. Do not second-guess unless you have good reason to believe the second answer is definitely more correct
11. Cross out original answer if you decide another answer is more accurate; do not erase until you are ready to hand your paper in
12. Answer all questions; guess unless instructed otherwise
13. Leave time for review

b. Essay questions
 1. Read each question carefully
 2. Determine exactly what is wanted. Underline key words or phrases.
 3. Decide on outline or paragraph answer
 4. Include many different points and elements unless asked to develop any one or two points or elements
 5. Show impartiality by giving pros and cons unless directed to select one side only
 6. Make and write down any assumptions you find necessary to answer the questions
 7. Watch your English, grammar, punctuation and choice of words
 8. Time your answers; don't crowd material

8) Answering the essay question

Most essay questions can be answered by framing the specific response around several key words or ideas. Here are a few such key words or ideas:

M's: manpower, materials, methods, money, management
P's: purpose, program, policy, plan, procedure, practice, problems, pitfalls, personnel, public relations

 a. Six basic steps in handling problems:
  1. Preliminary plan and background development
  2. Collect information, data and facts
  3. Analyze and interpret information, data and facts
  4. Analyze and develop solutions as well as make recommendations
  5. Prepare report and sell recommendations
  6. Install recommendations and follow up effectiveness

 b. Pitfalls to avoid
  1. *Taking things for granted* – A statement of the situation does not necessarily imply that each of the elements is necessarily true; for example, a complaint may be invalid and biased so that all that can be taken for granted is that a complaint has been registered

2. *Considering only one side of a situation* – Wherever possible, indicate several alternatives and then point out the reasons you selected the best one
3. *Failing to indicate follow up* – Whenever your answer indicates action on your part, make certain that you will take proper follow-up action to see how successful your recommendations, procedures or actions turn out to be
4. *Taking too long in answering any single question* – Remember to time your answers properly

IX. AFTER THE TEST

Scoring procedures differ in detail among civil service jurisdictions although the general principles are the same. Whether the papers are hand-scored or graded by machine we have described, they are nearly always graded by number. That is, the person who marks the paper knows only the number – never the name – of the applicant. Not until all the papers have been graded will they be matched with names. If other tests, such as training and experience or oral interview ratings have been given, scores will be combined. Different parts of the examination usually have different weights. For example, the written test might count 60 percent of the final grade, and a rating of training and experience 40 percent. In many jurisdictions, veterans will have a certain number of points added to their grades.

After the final grade has been determined, the names are placed in grade order and an eligible list is established. There are various methods for resolving ties between those who get the same final grade – probably the most common is to place first the name of the person whose application was received first. Job offers are made from the eligible list in the order the names appear on it. You will be notified of your grade and your rank as soon as all these computations have been made. This will be done as rapidly as possible.

People who are found to meet the requirements in the announcement are called "eligibles." Their names are put on a list of eligible candidates. An eligible's chances of getting a job depend on how high he stands on this list and how fast agencies are filling jobs from the list.

When a job is to be filled from a list of eligibles, the agency asks for the names of people on the list of eligibles for that job. When the civil service commission receives this request, it sends to the agency the names of the three people highest on this list. Or, if the job to be filled has specialized requirements, the office sends the agency the names of the top three persons who meet these requirements from the general list.

The appointing officer makes a choice from among the three people whose names were sent to him. If the selected person accepts the appointment, the names of the others are put back on the list to be considered for future openings.

That is the rule in hiring from all kinds of eligible lists, whether they are for typist, carpenter, chemist, or something else. For every vacancy, the appointing officer has his choice of any one of the top three eligibles on the list. This explains why the person whose name is on top of the list sometimes does not get an appointment when some of the persons lower on the list do. If the appointing officer chooses the second or third eligible, the No. 1 eligible does not get a job at once, but stays on the list until he is appointed or the list is terminated.

X. HOW TO PASS THE INTERVIEW TEST

The examination for which you applied requires an oral interview test. You have already taken the written test and you are now being called for the interview test – the final part of the formal examination.

You may think that it is not possible to prepare for an interview test and that there are no procedures to follow during an interview. Our purpose is to point out some things you can do in advance that will help you and some good rules to follow and pitfalls to avoid while you are being interviewed.

What is an interview supposed to test?

The written examination is designed to test the technical knowledge and competence of the candidate; the oral is designed to evaluate intangible qualities, not readily measured otherwise, and to establish a list showing the relative fitness of each candidate – as measured against his competitors – for the position sought. Scoring is not on the basis of "right" and "wrong," but on a sliding scale of values ranging from "not passable" to "outstanding." As a matter of fact, it is possible to achieve a relatively low score without a single "incorrect" answer because of evident weakness in the qualities being measured.

Occasionally, an examination may consist entirely of an oral test – either an individual or a group oral. In such cases, information is sought concerning the technical knowledges and abilities of the candidate, since there has been no written examination for this purpose. More commonly, however, an oral test is used to supplement a written examination.

Who conducts interviews?

The composition of oral boards varies among different jurisdictions. In nearly all, a representative of the personnel department serves as chairman. One of the members of the board may be a representative of the department in which the candidate would work. In some cases, "outside experts" are used, and, frequently, a businessman or some other representative of the general public is asked to serve. Labor and management or other special groups may be represented. The aim is to secure the services of experts in the appropriate field.

However the board is composed, it is a good idea (and not at all improper or unethical) to ascertain in advance of the interview who the members are and what groups they represent. When you are introduced to them, you will have some idea of their backgrounds and interests, and at least you will not stutter and stammer over their names.

What should be done before the interview?

While knowledge about the board members is useful and takes some of the surprise element out of the interview, there is other preparation which is more substantive. It *is* possible to prepare for an oral interview – in several ways:

1) Keep a copy of your application and review it carefully before the interview

This may be the only document before the oral board, and the starting point of the interview. Know what education and experience you have listed there, and the sequence and dates of all of it. Sometimes the board will ask you to review the highlights of your experience for them; you should not have to hem and haw doing it.

2) Study the class specification and the examination announcement

Usually, the oral board has one or both of these to guide them. The qualities, characteristics or knowledges required by the position sought are stated in these documents. They offer valuable clues as to the nature of the oral interview. For example, if the job involves supervisory responsibilities, the announcement will usually indicate that knowledge of modern supervisory methods and the qualifications of the candidate as a supervisor will be tested. If so, you can expect such questions, frequently in the form of a hypothetical situation which you are expected to solve. NEVER go into an oral without knowledge of the duties and responsibilities of the job you seek.

3) Think through each qualification required

Try to visualize the kind of questions you would ask if you were a board member. How well could you answer them? Try especially to appraise your own knowledge and background in each area, *measured against the job sought*, and identify any areas in which you are weak. Be critical and realistic – do not flatter yourself.

4) Do some general reading in areas in which you feel you may be weak

For example, if the job involves supervision and your past experience has NOT, some general reading in supervisory methods and practices, particularly in the field of human relations, might be useful. Do NOT study agency procedures or detailed manuals. The oral board will be testing your understanding and capacity, not your memory.

5) Get a good night's sleep and watch your general health and mental attitude

You will want a clear head at the interview. Take care of a cold or any other minor ailment, and of course, no hangovers.

What should be done on the day of the interview?

Now comes the day of the interview itself. Give yourself plenty of time to get there. Plan to arrive somewhat ahead of the scheduled time, particularly if your appointment is in the fore part of the day. If a previous candidate fails to appear, the board might be ready for you a bit early. By early afternoon an oral board is almost invariably behind schedule if there are many candidates, and you may have to wait. Take along a book or magazine to read, or your application to review, but leave any extraneous material in the waiting room when you go in for your interview. In any event, relax and compose yourself.

The matter of dress is important. The board is forming impressions about you – from your experience, your manners, your attitude, and your appearance. Give your personal appearance careful attention. Dress your best, but not your flashiest. Choose conservative, appropriate clothing, and be sure it is immaculate. This is a business interview, and your appearance should indicate that you regard it as such. Besides, being well groomed and properly dressed will help boost your confidence.

Sooner or later, someone will call your name and escort you into the interview room. *This is it.* From here on you are on your own. It is too late for any more preparation. But remember, you asked for this opportunity to prove your fitness, and you are here because your request was granted.

What happens when you go in?

The usual sequence of events will be as follows: The clerk (who is often the board stenographer) will introduce you to the chairman of the oral board, who will introduce you to the other members of the board. Acknowledge the introductions before you sit down. Do not be surprised if you find a microphone facing you or a stenotypist sitting by. Oral interviews are usually recorded in the event of an appeal or other review.

Usually the chairman of the board will open the interview by reviewing the highlights of your education and work experience from your application – primarily for the benefit of the other members of the board, as well as to get the material into the record. Do not interrupt or comment unless there is an error or significant misinterpretation; if that is the case, do not hesitate. But do not quibble about insignificant matters. Also, he will usually ask you some question about your education, experience or your present job – partly to get you to start talking and to establish the interviewing "rapport." He may start the actual questioning, or turn it over to one of the other members. Frequently, each member undertakes the questioning on a particular area, one in which he is perhaps most competent, so you can expect each member to participate in the examination. Because time is limited, you may also expect some rather abrupt switches in the direction the questioning takes, so do not be upset by it. Normally, a board member will not pursue a single line of questioning unless he discovers a particular strength or weakness.

After each member has participated, the chairman will usually ask whether any member has any further questions, then will ask you if you have anything you wish to add. Unless you are expecting this question, it may floor you. Worse, it may start you off on an extended, extemporaneous speech. The board is not usually seeking more information. The question is principally to offer you a last opportunity to present further qualifications or to indicate that you have nothing to add. So, if you feel that a significant qualification or characteristic has been overlooked, it is proper to point it out in a sentence or so. Do not compliment the board on the thoroughness of their examination – they have been sketchy, and you know it. If you wish, merely say, "No thank you, I have nothing further to add." This is a point where you can "talk yourself out" of a good impression or fail to present an important bit of information. Remember, *you close the interview yourself.*

The chairman will then say, "That is all, Mr. _____, thank you." Do not be startled; the interview is over, and quicker than you think. Thank him, gather your belongings and take your leave. Save your sigh of relief for the other side of the door.

How to put your best foot forward

Throughout this entire process, you may feel that the board individually and collectively is trying to pierce your defenses, seek out your hidden weaknesses and embarrass and confuse you. Actually, this is not true. They are obliged to make an appraisal of your qualifications for the job you are seeking, and they want to see you in your best light. Remember, they must interview all candidates and a non-cooperative candidate may become a failure in spite of their best efforts to bring out his qualifications. Here are 15 suggestions that will help you:

1) Be natural – Keep your attitude confident, not cocky

If you are not confident that you can do the job, do not expect the board to be. Do not apologize for your weaknesses, try to bring out your strong points. The board is interested in a positive, not negative, presentation. Cockiness will antagonize any board member and make him wonder if you are covering up a weakness by a false show of strength.

2) Get comfortable, but don't lounge or sprawl

Sit erectly but not stiffly. A careless posture may lead the board to conclude that you are careless in other things, or at least that you are not impressed by the importance of the occasion. Either conclusion is natural, even if incorrect. Do not fuss with your clothing, a pencil or an ashtray. Your hands may occasionally be useful to emphasize a point; do not let them become a point of distraction.

3) Do not wisecrack or make small talk

This is a serious situation, and your attitude should show that you consider it as such. Further, the time of the board is limited – they do not want to waste it, and neither should you.

4) Do not exaggerate your experience or abilities

In the first place, from information in the application or other interviews and sources, the board may know more about you than you think. Secondly, you probably will not get away with it. An experienced board is rather adept at spotting such a situation, so do not take the chance.

5) If you know a board member, do not make a point of it, yet do not hide it

Certainly you are not fooling him, and probably not the other members of the board. Do not try to take advantage of your acquaintanceship – it will probably do you little good.

6) Do not dominate the interview

Let the board do that. They will give you the clues – do not assume that you have to do all the talking. Realize that the board has a number of questions to ask you, and do not try to take up all the interview time by showing off your extensive knowledge of the answer to the first one.

7) Be attentive

You only have 20 minutes or so, and you should keep your attention at its sharpest throughout. When a member is addressing a problem or question to you, give him your undivided attention. Address your reply principally to him, but do not exclude the other board members.

8) Do not interrupt

A board member may be stating a problem for you to analyze. He will ask you a question when the time comes. Let him state the problem, and wait for the question.

9) Make sure you understand the question

Do not try to answer until you are sure what the question is. If it is not clear, restate it in your own words or ask the board member to clarify it for you. However, do not haggle about minor elements.

10) Reply promptly but not hastily

A common entry on oral board rating sheets is "candidate responded readily," or "candidate hesitated in replies." Respond as promptly and quickly as you can, but do not jump to a hasty, ill-considered answer.

11) Do not be peremptory in your answers

A brief answer is proper – but do not fire your answer back. That is a losing game from your point of view. The board member can probably ask questions much faster than you can answer them.

12) Do not try to create the answer you think the board member wants

He is interested in what kind of mind you have and how it works – not in playing games. Furthermore, he can usually spot this practice and will actually grade you down on it.

13) Do not switch sides in your reply merely to agree with a board member

Frequently, a member will take a contrary position merely to draw you out and to see if you are willing and able to defend your point of view. Do not start a debate, yet do not surrender a good position. If a position is worth taking, it is worth defending.

14) Do not be afraid to admit an error in judgment if you are shown to be wrong
The board knows that you are forced to reply without any opportunity for careful consideration. Your answer may be demonstrably wrong. If so, admit it and get on with the interview.

15) Do not dwell at length on your present job
The opening question may relate to your present assignment. Answer the question but do not go into an extended discussion. You are being examined for a *new* job, not your present one. As a matter of fact, try to phrase ALL your answers in terms of the job for which you are being examined.

Basis of Rating

Probably you will forget most of these "do's" and "don'ts" when you walk into the oral interview room. Even remembering them all will not ensure you a passing grade. Perhaps you did not have the qualifications in the first place. But remembering them will help you to put your best foot forward, without treading on the toes of the board members.

Rumor and popular opinion to the contrary notwithstanding, an oral board wants you to make the best appearance possible. They know you are under pressure – but they also want to see how you respond to it as a guide to what your reaction would be under the pressures of the job you seek. They will be influenced by the degree of poise you display, the personal traits you show and the manner in which you respond.

ABOUT THIS BOOK

This book contains tests divided into Examination Sections. Go through each test, answering every question in the margin. We have also attached a sample answer sheet at the back of the book that can be removed and used. At the end of each test look at the answer key and check your answers. On the ones you got wrong, look at the right answer choice and learn. Do not fill in the answers first. Do not memorize the questions and answers, but understand the answer and principles involved. On your test, the questions will likely be different from the samples. Questions are changed and new ones added. If you understand these past questions you should have success with any changes that arise. Tests may consist of several types of questions. We have additional books on each subject should more study be advisable or necessary for you. Finally, the more you study, the better prepared you will be. This book is intended to be the last thing you study before you walk into the examination room. Prior study of relevant texts is also recommended. NLC publishes some of these in our Fundamental Series. Knowledge and good sense are important factors in passing your exam. Good luck also helps. So now study this Passbook, absorb the material contained within and take that knowledge into the examination. Then do your best to pass that exam.

EXAMINATION SECTION

EXAMINATION SECTION
TEST 1

DIRECTIONS: Each question or incomplete statement is followed by several suggested answers or completions. Select the one that BEST answers the question or completes the statement. *PRINT THE LETTER OF THE CORRECT ANSWER IN THE SPACE AT THE RIGHT.*

Questions 1-5.

DIRECTIONS: Questions 1 to 5 refer to the table below.

TABLE 1: NEW HOUSING UNITS STARTED 2000-2005
(Hypothetical)

YEAR	TOTAL IN THOUSANDS	PERCENT CHANGE[1]	PRIVATELY OWNED (in thousands) TOTAL	1-UNIT STRUCTURE	PUBLICLY OWNED IN THOUSANDS
2000	1,398	-20.4	1,250	990	I
2001	II	4.9	1,370	1,120	96
2002	1,524	4.0	III	1,236	104
2003	1,420	-6.8	1,325	1,164	95
2004	1,380	-2.8	1,260	IV	120
2005	1,690	V	1,520	1,415	170

[1]Change from previous year
Minus sign (-) denotes decrease

1. What is the value of I?   1.____

   A. 148
   B. 150
   C. 146
   D. 248
   E. None of the above, or cannot be calculated from the data provided

2. What is the value of II?   2.____

   A. 1,216
   B. 2,495
   C. 1,466
   D. 1,464
   E. None of the above, or cannot be calculated from the data provided

3. What is the value of III?   3.____

   A. 288
   B. 1,420
   C. 1,132
   D. 1,430
   E. None of the above, or cannot be calculated from the data provided

4. What is the value of IV?

   A. 1,140
   B. 1,380
   C. 1,102
   D. 1,094
   E. None of the above, or cannot be calculated from the data provided

5. What is the value of V?

   A. 18.3
   B. 81.7
   C. 21.5
   D. 22.5
   E. None of the above, or cannot be calculated from the data provided

Questions 6-10.

DIRECTIONS: Questions 6 to 10 test the applicant's ability to determine whether or not conclusions are true based on a given set of premises. The examinee should first read the premises that are given; then, look at the conclusion. Assume that the premises are true and decide whether the conclusion is:
   A. Necessarily true
   B. Probably, but not necessarily true
   C. Indeterminable, cannot be determined
   D. Probably, but not necessarily false
   E. Necessarily false

6. *Premises:* If the Commission approves the new proposal, the agency will move to a new location immediately. If the agency moves, five new supervisors will be appointed immediately. The Commission approved the new proposal.

   Conclusion: No new supervisors were appointed.

7. *Premises:* If the director retires, John Jackson, the associate director, will not be transferred to another agency. Jackson will be promoted to director if he is not transferred. The director retired.

   Conclusion: Jackson will be promoted to director.

8. *Premises:* If the maximum allowable income for food stamp recipients is increased, the number of food stamp recipients will increase. If the number of food stamp recipients increases, more funds must be allocated to the food stamp program, which will require a tax increase. Taxes cannot be raised without the approval of Congress. Congress probably will not approve a tax increase.

   Conclusion: The maximum allowable income for food stamp recipients will increase.

9. *Premises:* If prices are raised and sales remain constant, profits will increase. Prices were raised and sales levels will probably be maintained.

   Conclusion: Profits will increase.

   9._____

10. *Premises:* Some employees in the personnel department are technicians. Most of the technicians working in the personnel department are test development specialists. Lisa Jones works in the personnel department.

    Conclusion: Lisa Jones is a technician.

    10._____

Questions 11-15.

DIRECTIONS: Many jobs require skill in analyzing, understanding, and interpreting written material of varying levels of difficulty. These questions are primarily designed to test the applicant's comprehension and interpretation abilities. Therefore, Questions 11 to 15 require examinees to understand a given paragraph and to choose an answer based on their comprehension of the general concept used in the written passage. The right answer is usually a repetition in different terminology of the main concept(s) found in the passage. It may also be a conclusion drawn from the content of the paragraph that is equivalent to a restatement. The applicant should read each passage and select the one of the five statements that is BEST supported by the contents of the passage.

11. *A viable affirmative action program must contain specific procedures designed to achieve equal employment opportunities for specified groups. Appropriate procedures, without necessary determination to carry them out, are useless. Determination, without well-defined procedures, will achieve only partial success.*
    The paragraph BEST supports the statement that:

    A. Well-defined procedures will assure the success of an affirmative action program
    B. A high degree of determination is necessary and sufficient for a highly successful affirmative action program
    C. It is impossible for an agency to develop a viable affirmative action program
    D. An agency may guarantee success of its affirmative action program by developing and implementing well-defined procedures
    E. Two important ingredients of a successful affirmative action program are well-defined procedures and a sincere resolve to implement those procedures

    11._____

12. *Claimants who have become unemployed by voluntarily leaving the job, by refusing to accept suitable work, or due to misconduct should be temporarily disqualified from receiving benefits. However, the disqualification period should never be longer than the average period required for a worker to find employment. Unemployment insurance is designed to alleviate hardship due to unemployment. Benefits should definitely be paid if unemployment continues beyond a certain point and the claimant can show that he has made an honest effort to find employment.*
    The paragraph BEST supports the statement that:

    A. If a claimant cannot find work after a certain period of time, he/she should no longer receive benefits
    B. In cases of willful misconduct, disqualification should continue indefinitely
    C. The reasons for unemployment change as the period of unemployment gets longer

    12._____

D. If a claimant cannot find employment after a certain period of time, he/she should be allowed to receive unemployment insurance benefits
E. If a claimant chooses voluntary unemployment, he/she should receive unemployment insurance benefits immediately

13. *Education in the United States is a state responsibility, a local function, and a federal concern. Unlike other social service programs, this arrangement also places state governments between the federal government and local governing bodies.*
The paragraph BEST supports the statement that:

    A. Enforcement of federal education policies is left to state discretion
    B. The federal government plays an advisory role only in matters concerning education
    C. Federal educational policies are generally implemented by local governments under the direction of the state
    D. No federal funds are used to support local educational programs
    E. Federal aid is often used to induce local school systems to implement federal policies

13.____

14. *Technological and psychological conditions are changing so rapidly that most agencies and organizations must continually adapt to new situations in order to remain viable.*
The paragraph BEST supports the statement that:

    A. Changes in general conditions determine the effectiveness of an organization
    B. The effectiveness of an organization depends more on technological advances than on psychological changes
    C. Organizations must be able to adapt to technological and psychological changes in order to maintain effectiveness
    D. The effectiveness of an organization is equally dependent upon technological advances and psychological changes
    E. The effectiveness of an organization is dependent upon its technological and psychological advances

14.____

15. *A disability may be defined as the inability to perform one or more activities essential to normal everyday living. Some examples are basic care of self, earning a living, and social competence. Some basic causes are physical impairment due to illness or injury, mental impairment, and physical or mental deprivation*
The paragraph BEST supports the statement that a disability is

    A. a term utilized to denote any lessening of an individual's ability to perform normal daily activities
    B. any acute or chronic condition that may be permanent or long-range in nature
    C. any physical or mental impairment which inhibits higher order intellectual pursuits
    D. an acute or chronic condition that can be described by the pathology underlying the condition
    E. defined as the inability to perform any activity essential to normal everyday living

15.____

Questions 16-20.

DIRECTIONS: Many occupations require skill in solving quantitative problems of varying degrees of difficulty. Questions 16 to 20 are designed to test these abilities. Read each statement carefully before attempting to solve the problem.

16. Angela Winston processed 300 applications for food stamps during the month of June. During the month of July, she processed 10% fewer applications. Determine the number she processed in July.

    A. 220 B. 240 C. 270
    D. 280 E. None of the above

    16.____

17. A personnel officer drove from Lake Charles to a conference in Baton Rouge. The total distance for the round trip was 240 miles. The time required to travel one way to Baton Rouge was two hours. Due to heavy traffic during the return trip to Lake Charles, an extra hour was required.
    How much *slower* was the personnel officer traveling on the return trip?

    A. 10 mph B. 15 mph C. 20 mph
    D. 25 mph E. None of the above

    17.____

18. Ten employment security interviewers interviewed a total of 800 applicants in five days. Sixty percent of those interviewed were placed on jobs.
    If each interviewer worked 8 hours each day, what was the AVERAGE number of applicants placed on jobs each hour by each interviewer?

    A. 1.2 B. 0.8 C. 0.5
    D. 1.5 E. None of the above

    18.____

19. A state park *is* budgeted at an amount 9 times the amount budgeted for a nearby city park.
    If the combined yearly budget of both parks is $1,000,000, what is the average monthly budget of the city park?

    A. $8,111.00 B. $8,222.22 C. $8,333.33
    D. $8,444.44 E.

    19.____

20. The estimated completion time for a 100-item test is 3 1/3 hours. Ten applicants actually took the test and completed it in 3 hours.
    What is the difference, in seconds, between the actual and estimated rate of completion per item?

    A. 10 B. 12 C. 14
    D. 16 E. None of the above

    20.____

KEY (CORRECT ANSWERS)

1.	A		11.	E
2.	C		12.	D
3.	B		13.	C
4.	E		14.	C
5.	D		15.	E
6.	E		16.	C
7.	A		17.	C
8.	D		18.	A
9.	B		19.	C
10.	C		20.	B

SOLUTIONS TO PROBLEMS

1. The answer is 148 or A. The figure represents the number of publicly-owned units which is obtained by subtracting the number of privately-owned units from the total: 1,398 - 1,250 = 148.

2. The answer is 1,466 or C. The figure represents the total number of housing units which is obtained by adding the total number of privately-owned units to the number of publicly-owned units: 1,370 + 96 = 1,466. Alternative A represents the sum of the total number of publicly-owned units and the number of 1-unit, privately-owned structures. Alternatives B and D are irrelevant values.

3. The answer is 1,420 or B. It is obtained by subtracting the number of publicly-owned units from the total number of housing units: 1,524 - 104 = 1,420. Alternative A is obtained by subtracting the number of 1-unit, privately-owned structures from the total number of units. Alternatives C and D are irrelevant values.

4. The answer is E. The number of privately-owned 1-unit structures cannot be calculated since the number of privately-owned multi-unit structures is not given in the table. Alternative A represents the difference between the number of privately-owned units and the number of publicly-owned units. Alternative B represents the sum of publicly-owned units and privately-owned units. Alternatives C and D are irrelevant values.

5. The answer is 22.5 or D. The percent change is calculated by computing the increase or decrease and dividing the result by the number that existed before the change: 1,690 - 1,380 = 310 and 310/1380 = 22.46 or 22.5. Alternative A erroneously divides 310 by 1,690, and Alternative B was found by erroneously dividing 1,380 by 1,690. Alternative C is an irrelevant value.

6. The correct answer is E. The new proposal was approved. According to the premises, approval means that the agency will move, and moving to a new location means that five new supervisors will be appointed.

7. The correct answer is A. According to the premises, the director retired, which means that Jackson will not be transferred and, therefore, will be promoted to director.

8. The correct answer is D (probably, but not necessarily false). Since Congress probably will not approve a tax increase, the maximum allowable income for food stamp recipients probably will not increase.

9. The correct answer is B (probably, but not necessarily true). According to the premises, profits will increase if prices are raised and sales remain constant. It is known that prices were raised. Although sales levels will probably be maintained, this is not certain.

10. The correct answer is C (indeterminable, cannot be determined). The premises give no indication of the proportion of employees who are technicians. Therefore, no conclusion can be drawn with respect to the probability that any one employee is a technician.

11. The correct alternative, E, restates the idea presented in the paragraph. Statements A and B each contain only one of the ingredients. Alternative D overstates the implications of the paragraph.

12. The correct alternative, D, summarizes the meaning of the passage as a whole. Alternative A concerns the length of time the claimant should receive benefits. Alternatives B and E contradict parts of the passage and the idea expressed in Alternative C is not addressed in the paragraph.

13. Correct alternative, C, is supported by the paragraph. The ideas expressed in Alternatives A, B, and D are not addressed in the paragraph. Although Alternative E is probably true, it is not mentioned in the paragraph.

14. Correct alternative, C, effectively restates the essence of the paragraph. In contrast to Alternatives A and B, the paragraph states that organizations must adapt to changes. Alternatives D and E imply that effectiveness of an organization depends on change; however, the paragraph states that effectiveness depends on an organization's ability to adapt to change.

15. Correct alternative E is supported by the first sentence of the paragraph. Alternatives B, C, and D are not supported by the paragraph. Although Alternative A is supported by the paragraph to some extent, its lack of specificity makes it less acceptable than Alternative

16. The answer is C. First, compute 10% of 300: 300 x .10 = 30. Second, subtract the result from 300: 300 - 30 = 270.

17. The answer is C. First, compute the distance one way: 1/2 x 240 = 120 miles. Second, calculate the rate going: 120 miles ÷ 2 hours = 60 mph. Third, calculate the rate returning: 120 miles ÷ 3 hours = 40 mph. Fourth, compute the difference: 60 mph - 40 mph = 20 mph.

18. The answer is A. The total number of applicants placed on jobs equals 60% of 800: .60 x 800 = 480. The total placed per day equals 480 divided by the number of days: 480 ÷ 5 = 96. The total placed per hour equals 96 divided by hours per day: 96 ÷ 8 = 12. The total placed per hour per interviewer equals the total placed per hour divided by the number of interviewers: 12 ÷ 10 = 1.2.

19. The correct answer is C. Let x = the annual city park budget and 9x = the annual state park budget. Therefore, 10x = $1,000,000, and x = $100,000. $100,000 divided by 12 = $8,333.33, the average monthly city park budget.

20. The answer is B. The estimated time per item equals the estimated time divided by the number of items:

$$\frac{3\,1/3 \times 60}{100} = \frac{10/3 \times 60}{100} = \frac{10 \times 20}{100} = \frac{200}{100} = 2 \text{ minutes}$$

The actual time equals 3 hours or 180 minutes. The actual time per item equals 180 minutes divided by the number of items: 180 ÷ 100 = 1.8 minutes. The difference in estimated time and actual time equals 2 minutes minus 1.8 minutes: 2.0 - 1.8 = .2 minutes or .2 x 60 seconds = 12 seconds.

EXAMINATION SECTION

DIRECTIONS: Each question or incomplete statement is followed by several suggested answers or completions. Select the one that BEST answers the question or completes the statement. *PRINT THE LETTER OF THE CORRECT ANSWER IN THE SPACE AT THE RIGHT.*

Questions 1-5.

DIRECTIONS: Each of Questions 1 through 5 consists of a passage which contains one word that is incorrectly used because it is not in keeping with the meaning that the quotation is evidently intended to convey. Determine which word is incorrectly used. Select from the choices lettered A, B, C, and D the word which, when substituted for the incorrectly used word, would BEST help to convey the meaning of the quotation.

1. Whatever the method, the necessity to keep up with the dynamics of an organization is the point on which many classification plans go awry. The budgetary approach to "positions," for example, often leads to using for recruitment and pay purposes a position authorized many years earlier for quite a different purpose than currently contemplated – making perhaps the title, the class, and the qualifications required inappropriate to the current need. This happens because executives overlook the stability that takes place in job duties and fail to reread an initial description of the job before saying, as they scan a list of titles, "We should fill this position right away." Once a classification plan is adopted, it is pointless to do anything less than provide for continuous, painstaking maintenance on a current basis, else once different positions that have actually become similar to each other remain in different classes, and some former cognates that have become quite different continue in the same class. Such a program often seems expensive. But to stint too much on this out-of-pocket cost may create still higher hidden costs growing out of lowered morale, poor production, delayed operating programs, excessive pay for simple work, and low pay for responsible work (resulting in poorly qualified executives and professional men) – all normal concomitants of inadequate, hasty, or out-of-date classification.

    A. evolution
    B. personnel
    C. disapproved
    D. forward

    1.____

2. At first sight, it may seem that there is little or no difference between the usableness of a manual and the degree of its use. But there is a difference. A manual may have all the qualities which make up the usable manual and still not be used. Take this instance as an example: Suppose you have a satisfactory manual but issue instructions from day to day through the avenue of bulletins, memorandums, and other informational releases. Which will the employee use, the manual or the bulletin which passes over his desk? He will, of course, use the latter, for some obsolete material will not be contained in this manual. Here we have a theoretically usable manual which is unused because of the other avenues by which procedural information may be issued.

    A. countermand
    B. discard
    C. intentional
    D. worthwhile

    2.____

3. By reconcentrating control over its operations in a central headquarters, a firm is able to extend the influence of automation to many, if not all, of its functions – from inventory and payroll to production, sales, and personnel. In so doing, businesses freeze all the elements of the corporate function in their relationship to one another and to the overall objectives of the firm. From this total systems concept, companies learn that computers can accomplish much more than clerical and accounting jobs. Their capabilities can be tapped to perform the traditional applications (payroll processing, inventory control, accounts payable, and accounts receivable) as well as newer applications such as spotting deviations from planned programs (exception reporting), adjusting planning schedules, forecasting business trends, simulating market conditions, and solving production problems. Since the office manager is a manager of information and each of these applications revolves around the processing of data, he must take an active role in studying and improving the system under his care.

3.____

    A. maintaining   B. inclusion
    C. limited   D. visualize

4. In addition to the formal and acceptance theories of the source of authority, although perhaps more closely related to the latter, is the belief that authority is generated by personal qualifies of technical competence. Under this heading is the individual who has made, in effect, subordinates of others through sheer force of personality, and the engineer or economist who exerts influence by furnishing answers or sound advice. These may have no actual organizational authority, yet their advice may be so eagerly sought and so unerringly followed that it appears to carry the weight of an order.
But, above all, one cannot discount the importance of formal authority with its institutional foundations. Buttressed by the qualities of leadership implicit in the acceptance theory, formal authority is basic to the managerial job. Once abrogated, it may be delegated or withheld, used or misused, and be effective in capable hands or be ineffective in inept hands.

4.____

    A. selected   B. delegation
    C. limited   D. possessed

5. Since managerial operations in organizing, staffing, directing, and controlling are designed to support the accomplishment of enterprise objectives, planning logically precedes the execution of all other managerial functions. Although all the functions intermesh in practice, planning is unique in that it establishes the objectives necessary for all group effort. Besides, plans must be made to accomplish these objectives before the manager knows what kind of organization relationships and personal qualifications are needed, along which course subordinates are to be directed, and what kind of control is to be applied. And, of course, each of the other managerial functions must be planned if they are to be effective.
Planning and control are inseparable – the Siamese twins of management. Unplanned action cannot be controlled, for control involves keeping activities on course by correcting deviations from plans. Any attempt to control without plans would be meaningless, since there is no way anyone can tell whether he is going where he wants to go – the task of control – unless first he knows where he wants to go – the task of planning. Plans thus preclude the standards of control.

5.____

    A. coordinating   B. individual
    C. furnish   D. follow

Questions 6-7.

DIRECTIONS: Answer Questions 6 and 7 SOLELY on the basis of information given in the following paragraph.

In-basket tests are often used to assess managerial potential. The exercise consists of a set of papers that would be likely to be found in the in-basket of an administrator or manager at any given time, and requires the individuals participating in the examination to indicate how they would dispose of each item found in the in-basket. In order to handle the in-basket effectively, they must successfully manage their time, refer and assign some work to subordinates, juggle potentially conflicting appointments and meetings, and arrange for follow-up of problems generated by the items in the in-basket. In other words, the in-basket test is attempting to evaluate the participants' abilities to organize their work, set priorities, delegate, control, and make decisions.

6. According to the above paragraph, to succeed in an in-basket test, an administrator must   6._____

    A. be able to read very quickly
    B. have a great deal of technical knowledge
    C. know when to delegate work
    D. arrange a lot of appointments and meetings

7. According to the above paragraph, all of the following abilities are indications of managerial potential EXCEPT the ability to   7._____

    A. organize and control   B. manage time
    C. write effective reports   D. make appropriate decisions

Questions 8-9.

DIRECTIONS: Answer Questions 8 and 9 SOLELY on the basis of information given in the following paragraph.

One of the biggest mistakes of government executives with substantial supervisory responsibility is failing to make careful appraisals of performance during employee probationary periods. Many a later headache could have been avoided by prompt and full appraisal during the early months of an employee's assignment. There is not much more to say about this except to emphasize the common prevalence of this oversight, and to underscore that for its consequences, which are many and sad, the offending managers have no one to blame but themselves.

8. According to the above passage, probationary periods are   8._____

    A. a mistake, and should not be used by supervisors with large responsibilities
    B. not used properly by government executives
    C. used only for those with supervisory responsibility
    D. the consequence of management mistakes

9. The one of the following conclusions that can MOST appropriately be drawn from the above passage is that

   A. management's failure to appraise employees during their probationary period is a common occurrence
   B. there is not much to say about probationary periods, because they are unimportant
   C. managers should blame employees for failing to use their probationary periods properly
   D. probationary periods are a headache to most managers

Questions 10-12.

DIRECTIONS: Answer Questions 10 through 12 SOLELY on the basis of information given in the following paragraph.

The common sense character of the merit system seems so natural to most Americans that many people wonder why it should ever have been inoperative. After all, the American economic system, the most phenomenal the world has ever known, is also founded on a rugged selective process which emphasizes the personal qualities of capacity, industriousness, and productivity. The criteria may not have always been appropriate and competition has not always been fair, but competition there was, and the responsibilities and the rewards – with exceptions, of course – have gone to those who could measure up in terms of intelligence, knowledge, or perseverance. This has been true not only in the economic area, in the money-making process, but also in achievement in the professions and other walks of life.

10. According to the above paragraph, economic rewards in the United States have

    A. always been based on appropriate, fair criteria
    B. only recently been based on a competitive system
    C. not gone to people who compete too ruggedly
    D. usually gone to those people with intelligence, knowledge, and perseverance

11. According to the above passage, a merit system is

    A. an unfair criterion on which to base rewards
    B. unnatural to anyone who is not American
    C. based only on common sense
    D. based on the same principles as the American economic system

12. According to the above passage, it is MOST accurate to say that

    A. the United States has always had a civil service merit system
    B. civil service employees are very rugged
    C. the American economic system has always been based on a merit objective
    D. competition is unique to the American way of life

Questions 13-15.

DIRECTIONS: The management study of employee absence due to sickness is an effective tool in planning. Answer Questions 13 through 15 SOLELY on the data given below.

Number of days absent per worker (sickness)	1	2	3	4	5	6	7	8 or Over
Number of workers	76	23	6	3	1	0	1	0

Total Number of Workers: 400
Period Covered: January 1 - December 31

13. The total number of man days lost due to illness was

    A. 110   B. 137   C. 144   D. 164

13._____

14. What percent of the workers had 4 or more days absence due to sickness?

    A. .25%   B. 2.5%   C. 1.25%   D. 12.5%

14._____

15. Of the 400 workers studied, the number who lost no days due to sickness was

    A. 190   B. 236   C. 290   D. 346

15._____

Questions 16-18.

DIRECTIONS: In the graph below, the lines labeled "A" and "B" represent the cumulative progress in the work of two file clerks, each of whom was given 500 consecutively numbered applications to file in the proper cabinets over a five-day work week. Answer Questions 16 through 18 SOLELY upon the data provided in the graph.

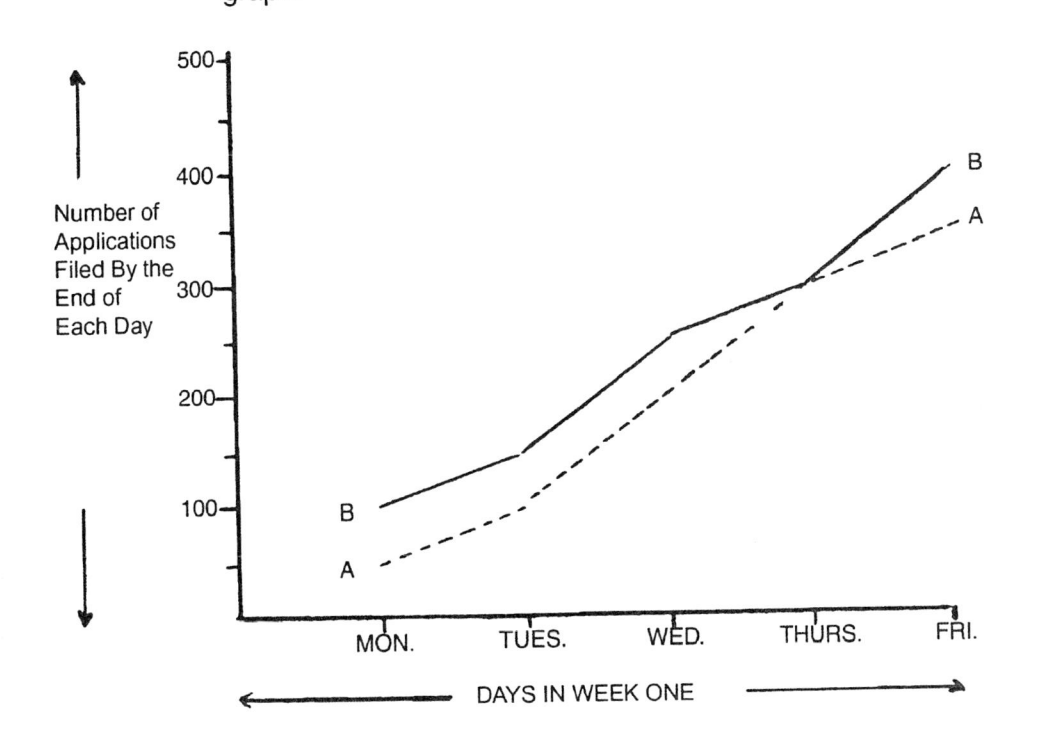

16. The day during which the LARGEST number of applications was filed by both clerks was   16.____
    A. Monday   B. Tuesday   C. Wednesday   D. Friday

17. At the end of the second day, the percentage of applications STILL to be filed was   17.____
    A. 25%   B. 50%   C. 66%   D. 75%

18. Assuming that the production pattern is the same the following week as the week shown in the chart, the day on which the file clerks will FINISH this assignment will be   18.____
    A. Monday   B. Tuesday   C. Wednesday   D. Friday

Questions 19-21.

DIRECTIONS: The following chart shows the differences between the rates of production of employees in Department D in 1996 and 2006. Answer Questions 19 through 21 SOLELY on the basis of the information given in the chart.

Number of Employees Producing Work-Units Within Range in 1996	Number of Work-Units Produced	Number of Employees Producing Work-Units Within Range in 2006
7	500 - 1000	4
14	1001 - 1500	11
26	1501 - 2000	28
22	2001 - 2500	36
17	2501 - 3000	39
10	3001 - 3500	23
4	3501 - 4000	9

19. Assuming that within each range of work-units produced the average production was at the mid-point at that range (e.g., category 500 - 1000 = 750), then the AVERAGE number of work-units produced per employee in 1996 fell into the range   19.____

    A. 1001 - 1500   B. 1501 - 2000
    C. 2001 - 2500   D. 2501 - 3000

20. The ratio of the number of employees producing more than 2000 work-units in 1996 to the number of employees producing more than 2000 work-units in 2006 is *most nearly*   20.____

    A. 1:2   B. 2:3   C. 3:4   D. 4:5

21. In Department D, which of the following were GREATER in 2006 than in 1996?   21.____
    I. Total number of employees
    II. Total number of work-units produced
    III. Number of employees producing 2000 or fewer work-units
    The CORRECT answer is:

    A. I, II, III   B. I, II
    C. I, III   D. II, III

22. Unit S's production fluctuated substantially from one year to another. In 2004, Unit S's production was 100% greater than in 2003. In 2005, production decreased by 25% from 2004. In 2006, Unit S's production was 10% greater than in 2005.
On the basis of this information, it is CORRECT to conclude that Unit S's production in 2006 exceeded Unit S's production in 2003 by

    A. 65%   B. 85%   C. 95%   D. 135%

23. Agency "X" is moving into a new building. It has 1500 employees presently on its staff and does not contemplate much variance from this level. The new building contains 100 available offices, each with a maximum capacity of 30 employees. It has been decided that only 2/3 of the maximum capacity of each office will be utilized. The TOTAL number of offices that will be occupied by Agency "X" is

    A. 30   B. 66   C. 75   D. 90

24. One typist completes a form letter every 5 minutes and another typist completes one every 6 minutes.
If the two typists start together, they will again start typing new letters simultaneously _____ minutes later and will have completed ____ letters by that time.

    A. 11; 30   B. 12; 24   C. 24; 12   D. 30; 11

25. During one week, a machine operator produces 10 fewer pages per hour of work than he usually does. If it ordinarily takes him six hours to produce a 300-page report, it will take him ____ hours LONGER to produce that same 300-page report during the week when he produces MORE slowly.

    A. $1\frac{1}{2}$ B. $1\frac{2}{3}$ C. 2   D. $2\frac{3}{4}$

KEY (CORRECT ANSWERS)

		Incorrect Words
1.	A	stability
2.	D	obsolete
3.	D	freeze
4.	D	abrogated
5.	C	preclude

6.	C	16.	C
7.	C	17.	D
8.	B	18.	B
9.	A	19.	C
10.	D	20.	A
11.	D	21.	B
12.	C	22.	A
13.	D	23.	C
14.	C	24.	D
15.	C	25.	A

EXAMINATION SECTION
TEST 1

DIRECTIONS: Each question or incomplete statement is followed by several suggested answers or completions. Select the one that BEST answers the question or completes the statement. *PRINT THE LETTER OF THE CORRECT ANSWER IN THE SPACE AT THE RIGHT.*

Questions 1–5.

DIRECTIONS: Questions 1 through 5 consist of sentences each of which contains one underlined word whose meaning you are to identify by marking your answer either A, B, C, or D.

EXAMPLE

Public employees should avoid unethical conduct.
The word unethical, as used in the sentence, means, most nearly,
 A. fine B. dishonest C. polite D. sleepy
The correct answer is dishonest (B). Therefore, you should mark your answer B.

1. Employees who can produce a considerable amount of good work are very valuable.
   The word *considerable,* as used in the sentence, means, most nearly,

   A. large   B. potential   C. necessary   D. frequent

2. No person should assume that he knows more than anyone else.
   The word *assume,* as used in the sentence, means, most nearly,

   A. verify   B. hope   C. suppose   D. argue

3. The parties decided to negotiate through the night.
   The word *negotiate,* as used in the sentence, means, most nearly,

   A. suffer   B. play   C. think   D. bargain

4. Employees who have severe emotional problems may create problems at work.
   The word *severe,* as used in the sentence, means, most nearly,

   A. serious   B. surprising   C. several   D. common

5. Supervisors should try to be as objective as possible when dealing with subordinates.
   The word *objective,* as used in the sentence, means, most nearly,

   A. pleasant   B. courteous   C. fair   D. strict

Questions 6–10.

DIRECTIONS: In each of Questions 6 through 10, *one* word is wrongly used because it is *NOT* in keeping with the intended meaning of the statement. First, decide which word is wrongly used; then select as your answer the right word which really belongs in its place.

EXAMPLE

The employee told ill and requested permission to leave early.
 A. felt B. considered C. cried D. spoke
The word *"told"* is clearly wrong and not in keeping with the intended meaning of the quotation.

The word *"felt"* (A), however, would clearly convey the intended meaning of the sentence. Option A is correct. Your answer space, therefore, would be marked A.

6. Only unwise supervisors would deliberately overload their subordinates in order to create themselves look good.   6.____

    A. delegate   B. make   C. reduce   D. produce

7. In a democratic organization each employee is seen as a special individual kind of fair treatment,   7.____

    A. granted   B. denial   C. perhaps   D. deserving

8. In order to function the work flow in an office you should begin by identifying each important procedure being performed in that office.   8.____

    A. uniformity   B. study   C. standards   D. reward

9. A wise supervisor tries to save employees' time by simplifying forms or adding forms where possible.   9.____

    A. taxing   B. supervising   C. eliminating   D. protecting

10. A public agency, whenever it changes its program, should give requirements to the need for retraining its employees.   10.____

    A. legislation   B. consideration   C. permission   D. advice

Questions 11-15.

DIRECTIONS: Answer each of Questions 11 through 15 ONLY on the basis of the reading passage preceding each question.

11. Things may not always be what they seem to be. Thus, the wise supervisor should analyze his problems and determine whether there is something there that does not meet the eye. For example, what may seem on the surface to be a personality clash between two subordinates may really be a problem of faulty organization, bad communication, or bad scheduling.   11.____
Which one of the following statements BEST supports this passage?

    A. The wise supervisor should avoid personality clashes.
    B. The smart supervisor should figure out what really is going on.
    C. Bad scheduling is the result of faulty organization.
    D. The best supervisor is the one who communicates effectively.

12. Some supervisors, under the pressure of meeting deadlines, become harsh and dictatorial to their subordinates. However, the supervisor most likely to be effective in meeting deadlines is one who absorbs or cushions pressures from above.
    According to the passage, if a supervisor wishes to meet deadlines, it is MOST important that he

    A. be informative to his superiors
    B. encourage personal initiative among his subordinates
    C. become harsh and dictatorial to his subordinates
    D. protects his subordinates from pressures from above

13. When giving instructions, a supervisor must always make clear his meaning, leaving no room for misunderstanding. For example, a supervisor who tells a subordinate to do a task "*as soon as possible*" might legitimately be understood to mean either "*it's top priority*" or "*do it when you can.*"
    Which of the following statements is BEST supported by the passage?

    A. Subordinates will attempt to avoid work by deliberately distorting instructions.
    B. Instructions should be short, since brief instructions are the clearest.
    C. Less educated subordinates are more likely to honestly misunderstand instructions.
    D. A supervisor should give precise instructions that cannot be misinterpreted.

14. Practical formulas are often suggested to simplify what a supervisor should know and how he should behave, such as the four F's (be firm, fair, friendly, and factual). But such simple formulas are really broad principles, not necessarily specific guides in a real situation.
    According to the passage, simple formulas for supervisory behavior

    A. are superior to complicated theories and principles
    B. not always of practical use in actual situations
    C. useful only if they are fair and factual
    D. would be better understood if written in clear language

15. Many management decisions are made far removed from the actual place of operations. Therefore, there is a great need for reliable reports and records and, the larger the organization, the greater is the need for such reports and records.
    According to the passage, management decisions made far from the place of operations are

    A. dependent to a great extent on reliable reports and records
    B. sometimes in error because of the great distances involved
    C. generally unreliable because of poor communications
    D. generally more accurate than on–the–scene decisions

16. Assume that you have just been advanced to a supervisory administrative position and have been assigned as supervisor to a new office with subordinates you do not know. The BEST way for you to establish good relations with these new subordinates would be to

    A. announce that all actions of the previous supervisor are now cancelled
    B. hold a meeting and warn them that you will not tolerate loafing on the job
    C. reassign all your subordinates to new tasks on the theory that a thorough shake-up is good for morale
    D. act fairly and show helpful interest in their work

16.____

17. One of your subordinates asks you to let her arrive at work 15 minutes later than usual but leave for the day 15 minutes later than she usually does. This is temporarily necessary, your subordinate states, because of early morning medication she must give her sick child.
Which of the following would be the MOST appropriate action for you to take?

    A. *Suggest* to your subordinate that she choose another family doctor
    B. *Warn* your subordinate that untruthful excuses are not acceptable
    C. *Tell* your subordinate that you will consider the request and let her know very shortly
    D. *Deny* the request since late arrival at work interferes with work performance

17.____

18. A young newly-hired employee asked his supervisor several times for advice on private financial matters. The supervisor commented, in a friendly manner, that he considered it undesirable to give such advice.
The supervisor's response was

    A. *unwise;* the supervisor missed an opportunity to advise the employee on an important matter
    B. *wise;* if the financial advice was wrong, it could damage the supervisor's relationship with the subordinate
    C. *unwise;* the subordinate will take up the matter with his fellow workers and probably get poor advice
    D. *wise;* the supervisor should never advise subordinates on any matter

18.____

19. Which of the following is the MOST justified reason for a supervisor to pay any serious attention to a subordinate's off-the-job behavior? The

    A. subordinate's life style is different from the supervisor's way of life
    B. subordinate has become well-known as a serious painter of fine art
    C. subordinate's work has become very poor as a result of his or her personal problems
    D. subordinate is a reserved person who, at work, seldom speaks of personal matters

19.____

20. One of your subordinates complains to you that you assign him to the least pleasant jobs more often than anyone else. You are disturbed by this complaint since you believe you have always rotated such assignments on a fair basis.
Of the following, it would be BEST for you to tell the complaining subordinate that

    A. you will review your past assignment records and discuss the matter with him further
    B. complaints to supervisors are not the wise way to get ahead on the job
    C. disciplinary action will follow if the complaint is not justified
    D. he may be correct, but you do not have sufficient time to verify the complaint

21. Assume that you have called one of your subordinates into your office to talk about the increasing number of careless errors in her work. Until recently, this subordinate had been doing good work, but this is no longer so. Your subordinate does not seem to respond to your questions about the reason for her poor work.
In these circumstances, your *next* step should be to tell her

    A. that her continued silence will result in severe disciplinary action
    B. to request an immediate transfer from your unit
    C. to return when she is ready to respond
    D. to be more open with you so that her work problem can be identified

22. Assume that you are given a complicated assignment with a tight deadline set by your superior. Shortly after you begin work you realize that, if you are to do a top quality job, you cannot possibly meet the deadline.
In these circumstances, what should be your FIRST course of action?

    A. *Continue* working as rapidly as possible, hoping that you will meet the deadline after all
    B. *Request* the assignment be given to an employee whom you believe works faster
    C. *Advise* your superior of the problem and see whether the deadline can be extended
    D. *Advise* your superior that the deadline cannot be met and, therefore, you will not start the job

23. Assume that a member of the public comes to you to complain about a long–standing practice of your agency. The complaint seems to be justified.
Which one of the following is the BEST way for you to handle this situation?

    A. *Inform* the complainant that you will have the agency practice looked into and that he will be advised of any action taken
    B. *Listen* politely, express sympathy, and state that you see no fault in the practice
    C. *Express* agreement with the practice on the ground that it has been in effect for many years
    D. *Advise* the complainant that things will work out well in good time

24. One of your subordinates tells you that he sees no good reason for having departmental safety rules.
Which one of the following replies would be BEST for you to make?

    A. Rules are meant to be obeyed without question.
    B. All types of rules are equally important.
    C. Safety rules are meant to protect people from injury.
    D. If a person is careful enough, he doesn't have to observe safety rules.

25. Assume that a supervisor, when he issues instructions to his subordinates, usually names his superior as the source of these instructions.
This practice is, generally,

    A. *wise,* since if things go wrong, the subordinates will know whom to blame
    B. *unwise,* since it may give the subordinates the impression that the supervisor doesn't really support the instructions
    C. *wise,* since it clearly invites the subordinates to go to higher authority if they don't like the instructions
    D. *unwise,* since the subordinates may thereby be given too much information

KEY (CORRECT ANSWERS)

1. A
2. C
3. D
4. A
5. C

6. B
7. D
8. B
9. C
10. B

11. B
12. D
13. D
14. B
15. A

16. D
17. C
18. B
19. C
20. A

21. D
22. C
23. A
24. C
25. B

TEST 2

DIRECTIONS: Each question or incomplete statement is followed by several suggested answers or completions. Select the one that BEST answers the question or completes the statement. PRINT THE LETTER OF THE CORRECT ANSWER IN THE SPACE AT THE RIGHT

1. An office aide is assigned as a receptionist in a busy office. The office aide often has stretches of idle time between visitors.
   In this situation, the supervisor should

   A. *give* the receptionist non-urgent clerical jobs which can quickly be done at the reception desk
   B. *offer* all office aides an opportunity to volunteer for this assignment
   C. *eliminate* the receptionist assignment
   D. *continue* the arrangement unchanged, because receptionist duties are so important nothing should interfere with them

   1.____

2. A supervisor can MOST correctly assume that an employee is not performing up to his usual standard when the employee does not handle a task as skillfully as

   A. do other employees who have received less training
   B. do similar employees having comparable work experience
   C. he has handled it in several recent instances
   D. the supervisor himself could handle it

   2.____

3. Assume that you receive a suggestion that you direct all the typists in a typing pool to complete the identical quantity of work each day.
   For you to adopt this suggestion would be

   A. *advisable;* it will demonstrate the absence of supervisory favoritism
   B. *advisable;* all employees in a given title should be treated identically
   C. *inadvisable;* a supervisor should decide on work standards without interference from others
   D. *inadvisable;* it ignores variations in specific assignments and individual skills

   3.____

4. A certain supervisor encouraged her subordinates to tell her if they become aware of possible job problems.
   This practice is *good* MAINLY because

   A. early awareness of job problems allows more time for seeking solutions
   B. such expected job problems may not develop
   C. the supervisor will be able to solve the job problem without consulting other people
   D. the supervisor will be able to place responsibility for poor work

   4.____

5. Some supervisors will discuss with a subordinate how he is doing on the job only when indicating his mistakes or faults.
   Which of the following is the MOST likely result of such a practice?

   A. The subordinate will become discouraged and frustrated.
   B. Management will set work standards too low.
   C. The subordinate will be favorably impressed by the supervisor's frankness.
   D. Supervisors will avoid creating any impression of favoritism.

   5.____

6. A supervisor calls in a subordinate he supervises to discuss the subordinate's annual work performance, indicating his work deficiencies and also praising his job strengths. The subordinate nods his head as if in agreement with his supervisor's comments on both his strengths and weaknesses, but actually says nothing, even after the supervisor has completed his comments. At this point, the supervisor should

    A. end the session and assume that the subordinate agrees completely with the evaluation
    B. end the session, since all the subordinate's good and bad points have been identified
    C. ask the subordinate whether the criticism is justified, and, if so, what he, the supervisor, can do to help
    D. thank the subordinate for being so fair–minded in accepting the criticism in a positive manner

7. The successful supervisor is often one who gives serious attention to his subordinates' needs for job satisfaction. A supervisor who believes this statement is MOST likely to

    A. treat all subordinates in an identical manner, irrespective of individual differences
    B. permit each subordinate to perform his work as he wishes, within reasonable limits
    C. give all subordinates both criticism and praise in equal measure
    D. provide each subordinate with as much direct supervision as possible

8. Assume that you are supervising seven subordinates and have been asked by your superior to prepare an especially complex report due today. Its completion will take the rest of the day. You break down the assignment into simple parts and give a different part to each subordinate.
    If you were to explain the work of each subordinate to more than one subordinate, your decision would be

    A. *wise;* this would prevent boredom
    B. *unwise;* valuable time would be lost
    C. *wise;* your subordinates would become well–rounded
    D. *unwise;* your subordinates would lose their competitive spirit

9. Suppose that an office associate whom you supervise has given you a well–researched report on a problem in an area in which he is expert. However, the report lacks solutions or recommendations. You know this office associate to be fearful of stating his opinions. In these circumstances, you should tell him that

    A. you will seek recommendations on the problem from other, even if less expert, office associates
    B. his work is unsatisfactory, in hope of arousing him to greater assertiveness
    C. you need his advise and expertise, to help you reach a decision on the problem
    D. his uncooperative behavior leaves you no choice but to speak to your superior

10. If a supervisor wishes to have the work of his unit completed on schedule, it is usually MOST important to

   A. avoid listening to employees' complaints, thereby discouraging dissatisfaction
   B. perform much of the work himself, since he is generally more capable
   C. observe employees continuously, so they do not slacken their efforts
   D. set up the work carefully, then stay informed as to how it is moving

11. Of the following agencies, the one MOST likely to work out a proposed budget close to its real needs is

   A. a newly-created agency staffed by inexperienced administrators
   B. funded with a considerable amount of money
   C. an existing agency which intends to install new, experimental systems for doing its work
   D. an existing agency which can base its estimate on its experience during the past few years

12. Assume that you are asked to prepare a report on the expected costs and benefits of a proposed new program to be installed in your office. However, you are aware that certain factors are not really measurable in dollars and cents.
As a result, you should

   A. *identify* the non-measurable factors and state why they are important
   B. *assign* a fixed money value to all factors that are not really measurable
   C. *recommend* that programs containing non-measurable factors should be dropped
   D. *assume* that the non-measurable factors are really unimportant

13. Assume that you are asked for your opinion as to the necessity for hiring more employees to perform certain revenue-producing work in your office.
The information that you will MOST likely need in giving an informed opinion is

   A. whether public opinion would favor hiring additional employees
   B. an estimate of the probable additional revenue compared with the additional personnel costs
   C. the total cots of all city operations in contrast to all city revenues
   D. the method by which present employees would be selected for promotion in an expanded operation

14. The *most* reasonable number of subordinates for a supervisor to have is BEST determined by the

   A. average number of subordinates other supervisors have
   B. particular responsibilities given to the supervisor
   C. supervisor's educational background
   D. personalities of the subordinates assigned to the supervisor

15. Most subordinates would need less supervision if they knew what they were supposed to do.
An ESSENTIAL first step in fixing in subordinates' minds exactly what is required of them is to

   A. *require* that supervisors be firm in their supervision of subordinates
   B. *encourage* subordinates to determine their own work standards
   C. *encourage* subordinates to submit suggestions to improve procedures
   D. *standardize* and simplify procedures and logically schedule activities

16. Assume that you have been asked to recommend an appropriate office layout to correspond with a just completed office reorganization.
Which of the following is it MOST advisable to recommend?

   A. *Allocate* most of the space for traffic flow
   B. *Use* the center area only for traffic flow
   C. *situate* close to each other those units whose work is closely related
   D. *Group* in an out–of–the–way corner the supply and file cabinets

17. Although an organization chart will illustrate the formal structure of an agency, it will seldom show a true picture of its actual workings.
Which of the following BEST explains this statement? Organization charts

   A. are often prepared by employees who may exaggerate their own importance
   B. usually show titles and sometimes names rather than the actual contacts and movements between employees
   C. are likely to discourage the use of official titles, and in so doing promote greater freedom in human relations
   D. usually show the informal arrangements and dealings between employees

18. Assume that a supervisor of a large unit has a variety of tasks to perform, and that he gives each of his subordinates just one set of tasks to do. He never rotates subordinates from one set of tasks to another.
Which one of the following is the MOST likely *advantage* to be gained by this practice?

   A. Each subordinate will get to know all the tasks of the unit.
   B. The subordinate will be encouraged to learn all they can about all the unit's tasks.
   C. Each subordinate will become an expert in his particular set of tasks.
   D. The subordinates will improve their opportunities for promotion.

19. Listed below are four steps commonly used in trying to solve administrative problems. These four steps are not listed in the order in which they normally would be taken. If they were listed in the proper order, which step should be taken FIRST?
   I. Choosing the most practical solution to the problem
   II. Analyzing the essential facts about the problem
   III. Correctly identifying the problem
   IV. Following up to see if the solution chosen really works

   The CORRECT answer is:

   A. III   B. I   C. II   D. IV

20. Assume that another agency informally tells you that most of your agency's reports are coming to them with careless errors made by many of your office aides.
    Which one of the following is MOST likely to solve this problem?

    A. *Require* careful review of all outgoing reports by the supervisors of the office aides
    B. *Request* the other agency to make necessary corrections whenever such errors come to their attention
    C. *Ask* the other agency to submit a written report on this situation
    D. *Establish* a small unit to review all reports received from other agencies

21. Assume that you supervise an office which gets two kinds of work. One kind is high-priority and must be done within two days. The other kind of work must be done within two weeks.
    Which one of the following instructions would be MOST reasonable for you to give to your subordinates in this office?

    A. If a backlog builds up during the day, clean the backlog up first, regardless of priority
    B. Spend half the day doing priority work and the other half doing non-priority work
    C. Generally do the priority work first as soon as it is received
    D. Usually do the work in the order in which it comes in, priority or non-priority

22. An experienced supervisor should do advance planning of his subordinates' work assignments and schedules.
    Which one of the following is the BEST reason for such advance planning? It

    A. enables the supervisor to do less supervision
    B. will assure the assignment of varied duties
    C. will make certain a high degree of discipline among subordinates
    D. helps make certain that essential operations are adequately covered

23. Agencies are required to evaluate the performance of their employees.
    Which one of the following would generally be POOR evaluation practice by an agency rater? The rater

    A. regularly observes the performance of the employee being rated
    B. in evaluating the employee, acquaints himself with the employee's job
    C. uses objective standards in evaluating the employee being rated
    D. uses different standards in evaluating men and women

24. A good supervisor should have a clear idea of the quantity and quality of his subordinates' work.
    Which one of the following sources would normally provide a supervisor with the LEAST reliable information about a subordinate's work performance?

    A. Discussion with a friend of the subordinate
    B. Comments by other supervisors who have worked recently with the subordinate
    C. Opinions of fellow workers who work closely with the subordinate on a daily basis
    D. Comparison with work records of others doing similar work during the same period of time

25. In order to handle the ordinary work of an office, a, supervisor sets up standard work procedures.
    The MOST likely benefit of this is to reduce the need to

    A. motivate employees to do superior work
    B. rethink what has to be done every time a routine matter comes up
    C. keep records and write reports
    D. change work procedures as new situations come up

KEY (CORRECT ANSWERS

1. A
2. C
3. D
4. A
5. A

6. C
7. B
8. B
9. C
10. D

11. D
12. A
13. B
14. B
15. D

16. C
17. B
18. C
19. A
20. A

21. C
22. D
23. D
24. A
25. B

EXAMINATION SECTION
TEST 1

DIRECTIONS: Each question or incomplete statement is followed by several suggested answers or completions. Select the one that BEST answers the question or completes the statement. *PRINT THE LETTER OF THE CORRECT ANSWER IN THE SPACE AT THE RIGHT.*

1. In almost every organization, there is a nucleus of highly important functions commonly designated as *management.* Which of the following statements BEST characterizes *management?*

    A. Getting things done through others
    B. The highest level of intelligence in any organization
    C. The process whereby democratic and participative activities are maximized
    D. The *first among equals*

    1._____

2. Strategies in problem-solving are important to anyone aspiring to advancement in the field of administration. Which of the following is BEST classified as the first step in the process of problem-solving?

    A. Collection and organization of data
    B. The formulation of a plan
    C. The definition of the problem
    D. The development of a method and methodology

    2._____

3. One of the objectives of preparing a budget is to

    A. create optimistic goals which each department can attempt to meet
    B. create an overall company goal by combining the budgets of the various departments
    C. be able to compare planned expenditures against actual expenditures
    D. be able to identify accounting errors

    3._____

4. The rise in demand for *systems* personnel in industrial and governmental organizations over the past five years has been extraordinary.
   In which of the following areas would a *systems* specialist assigned to an agency be LEAST likely to be of assistance?

    A. Developing, recommending, and establishing an effective cost and inventory system
    B. Development and maintenance of training manuals
    C. Reviewing existing work procedures and recommending improvements
    D. Development of aptitude tests for new employees

    4._____

5. Management experts have come to the conclusion that the traditional forms of motivation used in industry and government, which emphasize authority over and economic rewards for the employee, are no longer appropriate.
   To which of the following factors do such experts attribute the GREATEST importance in producing this change?

    A. The desire of employees to satisfy material needs has become greater and more complex.

    5._____

B. The desire for social satisfaction has become the most important aspect of the job for the average worker.
C. With greater standardization of work processes, there has been an increase in the willingness of workers to accept discipline.
D. In general, employee organizations have made it more difficult for management to fire an employee.

6. In preparing a budget, it is usually considered advisable to start the initial phases of preparation at the operational level of management.
Of the following, the justification that management experts usually advance as MOST reasonable for this practice is that operating managers, as a consequence of their involvement, will

   A. develop a background in finance or accounting
   B. have an understanding of the organizational structure
   C. tend to feel responsible for carrying out budget objectives
   D. have the ability to see the overall financial picture

7. An administrative officer has been asked by his superior to write a concise, factual report with objective conclusions and recommendations based on facts assembled by other researchers.
Of the following factors, the administrative officer should give LEAST consideration to

   A. the educational level of the person or persons for whom the report is being prepared
   B. the use to be made of the report
   C. the complexity of the problem
   D. his own feelings about the importance of the problem

8. In an agency, upon which of the following is a supervisor's effectiveness MOST likely to depend?
The

   A. degree to which a supervisor allows subordinates to participate in the decision-making process and the setting of objectives
   B. degree to which a supervisor's style meets management's objectives and subordinates' needs
   C. strength and forcefulness of the supervisor in pursuing his objectives
   D. expertise and knowledge the supervisor has about the specific work to be done

9. For authority to be effective, which of the following is the MOST basic requirement?
Authority must be

   A. absolute   B. formalized   C. accepted   D. delegated

10. Management no longer abhors the idea of employees taking daily work breaks, but prefers to schedule such breaks rather than to allot to each employee a standard amount of free time to be taken off during the day as he wishes. Which of the following BEST expresses the reason management theorists give for the practice of scheduling such breaks?

   A. Many jobs fall into natural work units which are scheduled, and the natural time to take a break is at the end of the unit.

B. Taking a scheduled break permits socialization and a feeling of accomplishment.
C. Managers have concluded that scheduling rest periods seems to reduce the incidence of unscheduled ones.
D. Many office workers who really need such breaks are hesitant about taking them unless they are scheduled.

11. The computer represents one of the major developments of modern technology. It is widely used in both scientific and managerial activities because of its many advantages. Which of the following is NOT an advantage gained by management in the use of the computer?
A computer

    A. provides the manager with a greatly enlarged memory so that he can easily be provided with data for decision making
    B. relieves the manager of basic decision-making responsibility, thereby giving him more time for directing and controlling
    C. performs routine, repetitive calculations with greater precision and reliability than employees
    D. provides a capacity for rapid simulations of alternative solutions to problem solving

12. A supervisor of a unit in a division is usually responsible for all of the following EXCEPT

    A. the conduct of subordinates in the achievement of division objectives
    B. maintaining quality standards in the unit
    C. the protection and care of materials and equipment in the unit
    D. performing the most detailed tasks in the unit himself

13. You have been assigned to teach a new employee the functions and procedures of your office.
In your introductory talk, which of the following approaches is PREFERABLE?

    A. Advise the new employee of the employee benefits and services available to him, over and above his salary.
    B. Discuss honestly the negative aspects of departmental procedures and indicate methods available to overcome them.
    C. Give the new employee an understanding of the general purpose of office procedures and functions and of their relevance to departmental objectives.
    D. Give a basic and detailed explanation of the operations of your office, covering all functions and procedures.

14. It is your responsibility to assign work to several clerks under your supervision. One of the clerks indignantly refuses to accept an assignment and asks to be given something else. He has not yet indicated why he does not want the assignment, but is sitting there glaring at you, awaiting your reaction.
Of the following, which is the FIRST action you should take?

    A. Ask the employee into your office in order to reprimand him and tell him emphatically that he must accept the assignment.
    B. Talk to the employee privately in an effort to find the reason for his indignation and refusal, and then base your action upon your findings.

4 (#1)

C. Let the matter drop for a day or two to allow the employee to cool off before you insist that he accept the assignment.
D. Inform the employee quietly and calmly that as his supervisor you have selected him for this assignment and that you fully expect him to accept it.

15. Administrative officers are expected to be able to handle duties delegated to them by their supervisors and to be able, as they advance in status, to delegate tasks to assistants.
When considering whether to delegate tasks to a subordinate, which of the following questions should be LEAST important to an administrative officer?
In the delegated tasks,

   A. how significant are the decisions to be made, and how much consultation will be involved?
   B. to what extent is uniformity and close coordination of activity required?
   C. to what extent must speedy-on-the-spot decisions be made?
   D. to what extent will delegation relieve the administrative officer of his burden of responsibility?

16. A functional forms file is a collection of forms which are grouped by

   A. purpose   B. department   C. title   D. subject

17. All of the following are reasons to consult a records retention schedule except one. Which one is that?
To determine

   A. whether something should be filed
   B. how long something should stay in file
   C. who should be assigned to filing
   D. when something on file should be destroyed

18. Listed below are four of the steps in the process of preparing correspondence for filing. If they were to be put in logical sequence, the SECOND step would be

   A. preparing cross-reference sheets or cards
   B. coding the correspondence using a classification system
   C. sorting the correspondence in the order to be filed
   D. checking for follow-up action required and preparing a follow-up slip

19. New material added to a file folder should USUALLY be inserted

   A. in the order of importance (the most important in front)
   B. in the order of importance (the most important in back)
   C. chronologically (most recent in front)
   D. chronologically (most recent in back)

20. An individual is looking for a name in the white pages of a telephone directory. Which of the following BEST describes the system of filing found there?
A(n)_____ file

   A. alphabetic   B. sequential
   C. locator   D. index

21. The MAIN purpose of a tickler file is to 21.____
    A. help prevent overlooking matters that require future attention
    B. check on adequacy of past performance
    C. pinpoint responsibility for recurring daily tasks
    D. reduce the volume of material kept in general files

22. Which of the following BEST describes the process of reconciling a bank statement? 22.____
    A. Analyzing the nature of the expenditures made by the office during the preceding month
    B. Comparing the statement of the bank with the banking records maintained in the office
    C. Determining the liquidity position by reading the bank statement carefully
    D. Checking the service charges noted on the bank statement

23. From the viewpoint of preserving agency or institutional funds, which of the following is the LEAST acceptable method for making a payment? 23.____
    A check made out to

    A. cash   B. a company
    C. an individual   D. a partnership

24. In general, the CHIEF economy of using multicopy forms is in 24.____
    A. the paper on which the form is printed   B. printing the form
    C. employee time   D. carbon paper

25. Suppose your supervisor has asked you to develop a form to record certain information needed. 25.____
    The FIRST thing you should do is to

    A. determine the type of data that will be recorded repeatedly so that it can be pre-printed
    B. study the relationship of the form to the job to be accomplished so that the form can be planned
    C. determine the information that will be recorded in the same place on each copy of the form so that it can be used as a check
    D. find out who will be responsible for supplying the information so that space can be provided for their signatures

26. An administrative officer in charge of a small fund for buying office supplies has just written a check to Charles Laird, a supplier, and has sent the check by messenger to him. A half-hour later, the messenger telephones the administrative officer. He has lost the check. 26.____
    Which of the following is the MOST important action for the administrative officer to take under these circumstances?

    A. Ask the messenger to return and write a report describing the loss of the check.
    B. Make a note on the performance record of the messenger who lost the check.
    C. Take the necessary steps to have payment stopped on the check.
    D. Refrain from doing anyting since the check may be found shortly.

27. A petty cash fund is set up PRIMARILY to

   A. take care of small investments that must be made from time to time
   B. take care of small expenses that arise from time to time
   C. provide a fund to be used as the office wants to use it with little need to maintain records
   D. take care of expenses that develop during emergencies, such as machine breakdowns and fires

28. Of the following, which is usually the MOST important guideline in writing business letters?
A letter should be

   A. neat
   B. written in a formalized style
   C. written in clear language intelligible to the reader
   D. written in the past tense

29. Suppose you are asked to edit a policy statement. You note that personal pronouns like *you, we,* and *I* are used freely.
Which of the following statements BEST applies to this use of personal pronouns?
It

   A. is proper usage because written business language should not be different from carefully spoken business language
   B. requires correction because it is ungrammatical
   C. is proper because it is clearer and has a warmer tone
   D. requires correction because policies should be expressed in an impersonal manner

30. Good business letters are coherent.
To be coherent means to

   A. keep only one unifying idea in the message
   B. present the total message
   C. use simple, direct words for the message
   D. tie together the various ideas in the message

31. Proper division of a letter into paragraphs requires that the writer of business letters should, as much as possible, be sure that

   A. each paragraph is short
   B. each paragraph develops discussion of just one topic
   C. each paragraph repeats the theme of the total message
   D. there are at least two paragraphs for every message

32. An editor is given a letter with this initial paragraph:
We have received your letter, which we read with interest, and we are happy to respond to your question. In fact, we talked with several people in our office to get ideas to send to you.
Which of the following is it MOST reasonable for the editor to conclude?
The paragraph is

A. concise
B. communicating something of value
C. unnecessary
D. coherent

33. As soon as you pick up the phone, a very angry caller begins immediately to complain about city agencies and *red tape*. He says that he has been shifted to two or three different offices. It turns out that he is seeking information which is not immediately available to you. You believe you know, however, where it can be found. Which of the following actions is the BEST one for you to take?

    A. To eliminate all confusion, suggest that the caller write the mayor stating explicitly what he wants.
    B. Apologize by telling the caller how busy city agencies now are, but also tell him directly that you do not have the information he needs.
    C. Ask for the caller's telephone number and assure him you will call back after you have checked further.
    D. Give the caller the name and telephone number of the person who might be able to help, but explain that you are not positive he will get results.

33.____

34. Suppose that one of your duties is to dictate responses to routine requests from the public for information. A letter writer asks for information which, as expressed in a one-sentence, explicit agency rule, cannot be given out to the public.
Of the following ways of answering the letter, which is the MOST efficient?

    A. Quote verbatim that section of the agency rules which prohibits giving this information to the public.
    B. Without quoting the rule, explain why you cannot accede to the request and suggest alternative sources.
    C. Describe how carefully the request was considered before classifying it as subject to the rule forbidding the issuance of such information.
    D. Acknowledge receipt of the letter and advise that the requested information is not released to the public.

34.____

35. Suppose you assist in supervising a staff which has rather high morale, and your own supervisor asks you to poll the staff to find out who will be able to work overtime this particular evening to help complete emergency work.
Which of the following approaches would be MOST likely to win their cooperation while maintaining their morale?

    A. Tell them that the better assignments will be given only to those who work overtime.
    B. Tell them that occasional overtime is a job requirement.
    C. Assure them they'll be doing you a personal favor.
    D. Let them know clearly why the overtime is needed.

35.____

36. Suppose that you have been asked to write and to prepare for reproduction new departmental vacation leave regulations.
After you have written the new regulations, all of which fit on one page, which one of the following would be the BEST method of reproducing 1000 copies?

    A. An outside private printer, because you can best maintain confidentiality using this technique
    B. Xeroxing, because the copies will have the best possible appearance

36.____

C. Typing copies, because you will be certain that there are the fewest possible errors
D. Including it in the next company newsletter

37. Administration is the center, but not necessarily the source, of all ideas for procedural improvement.
The MOST significant implication that this principle bears for the administrative officer is that

   A. before procedural improvements are introduced, they should be approved by a majority of the staff
   B. it is the unique function of the administrative officer to derive and introduce procedural improvements
   C. the administrative officer should derive ideas and suggestions for procedural improvement from all possible sources, introducing any that promise to be effective
   D. the administrative officer should view employee grievances as the chief source of procedural improvements

38. Your bureau is assigned an important task.
Of the following, the function that you, as an administrative officer, can LEAST reasonably be expected to perform under these circumstances is

   A. division of the large job into individual tasks
   B. establishment of *production lines* within the bureau
   C. performance personally of a substantial share of all the work
   D. check-up to see that the work has been well done

39. Suppose that you have broken a complex job into its smaller components before making assignments to the employees under your jurisdiction.
Of the following, the LEAST advisable procedure to follow from that point is to

   A. give each employee a picture of the importance of his work for the success of the total job
   B. establish a definite line of work flow and responsibility
   C. post a written memorandum of the best method for performing each job
   D. teach a number of alternative methods for doing each job

40. As an administrative officer, you are requested to draw up an organization chart of the whole department.
Of the following, the MOST important characteristic of such a chart is that it will

   A. include all peculiarities and details of the organization which distinguish it from any other
   B. be a schematic representation of purely administrative functions within the department
   C. present a modification of the actual departmental organization in the light of principles of scientific management
   D. present an accurate picture of the lines of authority and responsibility

KEY (CORRECT ANSWERS)

1.	A	11.	B	21.	A	31.	B
2.	C	12.	D	22.	B	32.	C
3.	C	13.	C	23.	A	33.	C
4.	D	14.	B	24.	C	34.	A
5.	D	15.	D	25.	B	35.	D
6.	C	16.	A	26.	C	36.	B
7.	D	17.	C	27.	B	37.	C
8.	B	18.	A	28.	C	38.	C
9.	C	19.	C	29.	D	39.	D
10.	C	20.	A	30.	D	40.	D

TEST 2

DIRECTIONS: Each question or incomplete statement is followed by several suggested answers or completions. Select the one that BEST answers the question or completes the statement. *PRINT THE LETTER OF THE CORRECT ANSWER IN THE SPACE AT THE RIGHT.*

Questions 1-10.

DIRECTIONS: In each of Questions 1 through 10, a pair of related words written in capital letters is followed by four other pairs of words. For each question, select the pair of words which MOST closely expresses a relationship similar to that of the pair in capital letters.

SAMPLE QUESTION:

BOAT - DOCK
- A. airplane - hangar
- B. rain - snow
- C. cloth - cotton
- D. hunger - food

Choice A is the answer to this sample question since, of the choices given, the relationship between airplane and hangar is most similar to the relationship between boat and dock.

1. AUTOMOBILE - FACTORY 1.___
   - A. tea - lemon
   - B. wheel - engine
   - C. pot - flower
   - D. paper - mill

2. GIRDER - BRIDGE 2.___
   - A. petal - flower
   - B. street - sidewalk
   - C. meat - vegetable
   - D. sun - storm

3. RADIUS - CIRCLE 3.___
   - A. brick - building
   - B. tie - tracks
   - C. spoke - wheel
   - D. axle - tire

4. DISEASE - RESEARCH 4.___
   - A. death - poverty
   - B. speech - audience
   - C. problem - conference
   - D. invalid - justice

5. CONCLUSION - INTRODUCTION 5.___
   - A. commencement - beginning
   - B. housing - motor
   - C. caboose - engine
   - D. train - cabin

6. SOCIETY - LAW 6.___
   - A. baseball - rules
   - B. jury - law
   - C. cell - prisoner
   - D. sentence - jury

7. PLAN - ACCOMPLISHMENT 7.___
   - A. deed - fact
   - B. method - success
   - C. graph - chart
   - D. rules - manual

8. ORDER - GOVERNMENT 8._____

   A. chaos - administration
   B. confusion - pandemonium
   C. rule - stability
   D. despair - hope

9. TYRANNY - FREEDOM 9._____

   A. despot - mob
   B. wealth - poverty
   C. nobility - commoners
   D. dictatorship - democracy

10. FAX - LETTER 10._____

    A. hare - tortoise
    B. lie - truth
    C. number - word
    D. report - research

Questions 11-16.

DIRECTIONS: Answer Questions 11 through 16 SOLELY on the basis of the information given in the passage below.

Inherent in all organized endeavors is the need to resolve the individual differences involved in conflict. Conflict may be either a positive or negative factor, since it may lead to creativity, innovation, and progress, on the one hand, or it may result, on the other hand, in a deterioration or even destruction of the organization. Thus, some forms of conflict are desirable, whereas others are undesirable and ethically wrong.

There are three management strategies which deal with interpersonal conflict. In the "divide-and-rule strategy", management attempts to maintain control by limiting the conflict to those directly involved and preventing their disagreement from spreading to the larger group. The "suppression-of-differences strategy" entails ignoring conflicts or pretending they are irrelevant. In the "working-through-differences strategy", management actively attempts to solve or resolve intergroup or interpersonal conflicts. Of the three strategies, only the last directly attacks and has the potential for eliminating the causes of conflict. An essential part of this strategy, however, is its employment by a committed and relatively mature management team.

11. According to the above passage, the *divide-and-rule strategy* for dealing with conflict is the attempt to 11._____

    A. involve other people in the conflict
    B. restrict the conflict to those participating in it
    C. divide the conflict into positive and negative factors
    D. divide the conflict into a number of smaller ones

12. The word *conflict* is used in relation to both positive and negative factors in this passage. Which one of the following words is MOST likely to describe the activity which the word *conflict*, in the sense of the passage, implies? 12._____

    A. Competition
    B. Cooperation
    C. Confusion
    D. Aggression

13. According to the above passage, which one of the following characteristics is shared by both the *suppression-of-differences strategy* and the *divide-and-rule strategy*? 13._____

    A. Pretending that conflicts are irrelevant
    B. Preventing conflicts from spreading to the group situation

C. Failure to directly attack the causes of conflict
D. Actively attempting to resolve interpersonal conflict

14. According to the above passage, the successful resolution of interpersonal conflict requires 14.___

    A. allowing the group to mediate conflicts between two individuals
    B. division of the conflict into positive and negative factors
    C. involvement of a committed, mature management team
    D. ignoring minor conflicts until they threaten the organization

15. Which can be MOST reasonably inferred from the above passage? 15.___
    A conflict between two individuals is LEAST likely to continue when management uses

    A. the *working-through-differences strategy*
    B. the *suppression-of-differences strategy*
    C. the *divide-and-rule strategy*
    D. a combination of all three strategies

16. According to the above passage, a desirable result of conflict in an organization is when conflict 16.___

    A. exposes production problems in the organization
    B. can be easily ignored by management
    C. results in advancement of more efficient managers
    D. leads to development of new methods

Questions 17-23.

DIRECTIONS: Answer Questions 17 through 23 SOLELY on the basis of the information given in the passage below.

Modern management places great emphasis on the concept of communication. The communication process consists of the steps through which an idea or concept passes from its inception by one person, the sender, until it is acted upon by another person, the receiver. Through an understanding of these steps and some of the possible barriers that may occur, more effective communication may be achieved. The first step in the communication process is ideation by the sender. This is the formation of the intended content of the message he wants to transmit. In the next step, encoding, the sender organizes his ideas into a series of symbols designed to communicate his message to his intended receiver. He selects suitable words or phrases that can be understood by the receiver, and he also selects the appropriate media to be used-for example, memorandum, conference, etc. The third step is transmission of the encoded message through selected channels in the organizational structure. In the fourth step, the receiver enters the process by tuning in to receive the message. If the receiver does not function, however, the message is lost. For example, if the message is oral, the receiver must be a good listener. The fifth step is decoding of the message by the receiver, as for example, by changing words into ideas. At this step, the decoded message may not be the same idea that the sender originally encoded because the sender and receiver have different perceptions regarding the meaning of certain words.

Finally, the receiver acts or responds. He may file the information, ask for more information, or take other action. There can be no assurance, however, that communication has taken place unless there is some type of feedback to the sender in the form of an acknowledgement that the message was received.

17. According to the above passage, *ideation* is the process by which the 17.____
	A. sender develops the intended content of the message
	B. sender organizes his ideas into a series of symbols
	C. receiver tunes in to receive the message
	D. receiver decodes the message

18. In the last sentence of the passage, the word *feedback* refers to the process by which the sender is assured that the 18.____
	A. receiver filed the information
	B. receiver's perception is the same as his own
	C. message was received
	D. message was properly interpreted

19. Which one of the following BEST shows the order of the steps in the communication process as described in the passage? 19.____

	A. 1- ideation 2- encoding
	   3- decoding 4- transmission
	   5- receiving 6- action
	   7- feedback to the sender

	B. 1- ideation 2- encoding
	   3- transmission 4- decoding
	   5- receiving 6- action
	   7- feedback to the sender

	C. 1- ideation 2- decoding
	   3- transmission 4- receiving
	   5- encoding 6- action
	   7- feedback to the sender

	D. 1- ideation 2- encoding
	   3- transmission 4- receiving
	   5- decoding 6- action
	   7- feedback to the sender

20. Which one of the following BEST expresses the main theme of the passage? 20.____
	A. Different individuals have the same perceptions regarding the meaning of words.
	B. An understanding of the steps in the communication process may achieve better communication.
	C. Receivers play a passive role in the communication process.
	D. Senders should not communicate with receivers who transmit feedback.

21. The above passage implies that a receiver does NOT function properly when he 21.____
	A. transmits feedback B. files the information
	C. is a poor listener D. asks for more information

22. Which of the following, according to the above passage, is included in the SECOND step of the communication process?

   A. Selecting the appropriate media to be used in transmission
   B. Formulation of the intended content of the message
   C. Using appropriate media to respond to the receiver's feedback
   D. Transmitting the message through selected channels in the organization

23. The above passage implies that the *decoding process* is MOST NEARLY the reverse of the _____ process.

   A. transmission   B. receiving
   C. feedback   D. encoding

Questions 24-27.

DIRECTIONS: Answer Questions 24 through 27 SOLELY on the basis of the information given in the paragraph below.

A personnel researcher has at his disposal various approaches for obtaining information, analyzing it, and arriving at conclusions that have value in predicting and affecting the behavior of people at work. The type of method to be used depends on such factors as the nature of the research problem, the available data, and the attitudes of those people being studied to the various kinds of approaches. While the experimental approach, with its use of control groups, is the most refined type of study, there are others that are often found useful in personnel research. Surveys, in which the researcher obtains facts on a problem from a variety of sources, are employed in research on wages, fringe benefits, and labor relations. Historical studies are used to trace the development of problems in order to understand them better and to isolate possible causative factors. Case studies are generally developed to explore all the details of a particular problem that is representative of other similar problems. A researcher chooses the most appropriate form of study for the problem he is investigating. He should recognize, however, that the experimental method, commonly referred to as the scientific method, if used validly and reliably, gives the most conclusive results.

24. The above statement discusses several approaches used to obtain information on particular problems.
    Which of the following may be MOST reasonably concluded from the paragraph? A(n)

   A. historical study cannot determine causative factors
   B. survey is often used in research on fringe benefits
   C. case study is usually used to explore a problem that is unique and unrelated to other problems
   D. experimental study is used when the scientific approach to a problem fails

25. According to the above paragraph, all of the following are factors that may determine the type of approach a researcher uses EXCEPT

   A. the attitudes of people toward being used in control groups
   B. the number of available sources
   C. his desire to isolate possible causative factors
   D. the degree of accuracy he requires

26. The words *scientific method*, used in the last sentence of the paragraph, refer to a type of study which, according to the paragraph, 26._____

    A. uses a variety of sources
    B. traces the development of problems
    C. uses control groups
    D. analyzes the details of a representative problem

27. Which of the following can be MOST reasonably concluded from the above paragraph? In obtaining and analyzing information on a particular problem, a researcher employs the method which is the 27._____

    A. most accurate
    B. most suitable
    C. least expensive
    D. least time-consuming

Questions 28-31.

DIRECTIONS: The graph below indicates at 5-year intervals the number of citations issued for various offenses from the year 1990 to the year 2010. Answer Questions 28 through 31 according to the information given in this graph.

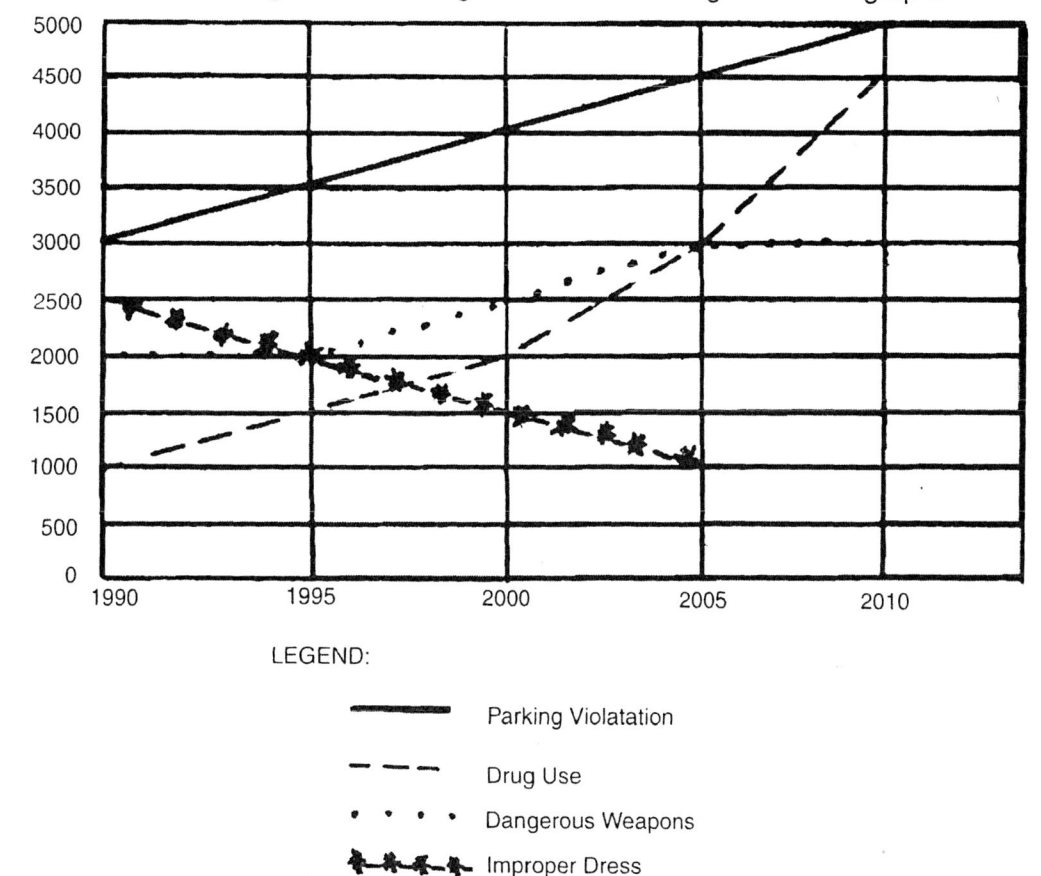

LEGEND:

— Parking Violatation
— — — Drug Use
• • • • Dangerous Weapons
🌸🌸🌸🌸 Improper Dress

28. Over the 20-year period, which offense shows an AVERAGE rate of increase of more than 150 citations per year? 28._____

    A. Parking Violations
    B. Dangerous Weapons
    C. Drug Use
    D. None of the above

29. Over the 20-year period, which offense shows a CONSTANT rate of increase or decrease?   29.___

    A. Parking Violations   B. Drug Use
    C. Dangerous Weapons   D. Improper Dress

30. Which offense shows a TOTAL INCREASE OR DECREASE of 50% for the full 20-year period?   30.___

    A. Parking Violations   B. Drug Use
    C. Dangerous Weapons   D. Improper Dress

31. The percentage increase in total citations issued from 1995 to 2000 is MOST NEARLY   31.___

    A. 7%   B. 11%   C. 21%   D. 41%

Questions 32-35.

DIRECTIONS: The chart below shows the annual average number of administrative actions completed for the four divisions of a bureau. Assume that the figures remain stable from year to year.

Answer Questions 32 through 35 SOLELY on the basis of information given in the chart.

Administrative Actions	DIVISIONS				Totals
	W	X	Y	Z	
Telephone Inquiries Answered	8,000	6,800	7,500	4,800	27,100
Interviews Conducted	500	630	550	500	2,180
Applications Processed	15,000	18,000	14,500	9,500	57,000
Letters Typed	2,500	4,400	4,350	3,250	14,500
Reports Completed	200	250	100	50	600
Totals	26,200	30,080	27,000	18,100	101,380

32. In which division is the number of Applications Processed the GREATEST percentage of the total Administrative Actions for that division?   32.___

    A. W   B. X   C. Y   D. Z

33. The bureau chief is considering a plan that would consolidate the typing of letters in a separate unit. This unit would be responsible for the typing of letters for all divisions in which the number of letters typed exceeds 15% of the total number of Administrative Actions. Under this plan, which of the following divisions would CONTINUE to type its own letters?   33.___

    A. W and X   B. W, X, and Y
    C. X and Y   D. X and Z

34. The setting up of a central information service that would be capable of answering 25% of the whole bureau's telephone inquiries is under consideration. Under such a plan, the divisions would gain for other activities that time previously spent on telephone inquiries. Approximately how much total time would such a service gain for all four divisions if it requires 5 minutes to answer the average telephone inquiry? _____ hours.

 A. 500   B. 515   C. 565   D. 585

35. Assume that the rate of production shown in the table can be projected as accurate for the coming year and that monthly output is constant for each type of administrative action within a division. Division Y is scheduled to work exclusively on a 4-month long special project during that year. During the period of the project, Division Y's regular workload will be divided evenly among the remaining divisions.
Using the figures in the table, what would be MOST NEARLY the percentage increase in the total Administrative Actions completed by Division Z for the year?

 A. 8%   B. 16%   C. 25%   D. 50%

36. You have conducted a traffic survey at 10 two-lane bridges and find the traffic between 4:30 and 5:30 P.M. averages 665 cars per bridge that hour. You can't find the tabulation sheet for Bridge #7, but you know that 6066 cars were counted at the other 9 bridges. Determine from this how many must have been counted at Bridge #7.

 A. 584   B. 674   C. 665   D. 607

37. You pay temporary help $11.20 per hour and regular employees $12.00 per hour. Your workload is temporarily heavy, so you need 20 hours of extra regular employees' time to catch up. If you do this on overtime, you must pay time-and-a-half. If you use temporary help, it takes 25% more time to do the job.
What is the difference in cost between the two alternatives?

 A. $20 more for temporary   B. $40 more for temporary
 C. $80 more for regular   D. $136 more for regular

38. An experienced clerk can process the mailing of annual forms in 9 days. A new clerk takes 14 days to process them.
If they work together, how many days MOST NEARLY will it take to do the processing?

 A. $4\frac{1}{2}$ B. $5\frac{1}{2}$ C. $6\frac{1}{2}$ D. 7

39. A certain administrative aide is usually able to successfully handle 27% of all telephone inquiries without assistance. In a particular month, he receives 1200 inquiries and handles 340 of them successfully on his own. How many more inquiries has he handled successfully in that month than would have been expected of him based on his usual rate?

 A. 10   B. 16   C. 24   D. 44

40. Suppose that on a scaled drawing of an office building floor, 1/2 inch represents three feet of actual floor dimensions.
A floor which is, in fact, 75 feet wide and 132 feet long has which of the following dimensions on this scaled drawing? _____ inches wide and _____ inches long.

 A. 9.5; 20.5   B. 12.5; 22
 C. 17; 32   D. 25; 44

9(#2)

41. In a division of clerks and stenographers, 15 people are currently employed, 20% of whom are stenographers.
    If management plans are to maintain the current number of stenographers, but to increase the clerical staff to the point where 12% of the total staff are stenographers, what is the MAXIMUM number of additional clerks that should be hired to meet these plans?

    A. 3   B. 8   C. 10   D. 12

41.___

42. Suppose that a certain agency had a 2005 budget of $1,100,500. The 2006 budget was 7% higher than that of 2005, and the 2007 budget was 8% higher than that of 2006. Of the following, which one is MOST NEARLY that agency's budget for 2007?

    A. $1,117,624   B. $1,261,737
    C. $1,265,575   D. $1,271,738

42.___

Question's 43-50.

DIRECTIONS: Your office keeps a file card record of the work assignments for all the employees in a certain bureau. On each card is the employee's name, a work assignment code number, and the date of this assignment. In this filing system, the employee's name is filed alphabetically, the work assignment code is filed numerically, and the date of the assignment is filed chronologically (earliest date first).

Each of Questions 43 through 50 represents five cards to be filed, numbered (1) through (5) shown in Column I. Each card is made up of the employee's name, a work assignment code number shown in parentheses, and the date of this assignment. The cards are to be filed according to the following rules:

First: File in alphabetical order;
Second: When two or more cards have the same employee's name, file according to the work assignment number, beginning with the lowest number.
Third: When two or more cards have the same employee's name and same assignment number, file according to the assignment date beginning with earliest date.

Column II shows the cards arranged in four different orders. Pick the answer (A, B, C, or D) in Column II which shows the cards arranged correctly according to the above filing rules.

SAMPLE QUESTION:

Column I				Column II				
(1) Cluney	(486503)	6/17/07	A.	2,	3,	4,	1,	5
(2) Roster	(246611)	5/10/06	B.	2,	5,	1,	3,	4
(3) Altool	(711433)	10/15/07	C.	3,	2,	1,	4,	5
(4) Cluney	(527610)	12/18/06	D.	3,	5,	1,	4,	2
(5) Cluney	(486500)	4/8/07						

The correct way to file the cards is:
(3) Altool   (711433)   10/15/07
(5) Cluney   (486500)   4/8/07
(1) Cluney   (486503)   6/17/07
(4) Cluney   (527610)   12/18/06
(2) Roster   (246611)   5/10/06

The correct filing order is shown by the numbers in front of each name (3, 5, 1, 4, 2). The answer to the sample question is the letter in Column II in front of the numbers 3, 5, 1, 4, 2. This answer is D.

43.

		Column I			Column II
(1)	Prichard	(013469)	4/6/06	A.	5, 4, 3, 2, 1
(2)	Parks	(678941)	2/7/06	B.	1, 2, 5, 3, 4
(3)	Williams	(551467)	3/6/05	C.	2, 1, 5, 3, 4
(4)	Wilson	(551466)	8/9/02	D.	1, 5, 4, 3, 2
(5)	Stanhope	(300014)	8/9/02		

43._____

44.

(1)	Ridgeway	(623809)	8/11/06	A.	5, 1, 3, 4, 2
(2)	Travers	(305439)	4/5/02	B.	5, 1, 3, 2, 4
(3)	Tayler	(818134)	7/5/03	C.	1, 5, 3, 2, 4
(4)	Travers	(305349)	5/6/05	D.	1, 5, 4, 2, 3
(5)	Ridgeway	(623089)	10/9/06		

44._____

45.

(1)	Jaffe	(384737)	2/19/06	A.	3, 5, 2, 4, 1
(2)	Inez	(859176)	8/8/07	B.	3, 5, 2, 1, 4
(3)	Ingrahm	(946460)	8/6/04	C.	2, 3, 5, 1, 4
(4)	Karp	(256146)	5/5/05	D.	2, 3, 5, 4, 1
(5)	Ingrahm	(946460)	6/4/05		

45._____

46.

(1)	Marrano	(369421)	7/24/04	A.	1, 5, 3, 4, 2
(2)	Marks	(652910)	2/23/06	B.	3, 5, 4, 2, 1
(3)	Netto	(556772)	3/10/07	C.	2, 4, 1, 5, 3
(4)	Marks	(652901)	2/17/07	D.	4, 2, 1, 5, 3
(5)	Netto	(556772)	6/17/05		

46._____

47.

(1)	Abernathy	(712467)	6/23/05	A.	5, 3, 1, 2, 4
(2)	Acevedo	(680262)	6/23/03	B.	5, 4, 2, 3, 1
(3)	Aaron	(967647)	1/17/04	C.	1, 3, 5, 2, 4
(4)	Acevedo	(680622)	5/14/02	D.	2, 4, 1, 5, 3
(5)	Aaron	(967647)	4/1/00		

47._____

48.

(1)	Simon	(645219)	8/19/05	A.	4, 1, 2, 5, 3
(2)	Simon	(645219)	9/2/03	B.	4, 5, 2, 1, 3
(3)	Simons	(645218)	7/7/05	C.	3, 5, 2, 1, 4
(4)	Simms	(646439)	10/12/06	D.	5, 1, 2, 3, 4
(5)	Simon	(645219)	10/16/02		

48._____

49.

(1)	Rappaport	(312230)	6/11/06	A.	4, 3, 1, 2, 5
(2)	Rascio	(777510)	2/9/05	B.	4, 3, 1, 5, 2
(3)	Rappaport	(312230)	7/3/02	C.	3, 4, 1, 5, 2
(4)	Rapaport	(312330)	9/6/05	D.	5, 2, 4, 3, 1
(5)	Rascio	(777501)	7/7/05		

49._____

50.
(1)	Johnson	(843250)	6/8/02	A.	1,	3,	2,	4,	5
(2)	Johnson	(843205)	4/3/05	B.	1,	3,	2,	5,	4
(3)	Johnson	(843205)	8/6/02	C.	3,	2,	1,	4,	5
(4)	Johnson	(843602)	3/8/06	D.	3,	2,	1,	5,	4
(5)	Johnson	(843602)	8/3/05						

50._____

KEY (CORRECT ANSWERS)

1.	D	11.	B	21.	C	31.	B	41.	C
2.	A	12.	A	22.	A	32.	B	42.	D
3.	C	13.	C	23.	D	33.	A	43.	C
4.	C	14.	C	24.	B	34.	C	44.	A
5.	C	15.	A	25.	D	35.	B	45.	C
6.	A	16.	D	26.	C	36.	A	46.	D
7.	B	17.	A	27.	B	37.	C	47.	A
8.	C	18.	C	28.	C	38.	B	48.	B
9.	D	19.	D	29.	A	39.	B	49.	B
10.	A	20.	B	30.	C	40.	B	50.	D

LOGICAL REASONING
EVALUATING CONCLUSIONS IN LIGHT OF KNOWN FACTS

EXAMINATION SECTION
TEST 1

COMMENTARY

This section is designed to provide practice questions in evaluating conclusions when you are given specific data to work with.

We suggest you do the questions three at a time, consulting the answer key and then the solution section for any questions you may have missed. It's a good idea to try the questions again a week before the exam.

In the validity of conclusion type of question, you are first given a reading passage which describes a particular situation. The passage may be on any topic, as it is not your knowledge of the topic that is being tested, but your reasoning abilities. The passage is likely to detail several proposed courses of action and factors affecting these proposals. The reading passage is followed by a conclusion based on the facts in the passage, or a description of a decision taken regarding the situation. The conclusion is followed by a number of statements which have a possible connection to the conclusion. For each statement, you are to determine whether:

- A. The statement proves the conclusion.
- B. The statement supports the conclusion but does not prove it.
- C. The statement disproves the conclusion.
- D. The statement weakens the conclusion but does not disprove it.
- E. The statement has no relevance to the conclusion.

Remember that the conclusion after the passage is to be accepted as the outcome of what actually happened, and that you are being asked to evaluate the impact each statement would have had on the conclusion.

Questions 1-8 are based on the following paragraph.

In May of 1993, Mr. Bryan inherited a clothing store on Main Street in a small New England town. The store has specialized in selling quality men's and women's clothing since 1885. Business has been stable throughout the years, neither increasing nor decreasing. He has an opportunity to buy two adjacent stores which would enable him to add a wider range and style of clothing. In order to do this, he would have to borrow a substantial amount of money. He also risks losing the goodwill of his present clientele.

CONCLUSION: On November 7, 1993, Mr. Bryan tells the owner of the two adjacent stores that he has decided not to purchase them. He feels that it would be best to simply maintain his present marketing position, as there would not be enough new business to support an expansion.

- A. The statement proves the conclusion.
- B. The statement supports the conclusion but does not prove it.
- C. The statement disproves the conclusion.
- D. The statement weakens the conclusion.
- E. The statement is irrelevant to the conclusion.

1. A large new branch of the county's community college holds its first classes in September of 1993. 1.___

2. The town's largest factory shuts down with no indication that it will reopen. 2.___

3. The 1990 United States Census showed that the number of children per household dropped from 2.4 to 2.1 since the 1980 census. 3.___

4. Mr. Bryan's brother tells him of a new clothing boutique specializing in casual women's clothing which is opening soon. 4.___

5. Mr. Bryan's sister buys her baby several items for Christmas at Mr. Bryan's store. 5.___

6. Mrs. McIntyre, the President of the Town Council, brings Mr. Bryan a home-baked pumpkin pie in honor of his store's 100th anniversary. They discuss the changes that have taken place in the town, and she comments on how his store has maintained the same look and feel over the years. 6.___

7. In October of 1993, Mr. Bryan's aunt lends him $50,000. 7.___

8. The Town Council has just announced that the town is eligible for funding from a federal project designed to encourage the location of new businesses in the central districts of cities and towns. 8.___

Questions 9-18 are based on the following paragraph.

A proposal has been put before the legislative body of a small European country to require air bags in all automobiles manufactured for domestic use in that country after 1999. The air bag, made of nylon or plastic, is designed to inflate automatically within a car at the impact of a collision, thus protecting front-seat occupants from being thrown forward. There has been much support of the measure from consumer groups, the insurance industry, key legislators, and the general public. The country's automobile manufacturers, who contend the new crash equipment would add up to $1,000 to car prices and provide no more protection than existing seat belts, are against the proposed legislation.

CONCLUSION: On April 21, 1994, the legislature passed legislation requiring air bags in all automobiles manufactured for domestic use in that country after 1999.

  A. The statement proves the conclusion.
  B. The statement supports the conclusion but does not prove it.
  C. The statement disproves the conclusion.
  D. The statement weakens the conclusion.
  E. The statement is irrelevant to the conclusion.

9. A study has shown that 59% of car occupants do not use seat belts. 9.___

10. The country's Department of Transportation has estimated that the crash protection equipment would save up to 5,900 lives each year. 10.___

11. On April 27, 1993, Augusta Raneoni was named head of an advisory committee to gather and analyze data on the costs, benefits, and feasibility of the proposed legislation on air bags in automobiles. 11.___

12. Consumer groups and the insurance industry accuse the legislature of rejecting passage of the regulation for political reasons. 12._____

13. A study by the Committee on Imports and Exports projected that the sales of imported cars would rise dramatically in 1999 because imported cars do not have to include air bags, and can be sold more cheaply. 13._____

14. Research has shown that air bags, if produced on a large scale, would cost about $200 apiece, and would provide more reliable protection than any other type of seat belt. 14._____

15. Auto sales in 1991 have increased 3% over the previous year. 15._____

16. A Department of Transportation report in July of 2000 credits a drop in automobile deaths of 4,100 to the use of air bags. 16._____

17. In June of 1994, the lobbyist of the largest insurance company receives a bonus for her work on the passage of the air bag legislation. 17._____

18. In 2000, the stock in crash protection equipment has risen three-fold over the previous year. 18._____

Questions 19-25 are based on the following paragraph.

On a national television talk show, Joan Rivera, a famous comedienne, has recently insulted the physical appearances of a famous actress and the dead wife of an ex-President. There has been a flurry of controversy over her comments, and much discussion of the incident has appeared in the press. Most of the comments have been negative. It appears that this time she might have gone too far. There have been cancellations of two of her five scheduled performances in the two weeks since the show was televised, and Joan's been receiving a lot of negative mail. Because of the controversy, she has an interview with a national news magazine at the end of the week, and her press agent is strongly urging her to apologize publicly. She feels strongly that her comments were no worse than any other she has ever made, and that the whole incident will *blow over* soon. She respects her press agent's judgment, however, as his assessment of public sentiment tends to be very accurate.

CONCLUSION: Joan does not apologize publicly, and during the interview she challenges the actress to a weight-losing contest. For every pound the actress loses, Joan says she will donate $1 to the Cellulite Prevention League.

  A. The statement proves the conclusion.
  B. The statement supports the conclusion but does not prove it.
  C. The statement disproves the conclusion.
  D. The statement weakens the conclusion.
  E. The statement is irrelevant to the conclusion.

19. Joan's mother, who she is very fond of, is very upset about Joan's comments. 19._____

20. Six months after the interview, Joan's income has doubled. 20._____

21. Joan's agent is pleased with the way Joan handles the interview. 21.___

22. Joan's sister has been appointed Treasurer of the Cellulite Prevention League. In her report, she states that Joan's $12 contribution is the only amount that has been donated to the League in its first six months. 22.___

23. The magazine receives many letters commending Joan for the courage it took for her to apologize publicly in the interview. 23.___

24. Immediately after the interview appears, another one of Joan's performances is cancelled. 24.___

25. Due to a printers strike, the article was not published until the following week. 25.___

Questions 26-30 are based on the following paragraph.

The law-making body of Country X must decide what to do about the issue of videotaping television shows for home use. There is currently no law against taping shows directly from the TV as long as the videotapes are not used for commercial purposes. The increasing popularity of pay TV and satellite systems, combined with the increasing number of homes that own video-cassette recorders, has caused a great deal of concern in some segments of the entertainment industry. Companies that own the rights to films, popular television shows, and sporting events feel that their copyright privileges are being violated, and they are seeking compensation or the banning of TV home videotaping. Legislation has been introduced to make it illegal to videotape television programs for home use. Separate proposed legislation is also pending that would continue to allow videotaping of TV shows for home use, but would place a tax of 10% on each videocassette that is purchased for home use. The income from that tax would then be proportionately distributed as royalties to those owning the rights to programs being aired. A weighted point system coupled with the averaging of several national viewing rating systems would be used to determine the royalties. There is a great deal of lobbying being done for both bills, as the manufacturers of videocassette recorders and videocassettes are against the passage of the bills.

CONCLUSION: The legislature of Country X rejects both bills by a wide margin.

- A. The statement proves the conclusion.
- B. The statement supports the conclusion but does not prove it.
- C. The statement disproves the conclusion.
- D. The statement weakens the conclusion.
- E. The statement is irrelevant to the conclusion.

26. Country X's Department of Taxation hires 500 new employees to handle the increased paperwork created by the new tax on videocassettes. 26.___

27. A study conducted by the country's most prestigious accounting firm shows that the cost of implementing the proposed new videocassette tax would be greater than the income expected from it. 27.___

28. It is estimated that 80% of all those working in the entertainment industry, excluding per-   28.____
formers, own video-cassette recorders.

29. The head of Country X's law enforcement agency states that legislation banning the   29.____
home taping of TV shows would be unenforceable.

30. Financial experts predict that unless a tax is placed on videocassettes, several large   30.____
companies in the entertainment industry will have to file for bankruptcy.

Questions 31-38.

DIRECTIONS: The following questions 31 through 38 are variations on the type of question you just had. It is important that you read the question very carefully to determine exactly what is required.

31. In this question, select the choice that is most relevant to the conclusion.   31.____

    1. The Buffalo Bills football team is in second place in its division.
    2. The New England Patriots are in first place in the same division.
    3. There are two games left to play in the season, and the Bills will not play the Patriots again.
    4. The New England Patriots won ten games and lost four games, and the Buffalo Bills have won eight games and lost six games.

    CONCLUSION: The Buffalo Bills win their division.

    A. The conclusion is proved by sentences 1-4.
    B. The conclusion is disproved by sentences 1-4.
    C. The facts are not sufficient to prove or disprove the conclusion.

32. In this question, select the choice that is most relevant to the conclusion.   32.____

    1. On the planet of Zeinon there are only two different eye colors and only two different hair colors.
    2. Half of those beings with purple hair have golden eyes.
    3. There are more inhabitants with purple hair than there are inhabitants with silver hair.
    4. One-third of those with silver hair have green eyes.

    CONCLUSION: There are more golden-eyed beings on Zeinon than green-eyed ones.

    A. The conclusion is proved by sentences 1-4.
    B. The conclusion is disproved by sentences 1-4.
    C. The facts are not sufficient to prove or disprove the conclusion.

33. In this question, select the choice that is most relevant to the conclusion.   33.____
John and Kevin are leaving Amaranth to go to school in Bethany. They've decided to rent a small truck to move their possessions. Joe's Truck Rental charges $100 plus 30¢ a mile. National Movers charges $50 more but gives free mileage for the first 100 miles. After the first 100 miles, they charge 25¢ a mile.

CONCLUSION: John and Kevin rent their truck from National Movers because it is cheaper.

- A. The conclusion is proved by the facts in the above paragraph.
- B. The conclusion is disproved by the facts in the above paragraph.
- C. The facts are not sufficient to prove or disprove the conclusion.

34. For this question, select the choice that supports the information given in the passage.
   Municipalities in Country X are divided into villages, towns, and cities. A village has a population of 5,000 or less. The population of a town ranges from 5,001 to 15,000. In order to be incorporated as a city, the municipality must have a population over 15,000. If, after a village becomes a town, or a town becomes a city, the population drops below the minimum required (for example, the population of a city goes below 15,000), and stays below the minimum for more than ten years, it loses its current status, and drops to the next category. As soon as a municipality rises in population to the next category (village to town, for example), however, it is immediately reclassified to the next category.
   In the 1970 census, Plainfield had a population of 12,000. Between 1970 and 1980, Plainfield grew 10%, and between 1980 and 1990 Plainfield grew another 20%. The population of Springdale doubled from 1970 to 1980, and increased 25% from 1980 to 1990. The city of Smallville's population, 20,283, has not changed significantly in the last twenty years. Granton had a population of 25,000 people in 1960, and has decreased 25% in each ten year period since then. Ellenville had a population of 4,283 in 1960, and grew 5% in each ten year period since 1960.
   In 1990,

- A. Plainfield, Smallville, and Granton are cities
- B. Smallville is a city, Granton is a town, and Ellenville is a village
- C. Springdale, Granton, and Ellenville are towns
- D. Plainfield and Smallville are cities, and Ellenville is a town

35. For this question, select the choice that is most relevant to the conclusion.
A study was done for a major food distributing firm to determine if there is any difference in the kind of caffeine containing products used by people of different ages. A sample of one thousand people between the ages of twenty and fifty were drawn from selected areas in the country. They were divided equally into three groups.
Those individuals who were 20-29 were designated Group A, those 30-39 were Group B, and those 40-50 were placed in Group C.
It was found that on the average, Group A drank 1.8 cups of coffee, Group B 3.1, and Group C 2.5 cups of coffee daily. Group A drank 2.1 cups of tea, Group B drank 1.2, and Group C drank 2.6 cups of tea daily. Group A drank 3.1 8-ounce glasses of cola, Group B drank 1.9, and Group C drank 1.5 glasses of cola daily.

CONCLUSION: According to the study, the average person in the 20-29 age group drinks less tea daily than the average person in the 40-50 age group, but drinks more coffee daily than the average person in the 30-39 age group drinks cola.

- A. The conclusion is proved by the facts in the above paragraph.
- B. The conclusion is disproved by the facts in the above paragraph.
- C. The facts are not sufficient to prove or disprove the conclusion.

36. For this question, select the choice that is most relevant to the conclusion. 36.____

   1. Mary is taller than Jane but shorter than Dale.
   2. Fred is taller than Mary but shorter than Steven.
   3. Dale is shorter than Steven but taller than Elizabeth.
   4. Elizabeth is taller than Mary but not as tall as Fred.

   CONCLUSION: Dale is taller than Fred.

   A. The conclusion is proved by sentences 1-4.
   B. The conclusion is disproved by sentences 1-4.
   C. The facts are not sufficient to prove or disprove the conclusion.

37. For this question, select the choice that is most relevant to the conclusion. 37.____

   1. Main Street is between Spring Street and Glenn Blvd.
   2. Hawley Avenue is one block south of Spring Street and three blocks north of Main Street.
   3. Glenn Street is five blocks south of Elm and four blocks south of Main.
   4. All the streets mentioned are parallel to one another.

   CONCLUSION: Elm Street is between Hawley Avenue and Glenn Blvd.

   A. The conclusion is proved by the facts in sentences 1-4.
   B. The conclusion is disproved by the facts in sentences 1-4.
   C. The facts are not sufficient to prove or disprove the conclusion.

38. For this question, select the choice that is most relevant to the conclusion. 38.____

   1. Train A leaves the town of Hampshire every day at 5:50 A.M. and arrives in New London at 6:42 A.M.
   2. Train A leaves New London at 7:00 A.M. and arrives in Kellogsville at 8:42 A.M.
   3. Train B leaves Kellogsville at 8:00 A.M. and arrives in Hampshire at 10:42 A.M.
   4. Due to the need for repairs, there is just one railroad track between New London and Hampshire.

   CONCLUSION: It is impossible for Train A and Train B to follow these schedules without colliding.

   A. The conclusion is proved by the facts in the above paragraph.
   B. The conclusion is disproved by the facts in the above passage.
   C. The facts are not sufficient to prove or disprove the conclusion.

KEY (CORRECT ANSWERS)

1.	D	11.	C	21.	D	31.	C
2.	B	12.	C	22.	A	32.	A
3.	E	13.	D	23.	C	33.	C
4.	B	14.	B	24.	B	34.	B
5.	C	15.	E	25.	E	35.	B
6.	D	16.	B	26.	C	36.	C
7.	B	17.	A	27.	B	37.	A
8.	A	18.	B	28.	E	38.	B
9.	B	19.	D	29.	B		
10.	B	20.	E	30.	D		

SOLUTIONS TO QUESTIONS

1. The answer is D. This statement weakens the conclusion, but does not disprove it. If a new branch of the community college opened in September, it could possibly bring in new business for Mr. Bryant. Since it states in the conclusion that Mr. Bryant felt there would not be enough new business to support the additional stores, this would tend to disprove the conclusion. Choice C would not be correct because it's possible that he felt that the students would not have enough additional money to support his new venture, or would not be interested in his clothing styles. It's also possible that the majority of the students already live in the area, so that they wouldn't really be a new customer population. This type of question is tricky, and can initially be very confusing, so don't feel badly if you missed it. Most people need to practice with a few of these types of questions before they feel comfortable recognizing exactly what they're being asked to do.

2. The answer is B. It supports the conclusion because the closing of the factory would probably take money and customers out of the town, causing Mr. Bryant to lose some of his present business. It doesn't prove the conclusion, however, because we don't know how large the factory was. It's possible that only a small percentage of the population was employed there, or that they found other jobs.

3. The answer is E. The fact that the number of children per household dropped slightly nationwide from 1970 to 1980 is irrelevant. Statistics showing a drop nationwide doesn't mean that there was a drop in the number of children per household in Mr. Bryant's hometown. This is a tricky question, as choice B, supporting the conclusion but not proving it, may seem reasonable. If the number of children per household declined nationwide, then it may not seem unreasonable to feel that this would support Mr. Bryant's decision not to expand his business. However, we're preparing you for promotional exams, not "real life." One of the difficult things about taking exams is that sometimes you're forced to make a choice between two statements that both seem like they could be the possible answer. What you need to do in that case is choose the best choice. Becoming annoyed or frustrated with the question won't really help much. If there's a review of the exam, you can certainly appeal the question. There have been many cases where, after an appeal, two possible choices have been allowed as correct answers. We've included this question, however, to help you see what to do should you get a question like this. It's most important not to get rattled, and to select the best choice. In this case, the connection between the statistical information and Mr. Bryant's decision is pretty remote. If the question had said that the number of children in Mr. Bryant's town had decreased, then choice B would have been a more reasonable choice. It could also help in this situation to visualize the situation. Picture Mr. Bryant in his armchair reading that, nationwide, the average number of children per household has declined slightly. How likely would this be to influence his decision, especially since he sells men's and women's clothing? It would take a while for this decline in population to show up, and we're not even sure if it applies to Mr. Bryant's hometown. Don't feel badly if you missed this, it was tricky. The more of these you do, the more comfortable you'll feel.

4. The answer is B. If a new clothing boutique specializing in casual women's clothing were to open soon, this would lend support to Mr. Bryant's decision not to expand, but would not prove that he had actually made the decision not to expand. A new women's clothing boutique would most likely be in competition with his existing business, thus making any possible expansion a riskier venture. We can't be sure from this, however, that he didn't go ahead and expand his business despite the increased competition. Choice A, proves the conclusion, would only be the answer if we could be absolutely sure from the statement that Mr. Bryant had actually not expanded his business.

5. The answer is C. This statement disproves the conclusion. In order for his sister to buy several items for her baby at Mr. Bryant's store, he would have to have changed his business to include children's clothing.

6. The answer is A. It definitely proves the conclusion. The passage states that Mr. Bryant's store had been in business since 1885. A pie baked in honor of his store's 100th anniversary would have to be presented sometime in 1985. The conclusion states that he made his decision not to expand on November 7, 1983. If, more than a year later Mrs. MacIntyre comments that his store has maintained the same look and feel over the years, it could not have been expanded, or otherwise significantly changed.

7. The answer is D. If Mr. Bryant's aunt lent him $50,000 in October, this would tend to weaken the conclusion, which took place in November. Because it was stated that Mr. Bryant would need to borrow money in order to expand his business, it would be logical to assume that if he borrowed money he had decided to expand his business, weakening the conclusion. The reason C, disproves the conclusion, is not the correct answer is because we can't be sure Mr. Bryant didn't borrow the money for another reason.

8. The answer is B. If Mr. Bryant's town is eligible for federal funds to encourage the location of new businesses in the central district, this would tend to support his decision not to expand his business. Funds to encourage new business would increase the likelihood of there being additional competition for Mr. Bryant's store to contend with. Since we can't say for sure that there would be direct competition from a new business, however, choice A would be incorrect. Note that this is also a tricky question. You might have thought that the new funds weakened the conclusion because it would mean that Mr. Bryant could easily get the money he needed. Mr. Bryant is expanding his present business, not creating a new business. Therefore he is not eligible for the funding.

9. The answer is B. This is a very tricky question. It's stated that 59% of car occupants don't use seat belts. The legislature is considering the use of air bags because of safety issues. The advantage of air bags over seat belts is that they inflate upon impact, and don't require car occupants to do anything with them ahead of time. Since the population has strongly resisted using seat belts, the air bags could become even more important in saving lives. Since saving lives is the purpose of the proposed legislation, the information that a small percentage of people use seat belts could be helpful to the passage of the legislation. We can't be sure that this is reason enough for the legislature to vote for the legislation, however, so choice A is incorrect.

10. The answer is B, as the information that 5,900 lives could be saved would tend to support the conclusion. Saving that many lives through the use of air bags could be a very persuasive reason to vote for the legislation. Since we don't know for sure that it's enough of a compelling reason for the legislature to vote for the legislation, however, choice A could not be the answer.

11. The answer is C, disproves the conclusion. If the legislation had been passed as stated in the conclusion, there would be no reason to appoint someone head of an advisory committee six days later to analyze the "feasibility of the proposed legislation." The key word here is "proposed." If it has been proposed, it means it hasn't been passed. This contradicts the conclusion and therefore disproves it.

12. The answer is C, disproves the conclusion. If the legislation had passed, there would be no reason for supporters of the legislation to accuse the legislature of rejecting the legislation for political reasons. This question may have seemed so obvious that you might have thought there was a trick to it. Exams usually have a few obvious questions, which will trip you up if you begin reading too much into them.

13. The answer is D, as this would tend to disprove the conclusion. A projected dramatic rise in imported cars could be very harmful to the country's economy and could be a very good reason for some legislators to vote against the proposed legislation. It would be assuming too much to choose C, however, because we don't know if they actually did vote against it.

14. The answer is B. This information would tend to support the passage of the legislation. The estimate of the cost of the air bags is $800 less than the cost estimated by opponents, and it's stated that the protection would be more reliable than any other type of seat belt. Both of these would be good arguments in favor of passing the legislation. Since we don't know for sure, however, how persuasive they actually were, choice A would not be the correct choice.

15. The answer is E, as this is irrelevant information. It really doesn't matter whether auto sales in 1981 have increased slightly over the previous year. If the air bag legislation were to go into effect in 1984, that might make the information somehow more relevant. But the air bag legislation would not take effect until 1989, so the information is irrelevant, since it tells us nothing about the state of the auto industry then.

16. The answer is B, supports the conclusion. This is a tricky question. While at first it might seem to prove the conclusion, we can't be sure that the air bag legislation is responsible for the drop in automobile deaths. It's possible air bags came into popular use without the legislation, or with different legislation. There's no way we can be sure that it was the proposed legislation mandating the use of air bags that was responsible.

17. The answer is A. If, in June of 1984, the lobbyist received a bonus "for her work on the air bag legislation," we can be sure that the legislation passed. This proves the conclusion.

18. The answer is B. This is another tricky question. A three fold stock increase would strongly suggest that the legislation had been passed, but it's possible that factors other than the air bag legislation caused the increase. Note that the stock is in "crash protection equipment." Nowhere in the statement does it say air bags. Seat belts, motorcycle helmets, and collapsible bumpers are all crash protection equipment and could have contributed to the increase. This is just another reminder to read carefully because the questions are often designed to mislead you.

19. The answer is D. This would tend to weaken the conclusion because Marsha is very fond of her mother and she would not want to upset her unnecessarily. It does not prove it, however, because if Marsha strongly feels she is right, she probably wouldn't let her mother's opinion sway her. Choice E would also not be correct, because we cannot assume that Marsha's mother's opinion is of so little importance to her as to be considered irrelevant.

20. The answer is E. The statement is irrelevant. We are told that Marsha's income has doubled but we are not told why. The phrase "six months after the interview" can be misleading in that it leads us to assume that the increase and the interview are related. Her income could have doubled because she regained her popularity but it could also have come from stocks or some other business venture. Because we are not given any reason for her income doubling, it would be impossible to say whether or not this statement proves or disproves the conclusion. Choice E is the best choice of the five possible choices. One of the problems with promotional exams is that sometimes you need to select a choice you're not crazy about. In this case, "not having enough information to make a determination" would be the best choice. However, that's not an option, so you're forced to work with what you've got. On these exams it's sometimes like voting for President, you have to pick the "lesser of the two evils" or the least awful choice. In this case, the information is more irrelevant to the conclusion than it is anything else.

21. The answer is D, weakens the conclusion. We've been told that Marsha's agent feels that she should apologize. If he is pleased with her interview, then it would tend to weaken the conclusion but not disprove it. We can't be sure that he hasn't had a change of heart, or that there weren't other parts of the interview he liked so much that they outweighed her unwillingness to apologize.

22. The answer is A. The conclusion states that Marsha will donate $1 to the Cellulite Prevention League for every pound the actress loses. Marsha's sister's financial report on the League's activities directly supports and proves the conclusion.

23. The answer is C, disproves the conclusion. If the magazine receives many letters commending Marsha for her courage in apologizing, this directly contradicts the conclusion, which states that Marsha didn't apologize.

24. The answer is B. It was stated in the passage that two of Marsha's performances were cancelled after the controversy first occurred. The cancellation of another performance immediately after her interview was published would tend to support the conclusion that she refused to apologize. Because we can't be sure, however, that her performance wasn't cancelled for another reason, choice A would be incorrect.

25. The answer is E, as this information is irrelevant. Postponing the article an extra week does not affect Marsha's decision or the public's reaction to it.

26. The answer is C. If 500 new employees are hired to handle the "increased paperwork created by the new tax on videocassettes", this would directly contradict the conclusion, which states that the legislature defeated both bills. (They should all be this easy.)

27. The answer is B. The results of the study would support the conclusion. If implementing the legislation was going to be so costly, it is likely that the legislature would vote against it. Choice A is not the answer, however, because we can't be sure that the legislature didn't pass it anyway.

28. The answer is E. It's irrelevant to the conclusion that 80% of all those working in the entertainment industry own videocassette recorders. Sometimes if you're not sure about these, it can help a lot to try and visualize the situation. Why would someone voting on this legislation care about this fact? It doesn't seem to be the kind of information that would make any difference or impact upon the conclusion.

29. The answer is B. The head of the law enforcement agency's statement that the legislation would be unenforceable would support the conclusion. It's possible that many legislators would question why they should bother to pass legislation that would be impossible to enforce. Choice A would be incorrect however, because we can't be sure that the legislation wasn't passed in spite of his statement.

30. The answer is D. This would tend to weaken the conclusion because the prospect of several large companies going bankrupt would seem to be a good argument in favor of the legislation. The possible loss of jobs and businesses would be a good reason for some people to vote for the legislation. We can't be sure, however, that this would be a compelling enough reason to ensure passage of the legislation so choice C is incorrect.

This concludes our section on the "Validity of Conclusion" type of questions.

We hope these weren't too horrible for you. It's important to keep in mind exactly what you've been given and exactly what they want you to do with it. It's also necessary to remember that you may have to choose between two possible answers. In that case you must choose the one that seems the best. Sometimes you may think there is no good answer. You will probably be right but you can't let that upset you. Just choose the one you dislike the least.

We want to repeat that it is unlikely that this exact format will appear on the exam. The skills required to answer these questions, however, are the same as those you'll need for the exam so we suggest that you review this section before taking the actual exam.

31. The answer is C. This next set of questions requires you to "switch gears" slightly, and get used to different formats. In this type of question, you have to decide whether the conclusion is proved by the facts given, disproved by the facts given, or neither because not enough information has been provided. Fortunately, unlike the previous questions, you don't have to decide whether particular facts support or don't support the conclusion. This type of question is more straight forward, but the reasoning behind it is the same. We are told that the Bills have won two games less than the Patriots, and that the Patriots are in first place and the Bills are in second place. We are also told that there are two games left to play, and that they won't play each other again. The conclusion states that the Bills won the division. Is there anything in the four statements that would prove this? We have no idea what the outcome of the last two games of the season was. The

Bills and Patriots could have ended up tied at the end of the season, or the Bills could have lost both or one of their last games while the Patriots did the same. There might even be another team tied for first or second place with the Bills or Patriots. Since we don't know for sure, Choice A is incorrect. Choice B is trickier. It might seem at first glance that the best the Bills could do would be to tie the Patriots if the Patriots lost their last two games and the Bills won their last two games. But it would be too much to assume that there is no procedure for a tiebreaker that wouldn't give the Bills the division championship. Since we don't know what the rules are in the event of a tie (for example, what if a tie was decided on the results of what happened when the two teams had played each other, or on the best record in the division, or on most points scored?), we can't say for sure that it would be impossible for the Bills to win their division. For this reason, choice C is the answer, as we don't have enough information to prove or disprove the conclusion. This question looked more difficult than it actually was. It's important to disregard any factors outside of the actual question, and to focus only on what you've been given. In this case, as on all of these types of questions, what you know or don't know about a subject is actually irrelevant. It's best to concentrate only on the actual facts given.

32. The answer is A. The conclusion is proved by the facts given.

In this type of problem it is usually best to pull as many facts as possible from the sentences and then put them into a simpler form. The phrasing and the order of exam questions are designed to be confusing so you need to restate things as clearly as possible by eliminating the extras.

Sentence 1 tells us that there are only two possible colors for eyes and two for hair. Looking at the other sentences we learn that eyes are either green or gold and that hair is either silver or purple. If half the beings with purple hair have golden eyes then the other half must have green eyes since it is the only other eye color. Likewise, if one-third of those with silver hair have green eyes the other two-thirds must have golden eyes.

This information makes it clear that there are more golden-eyed beings on Zeinon than green-eyed ones. It doesn't matter that we don't know exactly how many are actually living on the planet. The number of those with gold eyes (1/2 plus 2/3) will always be greater than the number of those with green eyes (1/2 plus 1/3), no matter what the actual figures might be. Sentence 3 is totally irrelevant because even if there were more silver-haired inhabitants it would not affect the conclusion.

33. The answer is C. The conclusion is neither proved nor disproved by the facts because we don't know how many miles Bethany is from Amoranth.

With this type of question, if you're not sure how to approach it you can always substitute in a range of "real numbers" to see what the result would be. If they were 200 miles apart Joe's Truck Rental would be cheaper because they would charge a total of $160 while National Movers would charge $175.

Joe's - $100 plus .30 x 200 (or $60) = $160
National - $150 plus .25 x 100 (or $25) = $175

If the towns were 600 miles apart, however, National Movers would be cheaper. The cost of renting from National would be $275 compared to the $280 charged by Joe's Trucking.

Joe's - $100 plus .30 x 600 (or $180) = $280
National - $150 plus .25 x 500 (or $125) = $275

34. The answer is B. We've varied the format once more, but the reasoning is similar. This is a tedious question that is more like a math question, but we wanted to give you some practice with this type, just in case. You won't be able to do this question if you've forgotten how to do percents. Many exams require this knowledge, so if you feel you need a review we suggest you read Booklets 1, 2 or 3 in this series.

The only way to attack this problem is to go through each choice until you find the one that is correct. Choice A states that Plainfield, Smallville and Granton are cities. Let's begin with Plainfield. The passage states that in 1960 Plainfield had a population of 12,000, and that it grew 10% between 1960 and 1970, and another 20% between 1970 and 1980. Ten percent of 12,000 is 1200 (12,000 x .10 = 1200). Therefore, the population grew from 12,000 in 1960 to 12,000 + 1200 between 1960 and 1970. At the time of the 1970 Census, Plainfield's population was 13,200. It then grew another 20% between 1970 and 1980, so, 13,200 x .20 = 2640. 13,200 plus the additional increase of 2640 would make the population of Plainfield 15,840. This would qualify it as a city, since its population is over 15,000. Since a change upward in the population of a municipality is re-classified immediately, Plainfield would have become a city right away. So far, statement A is true. The passage states that Smallville's population has not changed significantly in the last twenty years. Since Smallville's population was 20,283, Smallville would still be a city. Granton had a population of 25,000 (what a coincidence that so many of these places have such nice, even numbers) in 1950. The population has decreased 25% in each ten year period since that time. So from 1950 to 1960 the population decreased 25%. 25,000 x .25 = 6,250. 25,000 minus 6,250 = 18,750. So the population of Granton in 1960 would have been 18,750. (Or you could have saved a step and multiplied 25,000 by .75 to get 18,750.) The population from 1960 to 1970 decreased an additional 25%. So: 18,750 x .25 = 4687.50. 18,750 minus 4687.50 = 14,062.50. Or: 18,750 x .75 = 14,062.50. (Don't let the fact that a half of a person is involved confuse you, these are exam questions, not real life.) From 1970 to 1980 the population decreased an additional 25%. This would mean that Granton's population was below 15,000 for more than ten years, so it's status as a city would have changed to that of a town, which would make choice A incorrect, since it states that Granton is a city.

Choice B states that Smallville is a city and Granton is a town which we know to be true from the information above. Choice B is correct so far. We next need to determine if Ellenville is a village. Ellenville had a population of 4,283 in 1950, and increased 5% in each ten year period since 1950. 4,283 x .05 = 214.15. 4,283 plus 214.15 = 4,497.15, so Ellenville's population from 1950 to 1960 increased to 4,497.15. (Or: 4,283 x 1.05 - 4,497.15.) From 1960 to 1970 Ellenville's population increased another 5%: 4,497.15 x .05 = 224.86. 4,497.15 plus 224.86 = 4,772.01 (or: 4,497.15 x 1.05 = 4,722.01.) From 1970 to 1980, Ellenville's population increased another 5%: 4,722.01 x .05 = 236.1. 4722.01 plus 236.10 = 4958.11. (Or: 4,722.01 x 1.05 = 4958.11.).

Ellenville's population is still under 5,000 in 1980 so it would continue to be classified as a village. Since all three statements in choice B are true, Choice B must be the answer. However, we'll go through the other choices. Choice C states that Springdale is a town. The passage tells us that the population of Springdale doubled from 1960 to 1970, and increased

25% from 1970 to 1980. It doesn't give us any actual population figures, however, so it's impossible to know what the population of Springdale is, making Choice C incorrect. Choice C also states that Granton is a town, which is true, and that Ellenville is a town, which is false (from Choice B we know it's a village). Choice D states that Plainfield and Smallville are cities, which is information we already know is true, and that Ellenville is a town. Since Ellenville is a village, Choice D is also incorrect.

This was a lot of work for just one question and we doubt you'll get one like this on this section of the exam, but we included it just in case. On an exam, you can always put a check mark next to a question like this and come back to it later, if you feel you're pressed for time and could spend your time more productively on other, less time consuming problems.

35. The answer is B. This question requires very careful reading. It's best to break the conclusion down into smaller parts in order to solve the problem. The first half of the conclusion states that the average person in the 20-29 age group (Group A) drinks less tea daily than the average person in the 40-50 age group (Group C). The average person in Group A drinks 2.1 cups of tea daily, while the average person in Group C drinks 2.6 cups of tea daily. Since 2.1 is less than 2.6, the conclusion is correct so far. The second half of the conclusion states that the average person in Group A drinks more coffee daily than the average person in the 30-39 age group (Group B) drinks cola. The average person in Group A drinks 1.8 cups of coffee daily while the average person in Group B drinks 1.9 glasses of cola. This disproves the conclusion, which states that the average person in Group A drinks more coffee daily than the average person in Group B drinks cola.

36. The answer is C. The easiest way to approach a problem that deals with the relationship between a number of different people or things is to set up a diagram. This type of problem is usually too confusing to do in your head. For this particular problem the "diagram" could be a line, one end of which would be labelled tall and the other end labelled short. Then, taking one sentence at a time, place the people on the line to see where they fall in relation to one another.

The diagram of the first sentence would look like this:

```
Tall         Dale      Mary        Jane      Short
(left)                                       (right)
```

Mary is taller than Jane but shorter than Dale so she would fall somewhere between the two of them. We have placed tall on the left and labelled it left just to make the explanation easier. You could just as easily have reversed the position.

The second sentence places Fred somewhere to the left of Mary because he is taller than she is. Steven would be to the left of Fred for the same reason. At this point we don't know whether Steven and Fred are taller or shorter than Dale. The new diagram would look like this:

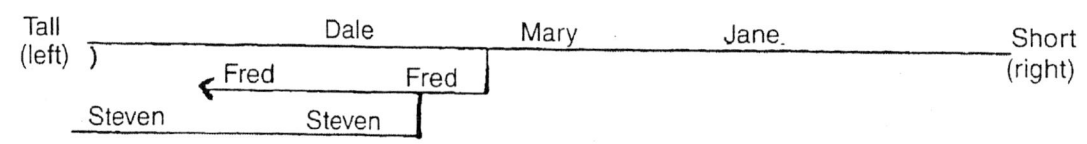

```
Tall                  Dale      Mary        Jane.       Short
(left)  )                                               (right)
          ← Fred          Fred
        Steven          Steven
```

The third stentence introduces Elizabeth, presenting a new problem. Elizabeth can be anywhere to the right of Dale. Don't make the mistake of assuming she falls between Dale and Mary. At this point we don't know where she fits in relation to Mary, Jane, or even Fred.

We do get information about Steven, however. He is taller than Dale so he would be to the left of Dale. Since he is also taller than Fred (see sentence two) we know that Steven is the tallest person thus far. The diagram would now look like this:

```
Tall        Dale        Mary        Jane        Short
(left)   ) ┌─Fred─────Fred─┐                    (right)
         ← 
         Steven      Steven
```

Fred's height is somewhere between Steven and Mary, Elizabeth's anywhere between Dale and the end of the line.

The fourth sentence tells us where Elizabeth stands, in relation to Fred and the others in the problem. The fact that she is taller than Mary means she is also taller than Jane. The final diagram would look like this:

```
Tall    Steven    Dale    Elizabeth    Mary    Jane    Short
(left)           └────Fred────┘                        (right)
```

We still don't know whether Dale or Fred is taller, however. Therefore, the conclusion that Dale is taller than Fred can't be proved. It also can't be disproved because we don't know for sure that he isn't. The answer has to be Choice C, as the conclusion can't be proved or disproved.

37. The answer is A. This is another problem that is easiest for most people if they make a diagram. Sentence 1 states that Main Street is between Spring Street and Glenn Blvd. At this point we don't know if they are next to each other or if they are separated by a number of streets. Therefore, you should leave space between streets as you plot your first diagram.

The order of the streets could go either:

        Spring St.   or   Glenn Blvd.
        Main St.   Main St.
        Glenn Blvd.   Spring St.

Sentence 2 states that Hawley Street is one block south of Spring Street and 3 blocks north of Main Street. Because most people think in terms of north as above and south as below and because it was stated that Hawley is one block south of Spring Street and three blocks north of Main Street, the next diagram could look like this:

        Spring
        Hawley

        ─────

        ─────
        Main
        Glenn

The third sentence states that Glenn Street is five blocks south of Elm and four blocks south of Main. It could look like this:

Spring
Hawley
_____
Elm
Main
_____
_____
Glenn

The conclusion states that Elm Street is between Hawley Avenue and Glenn Blvd. From the above diagram we can see that this is the case.

38. The answer is B. For most people the best way to do this problem is to draw a diagram, plotting the course of both trains. Sentence 1 states that train A leaves Hampshire at 5:50 a.m. and reaches New London at 6:42. Your first diagram might look like this:

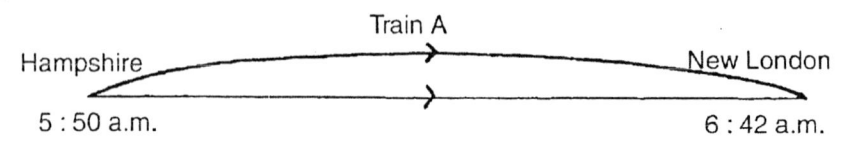

Train A: Hampshire (5:50 a.m.) → New London (6:42 a.m.)

Sentence 2 states that the train leaves New London at 7:00 a.m. and arrives in Kellogsville at 8:42 a.m. The diagram might now look like this:

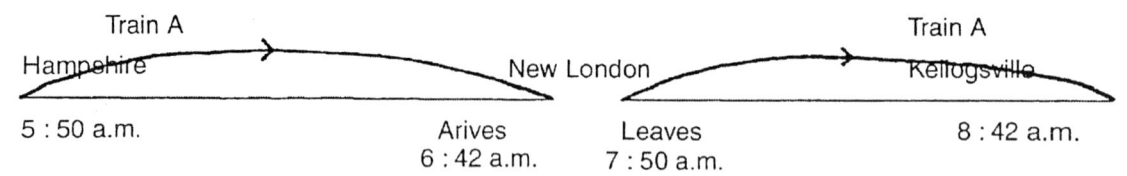

Train A: Hampshire (5:50 a.m.) → New London, Arrives 6:42 a.m., Leaves 7:50 a.m. → Train A: Kellogsville (8:42 a.m.)

Sentence 3 gives us the rest of the information that must be included in the diagram. It introduces Train B, which moves in the opposite direction, leaving Kellogsville at 8:00 a.m. and arriving at Hampshire at 10:42 a.m. The final diagram might look like this:

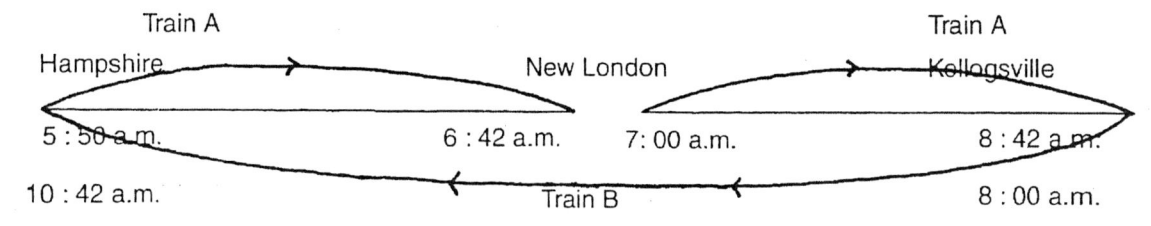

Train A: Hampshire (5:50 a.m.) → New London (6:42 a.m., 7:00 a.m.) → Kellogsville (8:42 a.m.); Train B: 10:42 a.m. ← ← 8:00 a.m.

As you can see from the diagram, the routes of the two trains will overlap somewhere between Kellogsville and New London. If you read sentence 4 quickly and assumed that that was the section with only one track, you probably would have assumed that there would have had to be a collision. Sentence 4 states, however, that there is only one railroad track between New London and Hampshire. That is the only section, then, where the two trains could collide. By the time Train B gets to that section, however, Train A will have passed it. The two trains will pass each other somewhere between New London and Kellogsville, not New London and Hampshire.

Evaluating Conclusions in Light of Known Facts

EXAMINATION SECTION
TEST 1

DIRECTIONS: Each question or incomplete statement is followed by several suggested answers or completions. Select the one that BEST answers the question or completes the statement. *PRINT THE LETTER OF THE CORRECT ANSWER IN THE SPACE AT THE RIGHT.*

Questions 1-9.

DIRECTIONS: In questions 1-9, you will read a set of facts and a conclusion drawn from them. The conclusion may be valid or invalid, based on the facts—it's your task to determine the validity of the conclusion.

For each question, select the letter before the statement that BEST expresses the relationship between the given facts and the conclusion that has been drawn from them. Your choices are:
A. The facts prove the conclusion
B. The facts disprove the conclusion; or
C. The facts neither prove nor disprove the conclusion.

1. FACTS: If the supervisor retires, James, the assistant supervisor, will not be transferred to another department. James will be promoted to supervisor if he is not transferred. The supervisor retired.

   CONCLUSION: James will be promoted to supervisor.

   A. The facts prove the conclusion.
   B. The facts disprove the conclusion.
   C. The facts neither prove nor disprove the conclusion.

2. FACTS: In the town of Luray, every player on the softball team works at Luray National Bank. In addition, every player on the Luray softball team wears glasses.

   CONCLUSION: At least some of the people who work at Luray National Bank wear glasses.

   A. The facts prove the conclusion.
   B. The facts disprove the conclusion.
   C. The facts neither prove nor disprove the conclusion.

3. FACTS: The only time Henry and June go out to dinner is on an evening when they have childbirth classes. Their childbirth classes meet on Tuesdays and Thursdays.

   CONCLUSION: Henry and June never go out to dinner on Friday or Saturday.

   A. The facts prove the conclusion.
   B. The facts disprove the conclusion.
   C. The facts neither prove nor disprove the conclusion.

4. FACTS: Every player on the field hockey team has at least one bruise. Everyone on the field hockey team also has scarred knees.

   CONCLUSION: Most people with both bruises and scarred knees are field hockey players.

   A. The facts prove the conclusion.
   B. The facts disprove the conclusion.
   C. The facts neither prove nor disprove the conclusion.

   4.___

5. FACTS: In the chess tournament, Lance will win his match against Jane if Jane wins her match against Mathias. If Lance wins his match against Jane, Christine will not win her match against Jane.

   CONCLUSION: Christine will not win her match against Jane if Jane wins her match against Mathias.

   A. The facts prove the conclusion.
   B. The facts disprove the conclusion.
   C. The facts neither prove nor disprove the conclusion.

   5.___

6. FACTS: No green lights on the machine are indicators for the belt drive status. Not all of the lights on the machine's upper panel are green. Some lights on the machine's lower panel are green.

   CONCLUSION: The green lights on the machine's lower panel may be indicators for the belt drive status.

   A. The facts prove the conclusion.
   B. The facts disprove the conclusion.
   C. The facts neither prove nor disprove the conclusion.

   6.___

7. FACTS: At a small, one-room country school, there are eight students: Amy, Ben, Carla, Dan, Elliot, Francine, Greg, and Hannah. Each student is in either the 6th, 7th, or 8th grade. Either two or three students are in each grade. Amy, Dan, and Francine are all in different grades. Ben and Elliot are both in the 7th grade. Hannah and Carl are in the same grade.

   CONCLUSION: Exactly three students are in the 7th grade.

   A. The facts prove the conclusion.
   B. The facts disprove the conclusion.
   C. The facts neither prove nor disprove the conclusion.

   7.___

8. FACTS: Two married couples are having lunch together. Two of the four people are German and two are Russian, but in each couple the nationality of a spouse is not necessarily the same as the other's. One person in the group is a teacher, the other a lawyer, one an engineer, and the other a writer. The teacher is a Russian man. The writer is Russian, and her husband is an engineer. One of the people, Mr. Stern, is German.

   CONCLUSION: Mr. Stern's wife is a writer.

   8.___

A. The facts prove the conclusion.
B. The facts disprove the conclusion.
C. The facts neither prove nor disprove the conclusion.

9. FACTS: The flume ride at the county fair is open only to children who are at least 36 inches tall. Lisa is 30 inches tall. John is shorter than Henry, but more than 10 inches taller than Lisa.

    CONCLUSION: Lisa is the only one who can't ride the flume ride.

    A. The facts prove the conclusion.
    B. The facts disprove the conclusion.
    C. The facts neither prove nor disprove the conclusion.

9.____

Questions 10-17.

DIRECTIONS: Questions 10-17 are based on the following reading passage. It is not your knowledge of the particular topic that is being tested, but your ability to reason based on what you have read. The passage is likely to detail several proposed courses of action and factors affecting these proposals. The reading passage is followed by a conclusion or outcome based on the facts in the passage, or a description of a decision taken regarding the situation. The conclusion is followed by a number of statements that have a possible connection to the conclusion. For each statement, you are to determine whether:

A. The statement proves the conclusion.
B. The statement supports the conclusion but does not prove it.
C. The statement disproves the conclusion.
D. The statement weakens the conclusion but does not disprove it.
E. The statement has no relevance to the conclusion.

Remember that the conclusion after the passage is to be accepted as the outcome of what actually happened, and that you are being asked to evaluate the impact each statement would have had on the conclusion.

PASSAGE:

The Grand Army of Foreign Wars, a national veteran's organization, is struggling to maintain its National Home, where the widowed spouses and orphans of deceased members are housed together in a small village-like community. The Home is open to spouses and children who are bereaved for any reason, regardless of whether the member's death was related to military service, but a new global conflict has led to a dramatic surge in the number of members' deaths: many veterans who re-enlisted for the conflict have been killed in action.

The Grand Army of Foreign Wars is considering several options for handling the increased number of applications for housing at the National Home, which has been traditionally supported by membership dues. At its national convention, it will choose only one of the following:

The first idea is a one-time $50 tax on all members, above and beyond the dues they pay already. Since the organization has more than a million members, this tax should be sufficient for the construction and maintenance of new housing for applicants on the existing grounds of the National Home. The idea is opposed, however, by some older members who live on fixed incomes. These members object in principle to the taxation of Grand Army members. The Grand Army has never imposed a tax on its members.

The second idea is to launch a national fund-raising drive and public relations campaign that will attract donations for the National Home. Several national celebrities are members of the organization, and other celebrities could be attracted to the cause. Many Grand Army members are wary of this approach, however: in the past, the net receipts of some fund-raising efforts have been relatively insignificant, given the costs of staging them.

A third approach, suggested by many of the younger members, is to have new applicants share some of the costs of construction and maintenance. The spouses and children would pay an up-front "enrollment" fee, based on a sliding scale proportionate to their income and assets, and then a monthly fee adjusted similarly to contribute to maintenance costs. Many older members are strongly opposed to this idea, as it is in direct contradiction to the principles on which the organization was founded more than a century ago.

The fourth option is simply to maintain the status quo, focus the organization's efforts on supporting the families who already live at the National Home, and wait to accept new applicants based on attrition.

CONCLUSION: At its annual national convention, the Grand Army of Foreign Wars votes to impose a one-time tax of $10 on each member for the purpose of expanding and supporting the National Home to welcome a larger number of applicants. The tax is considered to be the solution most likely to produce the funds needed to accommodate the growing number of applicants.

10. Actuarial studies have shown that because the Grand Army's membership consists mostly of older veterans from earlier wars, the organization's membership will suffer a precipitous decline in numbers in about five years.   10.___

   A.
   B.
   C.
   D.
   E.

11. After passage of the funding measure, a splinter group of older members appeals for the "sliding scale" provision to be applied to the tax, so that some members may be allowed to contribute less based on their income.   11.___

   A.
   B.
   C.
   D.
   E.

12. The original charter of the Grand Army of Foreign Wars specifically states that the organization will not levy any taxes or duties on its members beyond its modest annual dues. It takes a super-majority of attending delegates at the national convention to make alterations to the charter.

    A.
    B.
    C.
    D.
    E.

13. Six months before Grand Army of Foreign Wars' national convention, the Internal Revenue Service rules that because it is an organization that engages in political lobbying, the Grand Army must no longer enjoy its own federal tax-exempt status.

    A.
    B.
    C.
    D.
    E.

14. Two months before the national convention, Dirk Rockwell, arguably the country's most famous film actor, announces in a nationally televised interview that he has been saddened to learn of the plight of the National Home, and that he is going to make it his own personal crusade to see that it is able to house and support a greater number of widowed spouses and orphans in the future.

    A.
    B.
    C.
    D.
    E.

15. The Grand Army's final estimate is that the cost of expanding the National Home to accommodate the increased number of applicants will be about $61 million.

    A.
    B.
    C.
    D.
    E.

16. Just before the national convention, the federal Department of Veterans Affairs announces steep cuts in the benefits package that is currently offered to the widowed spouses and orphans of veterans.

    A.
    B.
    C.
    D.

17. After the national convention, the Grand Army of Foreign Wars begins charging a modest "start-up" fee to all families who apply for residence at the national home.   17.___

   A.
   B.
   C.
   D.
   E.

Questions 18-25.

DIRECTIONS: Questions 18-25 each provide four factual statements and a conclusion based on these statements. After reading the entire question, you will decide whether:
   A. The conclusion is proved by statements 1-4;
   B. The conclusion is disproved by statements 1-4; or
   C. The facts are not sufficient to prove or disprove the conclusion.

18. FACTUAL STATEMENTS: 18.___

   1. In the Field Day high jump competition, Martha jumped higher than Frank.
   2. Carl jumped higher than Ignacio.
   3. Ignacio jumped higher than Frank.
   4. Dan jumped higher than Carl.

   CONCLUSION: Frank finished last in the high jump competition.

   A. The conclusion is proved by statements 1-4.
   B. The conclusion is disproved by statements 1-4.
   C. The facts are not sufficient to prove or disprove the conclusion.

19. FACTUAL STATEMENTS: 19.___

   1. The door to the hammer mill chamber is locked if light 6 is red.
   2. The door to the hammer mill chamber is locked only when the mill is operating.
   3. If the mill is not operating, light 6 is blue.
   4. Light 6 is blue.

   CONCLUSION: The door to the hammer mill chamber is locked.

   A. The conclusion is proved by statements 1-4.
   B. The conclusion is disproved by statements 1-4.
   C. The facts are not sufficient to prove or disprove the conclusion.

7 (#1)

20. FACTUAL STATEMENTS:

   1. Ziegfried, the lion tamer at the circus, has demanded ten additional minutes of performance time during each show.
   2. If Ziegfried is allowed his ten additional minutes per show, he will attempt to teach Kimba the tiger to shoot a basketball.
   3. If Kimba learns how to shoot a basketball, then Ziegfried was not given his ten additional minutes.
   4. Ziegfried was given his ten additional minutes.

   CONCLUSION: Despite Ziegfried's efforts, Kimba did not learn how to shoot a basketball.

   A. The conclusion is proved by statements 1-4.
   B. The conclusion is disproved by statements 1-4.
   C. The facts are not sufficient to prove or disprove the conclusion.

21. FACTUAL STATEMENTS:

   1. If Stan goes to counseling, Sara won't divorce him.
   2. If Sara divorces Stan, she'll move back to Texas.
   3. If Sara doesn't divorce Stan, Irene will be disappointed.
   4. Stan goes to counseling.

   CONCLUSION: Irene will be disappointed.

   A. The conclusion is proved by statements 1-4.
   B. The conclusion is disproved by statements 1-4.
   C. The facts are not sufficient to prove or disprove the conclusion.

22. FACTUAL STATEMENTS:

   1. If Delia is promoted to district manager, Claudia will have to be promoted to team leader.
   2. Delia will be promoted to district manager unless she misses her fourth-quarter sales quota.
   3. If Claudia is promoted to team leader, Thomas will be promoted to assistant team leader.
   4. Delia meets her fourth-quarter sales quota.

   CONCLUSION: Thomas is promoted to assistant team leader.

   A. The conclusion is proved by statements 1-4.
   B. The conclusion is disproved by statements 1-4.
   C. The facts are not sufficient to prove or disprove the conclusion.

8 (#1)

23. FACTUAL STATEMENTS: 23.____

   1. Clone D is identical to Clone B.
   2. Clone B is not identical to Clone A.
   3. Clone D is not identical to Clone C.
   4. Clone E is not identical to the clones that are identical to Clone B.

   CONCLUSION: Clone E is identical to Clone D.

   A. The conclusion is proved by statements 1-4.
   B. The conclusion is disproved by statements 1-4.
   C. The facts are not sufficient to prove or disprove the conclusion.

24. FACTUAL STATEMENTS: 24.____

   1. In the Stafford Tower, each floor is occupied by a single business.
   2. Big G Staffing is on a floor between CyberGraphics and MainEvent.
   3. Gasco is on the floor directly below CyberGraphics and three floors above Treehorn Audio.
   4. MainEvent is five floors below EZ Tax and four floors below Treehorn Audio.

   CONCLUSION: EZ Tax is on a floor between Gasco and MainEvent.

   A. The conclusion is proved by statements 1-4.
   B. The conclusion is disproved by statements 1-4.
   C. The facts are not sufficient to prove or disprove the conclusion.

25. FACTUAL STATEMENTS: 25.____

   1. Only county roads lead to Nicodemus.
   2. All the roads from Hill City to Graham County are federal highways.
   3. Some of the roads from Plainville lead to Nicodemus.
   4. Some of the roads running from Hill City lead to Strong City.

   CONCLUSION: Some of the roads from Plainville are county roads.

   A. The conclusion is proved by statements 1-4.
   B. The conclusion is disproved by statements 1-4.
   C. The facts are not sufficient to prove or disprove the conclusion.

KEY (CORRECT ANSWERS)

1.	A		11.	A
2.	A		12.	D
3.	A		13.	E
4.	C		14.	D
5.	A		15.	B
6.	B		16.	B
7.	A		17.	C
8.	A		18.	A
9.	A		19.	B
10.	E		20.	A

21. A
22. A
23. B
24. A
25. A

TEST 2

DIRECTIONS: Each question or incomplete statement is followed by several suggested answers or completions. Select the one that BEST answers the question or completes the statement. *PRINT THE LETTER OF THE CORRECT ANSWER IN THE SPACE AT THE RIGHT.*

Questions 1-9.

DIRECTIONS: In questions 1-9, you will read a set of facts and a conclusion drawn from them. The conclusion may be valid or invalid, based on the facts-it's your task to determine the validity of the conclusion.

For each question, select the letter before the statement that BEST expresses the relationship between the given facts and the conclusion that has been drawn from them. Your choices are:
A. The facts prove the conclusion
B. The facts disprove the conclusion; or
C. The facts neither prove nor disprove the conclusion.

1. FACTS: Some employees in the testing department are statisticians. Most of the statisticians who work in the testing department are projection specialists. Tom Wilks works in the testing department.

   CONCLUSION: Tom Wilks is a statistician.

   A. The facts prove the conclusion.
   B. The facts disprove the conclusion.
   C. The facts neither prove nor disprove the conclusion.

2. FACTS: Ten coins are split among Hank, Lawrence, and Gail. If Lawrence gives his coins to Hank, then Hank will have more coins than Gail. If Gail gives her coins to Lawrence, then Lawrence will have more coins than Hank.

   CONCLUSION: Hank has six coins.

   A. The facts prove the conclusion.
   B. The facts disprove the conclusion.
   C. The facts neither prove nor disprove the conclusion.

3. FACTS: Nobody loves everybody. Janet loves Ken. Ken loves everybody who loves Janet.

   CONCLUSION: Everybody loves Janet.

   A. The facts prove the conclusion.
   B. The facts disprove the conclusion.
   C. The facts neither prove nor disprove the conclusion.

1.___

2.___

3.___

2 (#2)

4. FACTS: Most of the Torres family lives in East Los Angeles. Many people in East Los Angeles celebrate Cinco de Mayo. Joe is a member of the Torres family.

   CONCLUSION: Joe lives in East Los Angeles.
   - A. The facts prove the conclusion.
   - B. The facts disprove the conclusion.
   - C. The facts neither prove nor disprove the conclusion.

   4.____

5. FACTS: Five professionals each occupy one story of a five-story office building. Dr. Kane's office is above Dr. Assad's. Dr. Johnson's office is between Dr. Kane's and Dr. Conlon's. Dr. Steen's office is between Dr. Conlon's and Dr. Assad's. Dr. Johnson is on the fourth story.

   CONCLUSION: Dr. Kane occupies the top story.
   - A. The facts prove the conclusion.
   - B. The facts disprove the conclusion.
   - C. The facts neither prove nor disprove the conclusion.

   5.____

6. FACTS: To be eligible for membership in the Yukon Society, a person must be able to either tunnel through a snowbank while wearing only a T-shirt and shorts, or hold his breath for two minutes under water that is 50° F. Ray can only hold his breath for a minute and a half.

   CONCLUSION: Ray can still become a member of the Yukon Society by tunneling through a snowbank while wearing a T-shirt and shorts.
   - A. The facts prove the conclusion.
   - B. The facts disprove the conclusion.
   - C. The facts neither prove nor disprove the conclusion.

   6.____

7. FACTS: A mark is worth five plunks. You can exchange four sharps for a tinplot. It takes eight marks to buy a sharp.

   CONCLUSION: A sharp is the most valuable.
   - A. The facts prove the conclusion.
   - B. The facts disprove the conclusion.
   - C. The facts neither prove nor disprove the conclusion.

   7.____

8. FACTS: There are gibbons, as well as lemurs, who like to play in the trees at the monkey house. All those who like to play in the trees at the monkey house are fed lettuce and bananas.

   CONCLUSION: Lemurs and gibbons are types of monkeys.
   - A. The facts prove the conclusion.
   - B. The facts disprove the conclusion.
   - C. The facts neither prove nor disprove the conclusion.

   8.____

9. FACTS: None of the Blackfoot tribes is a Salishan Indian tribe. Sal-ishan Indians came from the northern Pacific Coast. All Salishan Indians live east of the Continental Divide.

    CONCLUSION: No Blackfoot tribes live east of the Continental Divide.
    A. The facts prove the conclusion.
    B. The facts disprove the conclusion.
    C. The facts neither prove nor disprove the conclusion.

Questions 10-17.

DIRECTIONS: Questions 10-17 are based on the following reading passage. It is not your knowledge of the particular topic that is being tested, but your ability to reason based on what you have read. The passage is likely to detail several proposed courses of action and factors affecting these proposals. The reading passage is followed by a conclusion or outcome based on the facts in the passage, or a description of a decision taken regarding the situation. The conclusion is followed by a number of statements that have a possible connection to the conclusion. For each statement, you are to determine whether:

    A. The statement proves the conclusion.
    B. The statement supports the conclusion but does not prove it.
    C. The statement disproves the conclusion.
    D. The statement weakens the conclusion but does not disprove it.
    E. The statement has no relevance to the conclusion.

Remember that the conclusion after the passage is to be accepted as the outcome of what actually happened, and that you are being asked to evaluate the impact each statement would have had on the conclusion.

PASSAGE:

On August 12, Beverly Willey reported that she was in the elevator late on the previous evening after leaving her office on the 16th floor of a large office building. In her report, she states that a man got on the elevator at the 11th floor, pulled her off the elevator, assaulted her, and stole her purse. Ms. Willey reported that she had seen the man in the elevators and hallways of the building before. She believes that the man works in the building. Her description of him is as follows: he is tall, unshaven, with wavy brown hair and a scar on his left cheek. He walks with a pronounced limp, often dragging his left foot behind his right.

CONCLUSION: After Beverly Willey makes her report, the police arrest a 43-year-man, Barton Black, and charge him with her assault.

10. Barton Black is a former Marine who served in Vietnam, where he sustained shrapnel wounds to the left side of his face and suffered nerve damage in his left leg.

    A.
    B.
    C.
    D.
    E.

4 (#2)

11. When they arrived at his residence to question him, detectives were greeted at the door by Barton Black, who was tall and clean-shaven.   11.____

    A.
    B.
    C.
    D.
    E.

12. Barton Black was booked into the county jail several days after Beverly Willey's assault.   12.____

    A.
    B.
    C.
    D.
    E.

13. Upon further investigation, detectives discover that Beverly Willey does not work at the office building.   13.____

    A.
    B.
    C.
    D.
    E.

14. Upon further investigation, detectives discover that Barton Black does not work at the office building.   14.____

    A.
    B.
    C.
    D.
    E.

15. In the spring of the following year, Barton Black is convicted of assaulting Beverly Willey on August 11.   15.____

    A.
    B.
    C.
    D.
    E.

16. During their investigation of the assault, detectives determine that Beverly Willey was assaulted on the 12th floor of the office building.   16.____

    A.
    B.
    C.
    D.
    E.

17. The day after Beverly Willey's assault, Barton Black fled the area and was never seen again.

    A.
    B.
    C.
    D.
    E.

Questions 18-25.

DIRECTIONS: Questions 18-25 each provide four factual statements and a conclusion based on these statements. After reading the entire question, you will decide whether:

    A. The conclusion is proved by statements 1-4;
    B. The conclusion is disproved by statements 1-4; or
    C. The facts are not sufficient to prove or disprove the conclusion.

18. FACTUAL STATEMENTS:

    1. Among five spice jars on the shelf, the sage is to the right of the parsley.
    2. The pepper is to the left of the basil.
    3. The nutmeg is between the sage and the pepper.
    4. The pepper is the second spice from the left.

    CONCLUSION: The sage is the farthest to the right.

    A. The conclusion is proved by statements 1-4.
    B. The conclusion is disproved by statements 1-4.
    C. The facts are not sufficient to prove or disprove the conclusion.

19. FACTUAL STATEMENTS:

    1. Gear X rotates in a clockwise direction if Switch C is in the OFF position
    2. Gear X will rotate in a counter-clockwise direction if Switch C is ON.
    3. If Gear X is rotating in a clockwise direction, then Gear Y will not be rotating at all.
    4. Switch C is ON.

    CONCLUSION: Gear X is rotating in a counter-clockwise direction.

    A. The conclusion is proved by statements 1-4.
    B. The conclusion is disproved by statements 1-4.
    C. The facts are not sufficient to prove or disprove the conclusion.

20. FACTUAL STATEMENTS:
    1. Lane will leave for the Toronto meeting today only if Terence, Rourke, and Jackson all file their marketing reports by the end of the work day.
    2. Rourke will file her report on time only if Ganz submits last quarter's data.
    3. If Terence attends the security meeting, he will attend it with Jackson, and they will not file their marketing reports by the end of the work day.
    4. Ganz submits last quarter's data to Rourke.

    CONCLUSION: Lane will leave for the Toronto meeting today.

    A. The conclusion is proved by statements 1-4.
    B. The conclusion is disproved by statements 1-4.
    C. The facts are not sufficient to prove or disprove the conclusion.

21. FACTUAL STATEMENTS:

    1. Bob is in second place in the Boston Marathon.
    2. Gregory is winning the Boston Marathon.
    3. There are four miles to go in the race, and Bob is gaining on Gregory at the rate of 100 yards every minute.
    4. There are 1760 yards in a mile, and Gregory's usual pace during the Boston Marathon is one mile every six minutes.

    CONCLUSION: Bob wins the Boston Marathon.

    A. The conclusion is proved by statements 1-4.
    B. The conclusion is disproved by statements 1-4.
    C. The facts are not sufficient to prove or disprove the conclusion.

22. FACTUAL STATEMENTS:

    1. Four brothers are named Earl, John, Gary, and Pete.
    2. Earl and Pete are unmarried.
    3. John is shorter than the youngest of the four.
    4. The oldest brother is married, and is also the tallest.

    CONCLUSION: Gary is the oldest brother.

    A. The conclusion is proved by statements 1-4.
    B. The conclusion is disproved by statements 1-4.
    C. The facts are not sufficient to prove or disprove the conclusion.

23. FACTUAL STATEMENTS:

    1. Brigade X is ten miles from the demilitarized zone.
    2. If General Woundwort gives the order, Brigade X will advance to the demilitarized zone, but not quickly enough to reach the zone before the conflict begins.
    3. Brigade Y, five miles behind Brigade X, will not advance unless General Woundwort gives the order.
    4. Brigade Y advances.

    CONCLUSION: Brigade X reaches the demilitarized zone before the conflict begins.

A. The conclusion is proved by statements 1-4.
B. The conclusion is disproved by statements 1-4.
C. The facts are not sufficient to prove or disprove the conclusion.

24. FACTUAL STATEMENTS: 24.___

    1. Jerry has decided to take a cab from Fullerton to Elverton.
    2. Chubby Cab charges $5 plus $3 a mile.
    3. Orange Cab charges $7.50 but gives free mileage for the first 5 miles.
    4. After the first 5 miles, Orange Cab charges $2.50 a mile.

    CONCLUSION: Orange Cab is the cheaper fare from Fullerton to Elverton.

    A. The conclusion is proved by statements 1-4.
    B. The conclusion is disproved by statements 1-4.
    C. The facts are not sufficient to prove or disprove the conclusion.

25. FACTUAL STATEMENTS: 25.___

    1. Dan is never in class when his friend Lucy is absent.
    2. Lucy is never absent unless her mother is sick.
    3. If Lucy is in class, Sergio is in class also
    4. Sergio is never in class when Dalton is absent.

    CONCLUSION: If Lucy is absent, Dalton may be in class.

    A. The conclusion is proved by statements 1-4.
    B. The conclusion is disproved by statements 1-4.
    C. The facts are not sufficient to prove or disprove the conclusion.

KEY (CORRECT ANSWERS)

1. C
2. B
3. B
4. C
5. C

6. A
7. B
8. C
9. C
10. B

11. E
12. B
13. D
14. E
15. A

16. E
17. C
18. C
19. A
20. C

21. C
22. A
23. B
24. C
25. B

READING COMPREHENSION
UNDERSTANDING AND INTERPRETING WRITTEN MATERIAL
EXAMINATION SECTION
TEST 1

DIRECTIONS: Each question or incomplete statement is followed by several suggested answers or completions. Select the one that BEST answers the question or completes the statement. *PRINT THE LETTER OF THE CORRECT ANSWER IN THE SPACE AT THE RIGHT.*

Questions 1-5.

DIRECTIONS: Questions 1 through 5 are to be answered SOLELY on the basis of the following passage.

    The most effective control mechanism to prevent gross incompetence on the part of public employees is a good personnel program. The personnel officer in the line departments and the central personnel agency should exert positive leadership to raise levels of performance. Although the key factor is the quality of the personnel recruited, staff members other than personnel officers can make important contributions to efficiency. Administrative analysts, now employed in many agencies, make detailed studies of organization and procedures, with the purpose of eliminating delays, waste, and other inefficiencies. Efficiency is, however, more than a question of good organization and procedures; it is also the product of the attitudes and values of the public employees. Personal motivation can provide the will to be efficient. The best management studies will not result in substantial improvement of the performance of those employees who feel no great urge to work up to their abilities.

1. The above passage indicates that the KEY factor in preventing gross incompetence of public employees is the

    A. hiring of administrative analysts to assist personnel people
    B. utilization of effective management studies
    C. overlapping of responsibility
    D. quality of the employees hired

1.____

2. According to the above passage, the central personnel agency staff SHOULD

    A. work more closely with administrative analysts in the line departments than with personnel officers
    B. make a serious effort to avoid jurisdictional conflicts with personnel officers in line departments
    C. contribute to improving the quality of work of public employees
    D. engage in a comprehensive program to change the public's negative image of public employees

2.____

3. The above passage indicates that efficiency in an organization can BEST be brought about by

    A. eliminating ineffective control mechanisms
    B. instituting sound organizational procedures

3.____

C. promoting competent personnel
D. recruiting people with desire to do good work

4. According to the above passage, the purpose of administrative analysis in a public agency is to

   A. prevent injustice to the public employee
   B. promote the efficiency of the agency
   C. protect the interests of the public
   D. ensure the observance of procedural due process

5. The above passage implies that a considerable rise in the quality of work of public employees can be brought about by

   A. encouraging positive employee attitudes toward work
   B. controlling personnel officers who exceed their powers
   C. creating warm personal associations among public employees in an agency
   D. closing loopholes in personnel organization and procedures

Questions 6-8.

DIRECTIONS: Questions 6 through 8 are to be answered SOLELY on the basis of the following passage on Employee Needs.

EMPLOYEE NEEDS

The greatest waste in industry and in government may be that of human resources. This waste usually derives not from employees' unwillingness or inability, but from management's ineptness to meet the maintenance and motivational needs of employees. Maintenance needs refer to such needs as providing employees with safe places to work, written work rules, job security, adequate salary, employer-sponsored social activities, and with knowledge of their role in the overall framework of the organization. However, of greatest significance to employees are the motivational needs of job growth, achievement, responsibility, and recognition.

Although employee dissatisfaction may stem from either poor maintenance or poor motivation factors, the outward manifestation of the dissatisfaction may be very much alike, i.e., negativism, complaints, deterioration of performance, and so forth. The improvement in the lighting of an employee's work area or raising his level of pay won't do much good if the source of the dissatisfaction is the absence of a meaningful assignment. By the same token, if an employee is dissatisfied with what he considers inequitable pay, the introduction of additional challenge in his work may simply make matters worse.

It is relatively easy for an employee to express frustration by complaining about pay, washroom conditions, fringe benefits, and so forth; but most people cannot easily express resentment in terms of the more abstract concepts concerning job growth, responsibility, and achievement.

It would be wrong to assume that there is no interaction between maintenance and motivational needs of employees. For example, conditions of high motivation often overshadow poor maintenance conditions. If an organization is in a period of strong growth and expansion, opportunities for job growth, responsibility, recognition, and achievement are usually abundant, but the rapid growth may have outrun the upkeep of maintenance factors. In this situation, motivation may be high, but only if employees recognize the poor maintenance conditions as unavoidable and temporary. The subordination of maintenance factors cannot go on indefinitely, even with the highest motivation.

Both maintenance and motivation factors influence the behavior of all employees, but employees are not identical and, furthermore, the needs of any individual do not remain constant. However, a broad distinction can be made between employees who have a basic orientation toward maintenance factors and those with greater sensitivity toward motivation factors.

A highly maintenance-oriented individual, preoccupied with the factors peripheral to his job rather than the job itself, is more concerned with comfort than challenge. He does not get deeply involved with his work but does with the condition of his work area, toilet facilities, and his time for going to lunch. By contrast, a strongly motivation-oriented employee is usually relatively indifferent to his surroundings and is caught up in the pursuit of work goals.

Fortunately, there are few people who are either exclusively maintenance-oriented or purely motivation-oriented. The former would be deadwood in an organization, while the latter might trample on those around him in his pursuit to achieve his goals.

6. With respect to employee motivational and maintenance needs, the management policies of an organization which is growing rapidly will probably result

   A. more in meeting motivational needs rather than maintenance needs
   B. more in meeting maintenance needs rather than motivational needs
   C. in meeting both of these needs equally
   D. in increased effort to define the motivational and maintenance needs of its employees

7. In accordance with the above passage, which of the following CANNOT be considered as an example of an employee maintenance need for railroad clerks?

   A. Providing more relief periods
   B. Providing fair salary increases at periodic intervals
   C. Increasing job responsibilities
   D. Increasing health insurance benefits

8. Most employees in an organization may be categorized as being interested in

   A. maintenance needs *only*
   B. motivational needs *only*
   C. both motivational and maintenance needs
   D. money only, to the exclusion of all other needs

Questions 9-11.

DIRECTIONS: Questions 9 through 11 are to be answered SOLELY on the basis of the following passage on Good Employee Practices.

GOOD EMPLOYEE PRACTICES

As a city employee, you will be expected to take an interest in your work and perform the duties of your job to the best of your ability and in a spirit of cooperation. Nothing shows an interest in your work more than coming to work on time, not only at the start of the day but also when returning from lunch. If it is necessary for you to keep a personal appointment at lunch hour which might cause a delay in getting back to work on time, you should explain the situation to your supervisor and get his approval to come back a little late before you leave for lunch.

You should do everything that is asked of you willingly and consider important even the small jobs that your supervisor gives you. Although these jobs may seem unimportant, if you forget to do them or if you don't do them right, trouble may develop later.

Getting along well with your fellow workers will add much to the enjoyment of your work. You should respect your fellow workers and try to see their side when a disagreement arises. The better you get along with your fellow workers and your supervisor, the better you will like your job and the better you will be able to do it.

9. According to the above passage, in your job as a city employee, you are expected to

   A. show a willingness to cooperate on the job
   B. get your supervisor's approval before keeping any personal appointments at lunch hour
   C. avoid doing small jobs that seem unimportant
   D. do the easier jobs at the start of the day and the more difficult ones later on

10. According to the above passage, getting to work on time shows that you

    A. need the job
    B. have an interest in your work
    C. get along well with your fellow workers
    D. like your supervisor

11. According to the above passage, the one of the following statements that is NOT true is

    A. if you do a small job wrong, trouble may develop
    B. you should respect your fellow workers
    C. if you disagree with a fellow worker, you should try to see his side of the story
    D. the less you get along with your supervisor, the better you will be able to do your job

Questions 12-15.

DIRECTIONS: Questions 12 through 15 are to be answered SOLELY on the basis of the following passage on Employee Suggestions.

EMPLOYEE SUGGESTIONS

To increase the effectiveness of the city government, the city asks its employees to offer suggestions when they feel an improvement could be made in some government operation. The Employees' Suggestions Program was started to encourage city employees to do this.

Through this Program, which is only for city employees, cash awards may be given to those whose suggestions are submitted and approved. Suggestions are looked for not only from supervisors but from all city employees as any city employee may get an idea which might be approved and contribute greatly to the solution of some problem of city government

Therefore, all suggestions for improvement are welcome, whether they be suggestions on how to improve working conditions, or on how to increase the speed with which work is done, or on how to reduce or eliminate such things as waste, time losses, accidents or fire hazards. There are, however, a few types of suggestions for which cash awards cannot be given. An example of this type would be a suggestion to increase salaries or a suggestion to change the regulations about annual leave or about sick leave. The number of suggestions sent in has increased sharply during the past few years. It is hoped that it will keep increasing in the future in order to meet the city's needs for more ideas for improved ways of doing things.

12. According to the above passage, the MAIN reason why the city asks its employees for suggestions about government operations is to

   A. increase the effectiveness of the city government
   B. show that the Employees' Suggestion Program is working well
   C. show that everybody helps run the city government
   D. have the employee win a prize

13. According to the above passage, the Employees' Suggestion Program can approve awards ONLY for those suggestions that come from

   A. city employees
   B. city employees who are supervisors
   C. city employees who are not supervisors
   D. experienced employees of the city

14. According to the above passage, a cash award cannot be given through the Employees' Suggestion Program for a suggestion about

   A. getting work done faster
   B. helping prevent accidents on the job
   C. increasing the amount of annual leave for city employees
   D. reducing the chance of fire where city employees work

15. According to the above passage, the suggestions sent in during the past few years have

   A. all been approved
   B. generally been well written
   C. been mostly about reducing or eliminating waste
   D. been greater in number than before

Questions 16-18.

DIRECTIONS: Questions 16 through 18 are to be answered SOLELY on the basis of the following passage.

The supervisor will gain the respect of the members of his staff and increase his influence over them by controlling his temper and avoiding criticizing anyone publicly. When a mistake is made, the good supervisor will talk it over with the employee quietly and privately. The supervisor will listen to the employee's story, suggest the better way of doing the job, and offer help so the mistake won't happen again. Before closing the discussion, the supervisor should try to find something good to say about other parts of the employee's work. Some praise and appreciation, along with instruction, is more likely to encourage an employee to improve in those areas where he is weakest.

16. A good title that would show the meaning of the above passage would be

   A. HOW TO CORRECT EMPLOYEE ERRORS
   B. HOW TO PRAISE EMPLOYEES
   C. MISTAKES ARE PREVENTABLE
   D. THE WEAK EMPLOYEE

17. According to the above passage, the work of an employee who has made a mistake is more likely to improve if the supervisor

   A. avoids criticizing him
   B. gives him a chance to suggest a better way of doing the work
   C. listens to the employee's excuses to see if he is right
   D. praises good work at the same time he corrects the mistake

18. According to the above passage, when a supervisor needs to correct an employee's mistake, it is important that he

   A. allow some time to go by after the mistake is made
   B. do so when other employees are not present
   C. show his influence with his tone of voice
   D. tell other employees to avoid the same mistake

Questions 19-23.

DIRECTIONS: Questions 19 through 23 are to be answered SOLELY on the basis of the following passage.

In studying the relationships of people to the organizational structure, it is absolutely necessary to identify and recognize the informal organizational structure. These relationships are necessary when coordination of a plan is attempted. They may be with *the boss,* line supervisors, staff personnel, or other representatives of the formal organization's hierarchy, and they may include the *liaison men* who serve as the leaders of the informal organization. An acquaintanceship with the people serving in these roles in the organization, and its formal counterpart, permits a supervisor to recognize sensitive areas in which it is simple to get a conflict reaction. Avoidance of such areas, plus conscious efforts to inform other people of his own objectives for various plans, will usually enlist their aid and support. Planning *without people* can lead to disaster because the individuals who must act together to make any plan a success are more important than the plans themselves.

19. Of the following titles, the one that MOST clearly describes the above passage is

   A. COORDINATION OF A FUNCTION
   B. AVOIDANCE OF CONFLICT
   C. PLANNING WITH PEOPLE
   D. PLANNING OBJECTIVES

20. According to the above passage, attempts at coordinating plans may fail unless

    A. the plan's objectives are clearly set forth
    B. conflict between groups is resolved
    C. the plans themselves are worthwhile
    D. informal relationships are recognized

21. According to the above passage, conflict

    A. may, in some cases, be desirable to secure results
    B. produces more heat than light
    C. should be avoided at all costs
    D. possibilities can be predicted by a sensitive supervisor

22. The above passage implies that

    A. informal relationships are more important than formal structure
    B. the weakness of a formal structure depends upon informal relationships
    C. liaison men are the key people to consult when taking formal and informal structures into account
    D. individuals in a group are at least as important as the plans for the group

23. The above passage suggests that

    A. some planning can be disastrous
    B. certain people in sensitive areas should be avoided
    C. the supervisor should discourage acquaintanceships in the organization
    D. organizational relationships should be consciously limited

Questions 24-25.

DIRECTIONS: Questions 24 and 25 are to be answered SOLELY on the basis of the following passage.

Good personnel relations of an organization depend upon mutual confidence, trust, and good will. The basis of confidence is understanding. Most troubles start with people who do not understand each other. When the organization's intentions or motives are misunderstood, or when reasons for actions, practices, or policies are misconstrued, complete cooperation from individuals is not forthcoming. If management expects full cooperation from employees, it has a responsibility of sharing with them the information which is the foundation of proper understanding, confidence, and trust. Personnel management has long since outgrown the days when it was the vogue to *treat them rough and tell them nothing.* Up-to-date personnel management provides all possible information about the activities, aims, and purposes of the organization. It seems altogether creditable that a desire should exist among employees for such information which the best-intentioned executive might think would not interest them and which the worst-intentioned would think was none of their business.

24. The above passage implies that one of the causes of the difficulty which an organization might have with its personnel relations is that its employees

    A. have not expressed interest in the activities, aims, and purposes of the organization
    B. do not believe in the good faith of the organization

C. have not been able to give full cooperation to the organization
D. do not recommend improvements in the practices and policies of the organization

25. According to the above passage, in order for an organization to have good personnel relations, it is NOT essential that

A. employees have confidence in the organization
B. the purposes of the organization be understood by the employees
C. employees have a desire for information about the organization
D. information about the organization be communicated to employees

KEY (CORRECT ANSWERS)

1.	D	11.	D
2.	C	12.	A
3.	D	13.	A
4.	B	14.	C
5.	A	15.	D
6.	A	16.	A
7.	C	17.	D
8.	C	18.	B
9.	A	19.	C
10.	B	20.	D

21. D
22. D
23. A
24. B
25. C

TEST 2

Questions 1-8.

DIRECTIONS: Questions 1 through 8 are to be answered SOLELY on the basis of the following passage.

Important figures in education and in public affairs have recommended development of a private organization sponsored in part by various private foundations which would offer installment payment plans to full-time matriculated students in accredited colleges and universities in the United States and Canada. Contracts would be drawn to cover either tuition and fees, or tuition, fees, room and board in college facilities, from one year up to and including six years. A special charge, which would vary with the length of the contract, would be added to the gross repayable amount. This would be in addition to interest at a rate which would vary with the income of the parents. There would be a 3% annual interest charge for families with total income, before income taxes, of $50,000 or less. The rate would increase by 1/10 of 1% for every $1,000 of additional net income in excess of $50,000 up to a maximum of 10% interest. Contracts would carry an insurance provision on the life of the parent or guardian who signs the contract; all contracts must have the signature of a parent or guardian. Payment would be scheduled in equal monthly installments.

1. Which of the following students would be eligible for the payment plan described in the above passage? A

   A. matriculated student taking six semester hours toward a graduate degree
   B. matriculated student taking seventeen semester hours toward an undergraduate degree
   C. graduate matriculated at the University of Mexico taking eighteen semester hours toward a graduate degree
   D. student taking eighteen semester hours in a special pre-matriculation program

2. According to the above passage, the organization described would be sponsored in part by

   A. private foundations
   B. colleges and universities
   C. persons in the field of education
   D. persons in public life

3. Which of the following expenses could NOT be covered by a contract with the organization described in the above passage?

   A. Tuition amounting to $20,000 per year
   B. Registration and laboratory fees
   C. Meals at restaurants near the college
   D. Rent for an apartment in a college dormitory

4. The total amount to be paid would include ONLY the

   A. principal
   B. principal and interest
   C. principal, interest, and special charge
   D. principal, interest, special charge, and fee

5. The contract would carry insurance on the
   A. life of the student
   B. life of the student's parents
   C. income of the parents of the student
   D. life of the parent who signed the contract

6. The interest rate for an annual loan of $25,000 from the organization described in the above passage for a student whose family's net income was $55,000 should be
   A. 3%   B. 3.5%   C. 4%   D. 4.5%

7. The interest rate for an annual loan of $35,000 from the organization described in the above passage for a student whose family's net income was $100,000 should be
   A. 5%   B. 8%   C. 9%   D. 10%

8. John Lee has submitted an application for the installment payment plan described in the above passage. John's mother and father have a store which grossed $500,000 last year, but the income which the family received from the store was $90,000 before taxes. They also had $5,000 income from stock dividends. They paid $10,000 in income taxes. The amount of income upon which the interest should be based is
   A. $85,000   B. $90,000   C. $95,000   D. $105,000

Questions 9-13.

DIRECTIONS: Questions 9 through 13 are to be answered SOLELY on the basis of the following passage.

Since an organization chart is pictorial in nature, there is a tendency for it to be drawn in an artistically balanced and appealing fashion, regardless of the realities of actual organizational structure. In addition to being subject to this distortion, there is the difficulty of communicating in any organization chart the relative importance or the relative size of various component parts of an organizational structure. Furthermore, because of the need for simplicity of design, an organization chart can never indicate the full extent of the interrelationships among the component parts of an organization.

These interrelationships are often just as vital as the specifications which an organization chart endeavors to indicate. Yet, if an organization chart were to be drawn with all the wide variety of criss-crossing communication and cooperation networks existent within a typical organization, the chart would probably be much more confusing than informative. It is also obvious that no organization chart as such can prove or disprove that the organizational structure it represents is effective in realizing the objectives of the organization. At best, an organization chart can only illustrate some of the various factors to be taken into consideration in understanding, devising, or altering organizational arrangements.

9. According to the above passage, an organization chart can be expected to portray the
   A. structure of the organization along somewhat ideal lines
   B. relative size of the organizational units quite accurately
   C. channels of information distribution within the organization graphically
   D. extent of the obligation of each unit to meet the organizational objectives

10. According to the above passage, those aspects of internal functioning which are NOT shown on an organization chart   10.____

    A. can be considered to have little practical application in the operations of the organization
    B. might well be considered to be as important as the structural relationships which a chart does present
    C. could be the cause of considerable confusion in the operations of an organization which is quite large
    D. would be most likely to provide the information needed to determine the overall effectiveness of an organization

11. In the above passage, the one of the following conditions which is NOT implied as being a defect of an organization chart is that an organization chart may   11.____

    A. present a picture of the organizational structure which is different from the structure that actually exists
    B. fail to indicate the comparative size of various organizational units
    C. be limited in its ability to convey some of the meaningful aspects of organizational relationships
    D. become less useful over a period of time during which the organizational facts which it illustrated have changed

12. The one of the following which is the MOST suitable title for the above passage is   12.____

    A. THE DESIGN AND CONSTRUCTION OF AN ORGANIZATION CHART
    B. THE INFORMAL ASPECTS OF AN ORGANIZATION CHART
    C. THE INHERENT DEFICIENCIES OF AN ORGANIZATION CHART
    D. THE UTILIZATION OF A TYPICAL ORGANIZATION CHART

13. It can be INFERRED from the above passage that the function of an organization chart is to   13.____

    A. contribute to the comprehension of the organization form and arrangements
    B. establish the capabilities of the organization to operate effectively
    C. provide a balanced picture of the operations of the organization
    D. eliminate the need for complexity in the organization's structure

Questions 14-16.

DIRECTIONS: Questions 14 through 16 are to be answered SOLELY on the basis of the following passage.

In dealing with visitors to the school office, the school secretary must use initiative, tact, and good judgment. All visitors should be greeted promptly and courteously. The nature of their business should be determined quickly and handled expeditiously. Frequently, the secretary should be able to handle requests, receipts, deliveries, or passes herself. Her judgment should determine when a visitor should see members of the staff or the principal. Serious problems or doubtful cases should be referred to a supervisor.

14. In general, visitors should be handled by the

    A. school secretary
    B. principal
    C. appropriate supervisor
    D. person who is free

15. It is wise to obtain the following information from visitors:

    A. Name
    B. Nature of business
    C. Address
    D. Problems they have

16. All visitors who wish to see members of the staff should

    A. be permitted to do so
    B. produce identification
    C. do so for valid reasons only
    D. be processed by a supervisor

Questions 17-19.

DIRECTIONS: Questions 17 through 19 are to be answered SOLELY on the basis of the following passage.

Information regarding payroll status, salary differentials, promotional salary increments, deductions, and pension payments should be given to all members of the staff who have questions regarding these items. On occasion, if the secretary is uncertain regarding the information, the staff member should be referred to the principal or the appropriate agency. No question by a staff member regarding payroll status should be brushed aside as immaterial or irrelevant. The school secretary must always try to handle the question or pass it on to the person who can handle it.

17. If a teacher is dissatisfied with information regarding her salary status, as given by the school secretary, the matter should be

    A. dropped
    B. passed on to the principal
    C. passed on by the secretary to proper agency or the principal
    D. made a basis for grievance procedures

18. The following is an adequate summary of the above passage:

    A. The secretary must handle all payroll matters
    B. The secretary must handle all payroll matters or know who can handle them
    C. The secretary or the principal must handle all payroll matters
    D. Payroll matters too difficult to handle must be followed up until they are solved

19. The above passage implies that

    A. many teachers ask immaterial questions regarding payroll status
    B. few teachers ask irrelevant pension questions
    C. no teachers ask immaterial salary questions
    D. no question regarding salary should be considered irrelevant

Questions 20-22.

DIRECTIONS: Questions 20 through 22 are to be answered SOLELY on the basis of the following passage.

The necessity for good speech on the part of the school secretary cannot be overstated. The school secretary must deal with the general public, the pupils, the members of the staff, and the school supervisors. In every situation which involves the general public, the secretary serves as a representative of the school. In dealing with pupils, the secretary's speech must serve as a model from which students may guide themselves. Slang, colloquialisms, malapropisms, and local dialects must be avoided.

20. The above passage implies that the speech pattern of the secretary must be 20.____

    A. perfect
    B. very good
    C. average
    D. on a level with that of the pupils

21. The last sentence indicates that slang 21.____

    A. is acceptable
    B. occurs in all speech
    C. might be used occasionally
    D. should be shunned

22. The above passage implies that the speech of pupils 22.____

    A. may be influenced   B. does not change readily
    C. is generally good   D. is generally poor

Questions 23-25.

DIRECTIONS: Questions 23 through 25 are to be answered SOLELY on the basis of the following passage.

The school secretary who is engaged in the task of filing records and correspondence should follow a general set of rules. Items which are filed should be available to other secretaries or to supervisors quickly and easily by means of the application of a modicum of common sense and good judgment. Items which, by their nature, may be difficult to find should be cross-indexed. Folders and drawers should be neatly and accurately labeled. There should never be a large accumulation of papers which have not been filed.

23. A good general rule to follow in filing is that materials should be 23.____

    A. placed in folders quickly
    B. neatly stored
    C. readily available
    D. cross-indexed

24. Items that are filed should be available to 24.____

    A. the secretary charged with the task of filing
    B. secretaries and supervisors
    C. school personnel
    D. the principal

25. A modicum of common sense means _____ common sense. 25.___

    A. an average amount of   B. a great deal of
    C. a little   D. no

KEY (CORRECT ANSWERS)

1. B   11. D
2. A   12. C
3. C   13. A
4. C   14. A
5. D   15. B

6. B   16. C
7. B   17. C
8. C   18. B
9. A   19. D
10. B   20. B

21. D
22. A
23. C
24. B
25. C

TEST 3

Questions 1-4.

DIRECTIONS: Questions 1 through 4 are to be answered SOLELY on the basis of the following passage.

The proposition that administrative activity is essentially the same in all organizations appears to underlie some of the practices in the administration of private higher education. Although the practice is unusual in public education, there are numerous instances of industrial, governmental, or military administrators being assigned to private institutions of higher education and, to a lesser extent, of college and university presidents assuming administrative positions in other types of organizations. To test this theory that administrators are interchangeable, there is a need for systematic observation and classification. The myth that an educational administrator must first have experience in the teaching profession is firmly rooted in a long tradition that has historical prestige. The myth is bound up in the expectations of the public and personnel surrounding the administrator. Since administrative success depends significantly on how well an administrator meets the expectations others have of him, the myth may be more powerful than the special experience in helping the administrator attain organizational and educational objectives. Educational administrators who have risen through the teaching profession have often expressed nostalgia for the life of a teacher or scholar, but there is no evidence that this nostalgia contributes to administrative success

1. Which of the following statements as completed is MOST consistent with the above passage? The greatest number of administrators has moved from   1._____

    A. industry and the military to government and universities
    B. government and universities to industry and the military
    C. government, the armed forces, and industry to colleges and universities
    D. colleges and universities to government, the armed forces, and industry

2. Of the following, the MOST reasonable inference from the above passage is that a specific area requiring further research is the   2._____

    A. place of myth in the tradition and history of the educational profession
    B. relative effectiveness of educational administrators from inside and outside the teaching profession
    C. performance of administrators in the administration of public colleges
    D. degree of reality behind the nostalgia for scholarly pursuits often expressed by educational administrators

3. According to the above passage, the value to an educational administrator of experience in the teaching profession   3._____

    A. lies in the firsthand knowledge he has acquired of immediate educational problems
    B. may lie in the belief of his colleagues, subordinates, and the public that such experience is necessary
    C. has been supported by evidence that the experience contributes to administrative success in educational fields
    D. would be greater if the administrator were able to free himself from nostalgia for his former duties

4. Of the following, the MOST suitable title for the above passage is 4.____
   A. EDUCATIONAL ADMINISTRATION, ITS PROBLEMS
   B. THE EXPERIENCE NEEDED FOR EDUCATIONAL ADMINISTRATION
   C. ADMINISTRATION IN HIGHER EDUCATION
   D. EVALUATING ADMINISTRATIVE EXPERIENCE

Questions 5-6.

DIRECTIONS: Questions 5 and 6 are to be answered SOLELY on the basis of the following passage.

Management by objectives (MBO) may be defined as the process by which the superior and the subordinate managers of an organization jointly define its common goals, define each individual's major areas of responsibility in terms of the results expected of him and use these measures as guides for operating the unit and assessing the contribution of each of its members.

The MBO approach requires that after organizational goals are established and communicated, targets must be set for each individual position which are congruent with organizational goals. Periodic performance reviews and a final review using the objectives set as criteria are also basic to this approach.

Recent studies have shown that MBO programs are influenced by attitudes and perceptions of the boss, the company, the reward-punishment system, and the program itself. In addition, the manner in which the MBO program is carried out can influence the success of the program. A study done in the late sixties indicates that the best results are obtained when the manager sets goals which deal with significant problem areas in the organizational unit, or with the subordinate's personal deficiencies. These goals must be clear with regard to what is expected of the subordinate. The frequency of feedback is also important in the success of a management-by-objectives program. Generally, the greater the amount of feedback, the more successful the MBO program.

5. According to the above passage, the expected output for individual employees should be determined 5.____
   A. after a number of reviews of work performance
   B. after common organizational goals are defined
   C. before common organizational goals are defined
   D. on the basis of an employee's personal qualities

6. According to the above passage, the management-by-objectives approach requires 6.____
   A. less feedback than other types of management programs
   B. little review of on-the-job performance after the initial setting of goals
   C. general conformance between individual goals and organizational goals
   D. the setting of goals which deal with minor problem areas in the organization

Questions 7-10.

DIRECTIONS: Questions 7 through 10 are to be answered SOLELY on the basis of the following passage.

Management, which is the function of executive leadership, has as its principal phases the planning, organizing, and controlling of the activities of subordinate groups in the accomplishment of organizational objectives. Planning specifies the kind and extent of the factors, forces, and effects, and the relationships among them, that will be required for satisfactory accomplishment. The nature of the objectives and their requirements must be known before determinations can be made as to what must be done, how it must be done and why, where actions should take place, who should be responsible, and similar problems pertaining to the formulation of a plan. Organizing, which creates the conditions that must be present before the execution of the plan can be undertaken successfully, cannot be done intelligently without knowledge of the organizational objectives. Control, which has to do with the constraint and regulation of activities entering into the execution of the plan, must be exercised in accordance with the characteristics and requirements of the activities demanded by the plan.

7. The one of the following which is the MOST suitable title for the above passage is

   A. THE NATURE OF SUCCESSFUL ORGANIZATION
   B. THE PLANNING OF MANAGEMENT FUNCTIONS
   C. THE IMPORTANCE OF ORGANIZATIONAL FUNCTIONS
   D. THE PRINCIPLE ASPECTS OF MANAGEMENT

8. It can be inferred from the above passage that the one of the following functions whose existence is essential to the existence of the other three is the

   A. regulation of the work needed to carry out a plan
   B. understanding of what the organization intends to accomplish
   C. securing of information of the factors necessary for accomplishment of objectives
   D. establishment of the conditions required for successful action

9. The one of the following which would NOT be included within any of the principal phases of the function of executive leadership as defined in the above passage is

   A. determination of manpower requirements
   B. procurement of required material
   C. establishment of organizational objectives
   D. scheduling of production

10. The conclusion which can MOST reasonably be drawn from the above passage is that the control phase of managing is most directly concerned with the

    A. influencing of policy determinations
    B. administering of suggestion systems
    C. acquisition of staff for the organization
    D. implementation of performance standards

Questions 11-12.

DIRECTIONS: Questions 11 and 12 are to be answered SOLELY on the basis of the following passage.

Under an open-and-above-board policy, it is to be expected that some supervisors will gloss over known shortcomings of subordinates rather than face the task of discussing them face-to-face. It is also to be expected that at least some employees whose job performance is below par will reject the supervisor's appraisal as biased and unfair. Be that as it may, these are inescapable aspects of any performance appraisal system in which human beings are involved. The supervisor who shies away from calling a spade a spade, as well as the employee with a chip on his shoulder, will each in his own way eventually be revealed in his true light--to the benefit of the organization as a whole.

11. The BEST of the following interpretations of the above passage is that

    A. the method of rating employee performance requires immediate revision to improve employee acceptance
    B. substandard performance ratings should be discussed with employees even if satisfactory ratings are not
    C. supervisors run the risk of being called unfair by their subordinates even though their appraisals are accurate
    D. any system of employee performance rating is satisfactory if used properly

11.___

12. The BEST of the following interpretations of the above passage is that

    A. supervisors generally are not open-and-above-board with their subordinates
    B. it is necessary for supervisors to tell employees objectively how they are performing
    C. employees complain when their supervisor does not keep them informed
    D. supervisors are afraid to tell subordinates their weaknesses

12.___

Questions 13-15.

DIRECTIONS: Questions 13 through 15 are to be answered SOLELY on the basis of the following passage.

During the last decade, a great deal of interest has been generated around the phenomenon of *organizational development,* or the process of developing human resources through conscious organization effort. Organizational development (OD) stresses improving interpersonal relationships and organizational skills, such as communication, to a much greater degree than individual training ever did. The kind of training that an organization should emphasize depends upon the present and future structure of the organization. If future organizations are to be unstable, shifting coalitions, then individual skills and abilities, particularly those emphasizing innovativeness, creativity, flexibility, and the latest technological knowledge, are crucial and individual training is most appropriate.

But if there is to be little change in organizational structure, then the main thrust of training should be group-oriented or organizational development. This approach seems better designed for overcoming hierarchical barriers, for developing a degree of interpersonal relationships which make communication along the chain of command possible, and for retaining a modicum of innovation and/or flexibility.

13. According to the above passage, group-oriented training is MOST useful in

    A. developing a communications system that will facilitate understanding through the chain of command
    B. highly flexible and mobile organizations
    C. preventing the crossing of hierarchical barriers within an organization
    D. saving energy otherwise wasted on developing methods of dealing with rigid hierarchies

13.___

14. The one of the following conclusions which can be drawn MOST appropriately from the above passage is that

    A. behavioral research supports the use of organizational development training methods rather than individualized training
    B. it is easier to provide individualized training in specific skills than to set up sensitivity training programs
    C. organizational development eliminates innovative or flexible activity
    D. the nature of an organization greatly influences which training methods will be most effective

15. According to the above passage, the one of the following which is LEAST important for large-scale organizations geared to rapid and abrupt change is

    A. current technological information
    B. development of a high degree of interpersonal relationships
    C. development of individual skills and abilities
    D. emphasis on creativity

Questions 16-18.

DIRECTIONS: Questions 16 through 18 are to be answered SOLELY on the basis of the following passage.

The increase in the extent to which each individual is personally responsible to others is most noticeable in a large bureaucracy. No one person *decides* anything; each decision of any importance, is the product of an intricate process of brokerage involving individuals inside and outside the organization who feel some reason to be affected by the decision, or who have special knowledge to contribute to it. The more varied the organization's constituency, the more outside *veto-groups* will need to be taken into account. But even if no outside consultations were involved, sheer size would produce a complex process of decision. For a large organization is a deliberately created system of tensions into which each individual is expected to bring work-ways, viewpoints, and outside relationships markedly different from those of his colleagues. It is the administrator's task to draw from these disparate forces the elements of wise action from day to day, consistent with the purposes of the organization as a whole.

16. The above passage is essentially a description of decision making as

    A. an organization process
    B. the key responsibility of the administrator
    C. the one best position among many
    D. a complex of individual decisions

17. Which one of the following statements BEST describes the responsibilities of an administrator?

    A. He modifies decisions and goals in accordance with pressures from within and outside the organization.
    B. He creates problem-solving mechanisms that rely on the varied interests of his staff and *veto-groups*.
    C. He makes determinations that will lead to attainment of his agency's objectives.
    D. He obtains agreement among varying viewpoints and interests.

18. In the context of the operations of a central public personnel agency, a *veto group* would LEAST likely consist of

   A. employee organizations
   B. professional personnel societies
   C. using agencies
   D. civil service newspapers

Questions 19-25.

DIRECTIONS: Questions 19 through 25 are to be answered SOLELY on the basis of the following passage, which is an extract from a report prepared for Department X, which outlines the procedure to be followed in the case of transfers of employees.

Every transfer, regardless of the reason therefore, requires completion of the record of transfer, Form DT 411. To denote consent to the transfer, DT 411 should contain the signatures of the transferee and the personnel officer(s) concerned, except that, in the case of an involuntary transfer, the signatures of the transferee's present and prospective supervisors shall be entered in Boxes 8A and 8B, respectively, since the transferee does not consent. Only a permanent employee may request a transfer; in such cases, the employee's attendance record shall be duly considered with regard to absences, latenesses, and accrued overtime balances. In the case of an inter-district transfer, the employee's attendance record must be included in Section 8A of the transfer request, Form DT 410, by the personnel officer of the district from which the transfer is requested. The personnel officer of the district to which the employee requested transfer may refuse to accept accrued overtime balances in excess of ten days.

An employee on probation shall be eligible for transfer. If such employee is involuntarily transferred, he shall be credited for the period of time already served on probation. However, if such transfer is voluntary, the employee shall be required to serve the entire period of his probation in the new position. An employee who has occurred a disability which prevents him from performing his normal duties may be transferred during the period of such disability to other appropriate duties. A disability transfer requires the completion of either Form DT 414 if the disability is job-connected, or Form DT 415 if it is not a job-connected disability. In either case, the personnel officer of the district from which the transfer is made signs in Box 6A of the first two copies and the personnel officer of the district to which the transfer is made signs in Box 6B of the last two copies, or, in the case of an intra-district disability transfer, the personnel officer must sign in Box 6A of the first two copies and Box 6B of the last two copies.

19. When a personnel officer consents to an employee's request for transfer from his district, this procedure requires that the personnel officer sign Form(s)

   A. DT 411
   B. DT 410 and DT 411
   C. DT 411 and either Form DT 414 or DT 415
   D. DT 410 and DT 411, and either Form DT 414 or DT 415

20. With respect to the time record of an employee transferred against his wishes during his probationary period, this procedure requires that

   A. he serve the entire period of his probation in his present office
   B. he lose his accrued overtime balance

C. his attendance record be considered with regard to absences and latenesses
D. he be given credit for the period of time he has already served on probation

21. Assume you are a supervisor and an employee must be transferred into your office against his wishes. According to the this procedure, the box you must sign on the record of transfer is

    A. 6A   B. 8A   C. 6B   D. 8B

21.____

22. Under this procedure, in the case of a disability transfer, when must Box 6A on Forms DT 414 and DT 415 be signed by the personnel officer of the district to which the transfer is being made?

    A. In all cases when either Form DT 414 or Form DT 415 is used
    B. In all cases when Form DT 414 is used and only under certain circumstances when Form DT 415 is used
    C. In all cases when Form DT 415 is used and only under certain circumstances when Form DT 414 is used
    D. Only under certain circumstances when either Form DT 414 or Form DT 415 is used

22.____

23. From the above passage, it may be inferred MOST correctly that the number of copies of Form DT 414 is

    A. no more than 2
    B. at least 3
    C. at least 5
    D. more than the number of copies of Form DT 415

23.____

24. A change in punctuation and capitalization only which would change one sentence into two and possibly contribute to somewhat greater ease of reading this report extract would be MOST appropriate in the

    A. 2nd sentence, 1st paragraph
    B. 3rd sentence, 1st paragraph
    C. next to he last sentence, 2nd paragraph
    D. 2nd sentence, 2nd paragraph

24.____

25. In the second paragraph, a word that is INCORRECTLY used is

    A. *shall* in the 1st sentence
    B. *voluntary* in the 3rd sentence
    C. *occurred* in the 4th sentence
    D. *intra-district* in the last sentence

25.____

KEY (CORRECT ANSWERS)

1.	C	11.	C
2.	B	12.	B
3.	B	13.	A
4.	B	14.	D
5.	B	15.	B
6.	C	16.	A
7.	D	17.	C
8.	B	18.	B
9.	C	19.	A
10.	D	20.	D

21. D
22. D
23. B
24. B
25. C

PREPARING WRITTEN MATERIAL

PARAGRAPH REARRANGEMENT
COMMENTARY

The sentences which follow are in scrambled order. You are to rearrange them in proper order and indicate the letter choice containing the correct answer at the space at the right.

Each group of sentences in this section is actually a paragraph presented in scrambled order. Each sentence in the group has a place in that paragraph; no sentence is to be left out. You are to read each group of sentences and decide upon the best order in which to put the sentences so as to form as well-organized paragraph.

The questions in this section measure the ability to solve a problem when all the facts relevant to its solution are not given.

More specifically, certain positions of responsibility and authority require the employee to discover connections between events sometimes, apparently, unrelated. In order to do this, the employee will find it necessary to correctly infer that unspecified events have probably occurred or are likely to occur. This ability becomes especially important when action must be taken on incomplete information.

Accordingly, these questions require competitors to choose among several suggested alternatives, each of which presents a different sequential arrangement of the events. Competitors must choose the MOST logical of the suggested sequences.

In order to do so, they may be required to draw on general knowledge to infer missing concepts or events that are essential to sequencing the given events. Competitors should be careful to infer only what is essential to the sequence. The plausibility of the wrong alternatives will always require the inclusion of unlikely events or of additional chains of events which are NOT essential to sequencing the given events.

It's very important to remember that you are looking for the best of the four possible choices, and that the best choice of all may not even be one of the answers you're given to choose from.

There is no one right way to these problems. Many people have found it helpful to first write out the order of the sentences, as they would have arranged them, on their scrap paper before looking at the possible answers. If their optimum answer is there, this can save them some time. If it isn't, this method can still give insight into solving the problem. Others find it most helpful to just go through each of the possible choices, contrasting each as they go along. You should use whatever method feels comfortable, and works, for you.

While most of these types of questions are not that difficult, we've added a higher percentage of the difficult type, just to give you more practice. Usually there are only one or two questions on this section that contain such subtle distinctions that you're unable to answer confidently, and you then may find yourself stuck deciding between two possible choices, neither of which you're sure about.

EXAMINATION SECTION
TEST 1

DIRECTIONS: The sentences that follow are in scrambled order. You are to rearrange them in proper order and indicate the letter choice containing the correct answer. *PRINT THE LETTER OF THE CORRECT ANSWER IN THE SPACE AT THE RIGHT.*

1. Below are four statements labeled W., X., Y., and Z. 1.____
   - W. He was a strict and fanatic drillmaster.
   - X. The word is always used in a derogatory sense and generally shows resentment and anger on the part of the user.
   - Y. It is from the name of this Frenchman that we derive our English word, martinet.
   - Z. Jean Martinet was the Inspector-General of Infantry during the reign of King Louis XIV.

   The *PROPER* order in which these sentences should be placed in a paragraph is:

   A. X, Z, W, Y   B. X, Z, Y, W   C. Z, W, Y, X   D. Z, Y, W, X

2. In the following paragraph, the sentences which are numbered, have been jumbled. 2.____
   1. Since then it has undergone changes.
   2. It was incorporated in 1955 under the laws of the State of New York.
   3. Its primary purpose, a cleaner city, has, however, remained the same.
   4. The Citizens Committee works in cooperation with the Mayor's Inter-departmental Committee for a Clean City.

   The order in which these sentences should be arranged to form a well-organized paragraph is:

   A. 2, 4, 1, 3   B. 3, 4, 1, 2   C. 4, 2, 1, 3   D. 4, 3, 2, 1

Questions 3-5.

DIRECTIONS: The sentences listed below are part of a meaningful paragraph but they are not given in their proper order. You are to decide what would be the *best order* in which to put the sentences so as to form a well-organized paragraph. Each sentence has a place in the paragraph; there are no extra sentences. You are then to answer questions 3 to 5 inclusive on the basis of your rearrangements of these secrambled sentences into a properly organized paragraph.

In 1887 some insurance companies organized an Inspection Department to advise their clients on all phases of fire prevention and protection. Probably this has been due to the smaller annual fire losses in Great Britain than in the United States. It tests various fire prevention devices and appliances and determines manufacturing hazards and their safeguards. Fire research began earlier in the United States and is more advanced than in Great Britain. Later they established a laboratory specializing in electrical, mechanical, hydraulic, and chemical fields.

3. When the five sentences are arranged in proper order, the paragraph starts with the sentence which begins

    A. "In 1887 ..."   B. "Probably this ..."   C. "It tests ..."
    D. "Fire research ..."   E. "Later they ..."

3.____

4. In the last sentence listed above, "they" refers to

    A. insurance companies
    B. the United States and Great Britain
    C. the Inspection Department
    D. clients
    E. technicians

4.____

5. When the above paragraph is properly arranged, it ends with the words

    A. "... and protection."   B. "... the United States."
    C. "... their safeguards."   D. "... in Great Britain."
    E. "... chemical fields."

5.____

KEY (CORRECT ANSWERS)

1. C
2. C
3. D
4. A
5. C

TEST 2

DIRECTIONS: In each of the questions numbered 1 through 5, several sentences are given. For each question, choose as your answer the group of numbers that represents the *most logical* order of these sentences if they were arranged in paragraph form. *PRINT THE LETTER OF THE CORRECT ANSWER IN THE SPACE AT THE RIGHT.*

1.
   1. It is established when one shows that the landlord has prevented the tenant's enjoyment of his interest in the property leased.
   2. Constructive eviction is the result of a breach of the covenant of quiet enjoyment implied in all leases.
   3. In some parts of the United States, it is not complete until the tenant vacates within a reasonable time.
   4. Generally, the acts must be of such serious and permanent character as to deny the tenant the enjoyment of his possessing rights.
   5. In this event, upon abandonment of the premises, the tenant's liability for that ceases.

   The CORRECT answer is:

   A. 2, 1, 4, 3, 5   B. 5, 2, 3, 1, 4   C. 4, 3, 1, 2, 5
   D. 1, 3, 5, 4, 2

1.____

2.
   1. The powerlessness before private and public authorities that is the typical experience of the slum tenant is reminiscent of the situation of blue-collar workers all through the nineteenth century.
   2. Similarly, in recent years, this chapter of history has been reopened by anti-poverty groups which have attempted to organize slum tenants to enable them to bargain collectively with their landlords about the conditions of their tenancies.
   3. It is familiar history that many of the workers remedied their condition by joining together and presenting their demands collectively.
   4. Like the workers, tenants are forced by the conditions of modern life into substantial dependence on these who possess great political arid economic power.
   5. What's more, the very fact of dependence coupled with an absence of education and self-confidence makes them hesitant and unable to stand up for what they need from those in power.

   The CORRECT answer is:

   A. 5, 4, 1, 2, 3   B. 2, 3, 1, 5, 4   C. 3, 1, 5, 4, 2
   D. 1, 4, 5, 3, 2

2.____

3.
   1. A railroad, for example, when not acting as a common carrier may contract; away responsibility for its own negligence.
   2. As to a landlord, however, no decision has been found relating to the legal effect of a clause shifting the statutory duty of repair to the tenant.
   3. The courts have not passed on the validity of clauses relieving the landlord of this duty and liability.
   4. They have, however, upheld the validity of exculpatory clauses in other types of contracts.
   5. Housing regulations impose a duty upon the landlord to maintain leased premises in safe condition.

3.____

6. As another example, a bailee may limit his liability except for gross negligence, willful acts, or fraud.

The CORRECT answer is:

A. 2, 1, 6, 4, 3, 5 B. 1, 3, 4, 5, 6, 2 C. 3, 5, 1, 4, 2, 6
D. 5, 3, 4, 1, 6, 2

4.
1. Since there are only samples in the building, retail or consumer sales are generally eschewed by mart occupants, and, in some instances, rigid controls are maintained to limit entrance to the mart only to those persons engaged in retailing.
2. Since World War I, in many larger cities, there has developed a new type of property, called the mart building.
3. It can, therefore, be used by wholesalers and jobbers for the display of sample merchandise.
4. This type of building is most frequently a multi-storied, finished interior property which is a cross between a retail arcade and a loft building.
5. This limitation enables the mart occupants to ship the orders from another location after the retailer or dealer makes his selection from the samples.

The CORRECT answer is:

A. 2, 4, 3, 1, 5 B. 4, 3, 5, 1, 2 C. 1, 3, 2, 4, 5
D. 1, 4, 2, 3, 5

5.
1. In general, staff-line friction reduces the distinctive contribution of staff personnel.
2. The conflicts, however, introduce an uncontrolled element into the managerial system.
3. On the other hand, the natural resistance of the line to staff innovations probably usefully restrains over-eager efforts to apply untested procedures on a large scale.
4. Under such conditions, it is difficult to know when valuable ideas are being sacrificed.
5. The relatively weak position of staff, requiring accommodation to the line, tends to restrict their ability to engage .in free, experimental innovation.

The CORRECT answer is:

A. 4, 2, 3, 1, 3 B. 1, 5, 3, 2, 4 C. 5, 3, 1, 2, 4
D. 2, 1, 4, 5, 3

KEY (CORRECT ANSWERS)

1. A
2. D
3. D
4. A
5. B

TEST 3

DIRECTIONS: Questions 1 through 4 consist of six sentences which can be arranged in a logical sequence. For each question, select the choice which places the numbered sentences in the *most logical* sequence. *PRINT THE LETTER OF THE CORRECT ANSWER IN THE SPACE AT THE RIGHT.*

1.
    1. The burden of proof as to each issue is determined before trial and remains upon the same party throughout the trial.
    2. The jury is at liberty to believe one witness' testimony as against a number of contradictory witnesses.
    3. In a civil case, the party bearing the burden of proof is required to prove his contention by a fair preponderance of the evidence.
    4. However, it must be noted that a fair preponderance of evidence does not necessarily mean a greater number of witnesses.
    5. The burden of proof is the burden which rests upon one of the parties to an action to persuade the trier of the facts, generally the jury, that a proposition he asserts is true.
    6. If the evidence is equally balanced, or if it leaves the jury in such doubt as to be unable to decide the controversy either way, judgment must be given against the party upon whom the burden of proof rests.

    The CORRECT answer is:

    A. 3, 2, 5, 4, 1, 6   B. 1, 2, 6, 5, 3, 4   C. 3, 4, 5, 1, 2, 6
    D. 5, 1, 3, 6, 4, 2

    1.____

2.
    1. If a parent is without assets and is unemployed, he cannot be convicted of the crime of non-support of a child.
    2. The term "sufficient ability" has been held to mean sufficient financial ability.
    3. It does not matter if his unemployment is by choice or unavoidable circumstances.
    4. If he fails to take any steps at all, he may be liable to prosecution for endangering the welfare of a child.
    5. Under the penal law, a parent is responsible for the support of his minor child only if the parent is "of sufficient ability."
    6. An indigent parent may meet his obligation by borrowing money or by seeking aid under the provisions of the Social Welfare Law.

    The CORRECT answer is:

    A. 6, 1, 5, 3, 2, 4   B. 1, 3, 5, 2, 4, 6   C. 5, 2, 1, 3, 6, 4
    D. 1, 6, 4, 5, 2, 3

    2.____

3.
1. Consider, for example, the case of a rabble rouser who urges a group of twenty people to go out and break the windows of a nearby factory.
2. Therefore, the law fills the indicated gap with the crime of inciting to riot."
3. A person is considered guilty of inciting to riot when he urges ten or more persons to engage in tumultuous and violent conduct of a kind likely to create public alarm.
4. However, if he has not obtained the cooperation of at least four people, he cannot be charged with unlawful assembly.
5. The charge of inciting to riot was added to the law to cover types of conduct which cannot be classified as either the crime of "riot" or the crime of "unlawful assembly."
6. If he acquires the acquiescence of at least four of them, he is guilty of unlawful assembly even if the project does not materialize.

The CORRECT answer is:

A. 3, 5, 1, 6, 4, 2   B. 5, 1, 4, 6, 2, 3   C. 3, 4, 1, 5, 2, 6
D. 5, 1, 4, 6, 3, 2

3.____

4.
1. If, however, the rebuttal evidence presents an issue of credibility, it is for the jury to determine whether the presumption has, in fact, been destroyed.
2. Once sufficient evidence to the contrary is introduced, the presumption disappears from the trial.
3. The effect of a presumption is to place the burden upon the adversary to come forward with evidence to rebut the presumption.
4. When a presumption is overcome and ceases to exist in the case, the fact or facts which gave rise to the presumption still remain.
5. Whether a presumption has been overcome is ordinarily a question for the court.
6. Such information may furnish a basis for a logical inference.

The CORRECT answer is:

A. 4, 6, 2, 5, 1, 3   B. 3, 2, 5, 1, 4, 6   C. 5, 3, 6, 4, 2, 1
D. 5, 4, 1, 2, 6, 3

4.____

KEY (CORRECT ANSWERS)

1. D
2. C
3. A
4. B

EXAMINATION SECTION
TEST 1

DIRECTIONS: Each question or incomplete statement is followed by several suggested answers or completions. Select the one that BEST answers the question or completes the statement. *PRINT THE LETTER OF THE CORRECT ANSWER IN THE SPACE AT THE RIGHT.*

Questions 1-4.

DIRECTIONS: Questions 1 through 4 are to be answered on the basis of the following passage.

A State department which is interested in finding acceptable solutions to the operational problems of specific types of community self-help organizations recently sent two of its staff members to meet with one such organization. At that meeting, the leaders of the community organization voiced the need for increased activity planning input of a more detailed nature from the citizens regularly served by that organization. There followed a discussion of a number of information-gathering methods, including surveys by telephone, questionnaires mailed to the citizens' residences, in-person interviews with the citizens, and the placing of suggestion boxes in the organization's headquarters building. Concern was expressed by one of the leaders that the organization's funds be spent judiciously. The State department representatives present promised to investigate the possibility of a matching fund grant of money to the organization.

Later, the proposed survey was conducted using questionnaires completed by those citizens who visited the organization's headquarters. The results of the survey included the information that twice as many citizens wanted more educational activities scheduled than wanted more social activities scheduled, whereas one-half of those who wanted more educational activities scheduled were interested mainly in special job training.

1. A similar survey conducted by a State department employee involved special job training. That survey uncovered the information below. The following four sentences are to be rearranged to form the most effective and logical paragraph. Select the letter representing the best sequence for these sentences.
   I. The majority of those who are still in this group are ethnic minorities.
   II. The number of economically disadvantaged people who enjoyed their special job training is larger than the number of economically disadvantaged people who did not enjoy it.
   III. Thirty-five percent of all those who are economically disadvantaged are not ethnic minorities.
   IV. Eighty percent of those who have completed special job training in the past ten years are economically disadvantaged.
   The CORRECT answer is:
   A. IV, I, III, II
   B. I, III, II, IV
   C. IV, II, I, III
   D. I, II, III, IV

1.____

2. In the reading passage above, the word *judiciously* means MOST NEARLY
   A. legally
   B. immediately
   C. prudently
   D. uniformly

2.____

3. Based *only* on the information in the reading passage, which one of the following statements is MOST fully supported?
    A. The leaders of the community organization in question wanted to increase the quantity and quality of feedback about that organization's suggestion boxes.
    B. The number of citizens surveyed who wanted more educational activities scheduled and were mainly interested in special job training was the same as the number of citizens surveyed who wanted more social activities to be scheduled.
    C. At the meeting concerned, matching funds were promised to the community organization in question by the two State department representatives present.
    D. Telephone surveys generally yield more accurate information than do surveys conducted through the use of mailed questionnaires.

4. The following four sentences are to be rearranged to form the most effective and logical paragraph. Select the letter representing the best sequence for these sentences.
    I. Formal surveys of citizens within a community also convey to those citizens the interest of the community leadership in hearing the citizens' ideas about community improvement.
    II. Such surveys can provide needed input into the process of establishing specific community program goals.
    III. Formally conducted surveys of community residents often yield valuable information to the local area leaders responsible for community-based programs.
    IV. No community should formulate these goals without attempting to obtain the views of its citizenry.

    The CORRECT answer is:

    A. III, I, IV, II   B. I, III, II, IV
    C. III, II, IV, I   D. IV, III, II, I

Questions 5-8.

DIRECTIONS: Questions 5 through 8 are to be answered on the basis of the following passage.

The Smith Paint Company, which currently employs 2,000 persons, has been in existence for 20 years. A new chemical paint, Futuron, was recently developed by an employee of that company. This paint was released for public use a month ago on a trial basis. The sales were phenomenal, and there is a great demand for more Futuron to be manufactured. The profits to be made by increased manufacturing and sale of Futuron could place the Smith Paint Company in a leading role in the paint industry.

The Smith Paint Company currently produces 2 million gallons of the more traditional paint per year. The Smith Paint Company's Board of Directors wishes to reduce its production of this traditional paint by 50%, and to produce 1 million gallons of Futuron per year.

The employees are quite concerned about this potential production change. A public nonprofit research group has been investigating the chemical make-up of Futuron. Initial research indicates that negative physical reactions may result from working closely with the chemicals necessary to manufacture Futuron. For this reason, most of the company employees do not want the proposed change in production to occur. The members of the Board of Directors, however, argue that the research results are too inconclusive to cause great concern. They say that the company would lose 25% to 50% of its potential profit if the large-scale manufacturing of Futuron is not initiated immediately.

5. Seventy-five percent of the Smith Paint Company's current employees were hired during its first 10 years of operation. Fifteen percent were hired in the past five years. During the five-year interval between the first ten years and the most recent five years, 40 persons were hired per year.
   What percentage of its total employees were hired during the Smith Paint Company's first 13 years of operation?

   A. 75%   B. 81%   C. 85%   D. 90%

6. Assume that the total possible profit the Smith Paint Company could make during its first year of manufacturing the proposed amount of Futuron would be $1.00 per gallon. The purchase of new machinery would reduce this first-year profit by 50%. The anticipated delay, during the first production year, in establishing large-scale manufacturing facilities would reduce the total possible profit by an additional 25%.
   Given this information, what would be the actual profit made from the first year of manufacturing Futuron?

   A. $250,000   B. $375,000   C. $500,000   D. $750,000

7. In the reading passage, the word *inconclusive* means MOST NEARLY

   A. ineluctable   B. incorrect
   C. unreasonable   D. indeterminate

8. Based on the information in the reading passage, which of the following statements represents the MOST accurate conclusion?

   A. The proposed reduction in the production of its traditional paint would not financially injure the Smith Paint Company.
   B. A greater proportion of the Smith Paint Company's employees are in favor of the proposed increase in Futuron production than are opposed to it.
   C. The increased Futuron production proposed by the Smith Paint Company's Board of Directors would cause that company's employees considerable health damage.
   D. Positive public response to the sale of Futuron suggests that considerable profit can be made by increasing the manufacturing and sale of Futuron.

KEY (CORRECT ANSWERS)

1. A
2. C
3. B
4. C
5. B
6. A
7. D
8. D

SOLUTIONS TO PROBLEMS

1. For the following reasons, Choice A is correct and the other three choices are incorrect:

    1. Both Choice B and Choice D begin with Sentence I, which states, *The majority of those who are still in this group are ethnic minorities.* The paragraph cannot logically begin with a statement such as Sentence I, because no one reading the paragraph would know what *this group* refers to. Therefore, Choice B and Choice D are not correct and may be eliminated from consideration.

    2. Both Choice A and Choice C begin with Sentence IV, which states, *Eighty percent of those who have completed special job training in the past ten years are economically disadvantaged.* The problem then becomes selecting the best sequence of the other three sentences so that they most logically follow the initial Sentence IV.

    3. If you select Choice C, then you are choosing Sentence II as the correct second sentence. Sentence II states, *The number of economically disadvantaged people who enjoyed their special job training is larger than the number of economically disadvantaged people who did not enjoy it.* Then Sentence I would be the third sentence. However, that would not be logical, because you could not tell whether *this group* in Sentence I refers to *economically disadvantaged people who enjoyed their special job training* or whether *this group* refers to *economically disadvantaged people who did not enjoy it*. Therefore, Choice C is not correct.

    4. By the process of elimination, only Choice A remains. Choice A specifies Sentence I as the second sentence, which is logically correct in that *this group* in Sentence I will then refer to those who *are economically disadvantaged* in Sentence IV. The two remaining sentences also refer back to *economically disadvantaged,* thus creating a paragraph that reads logically from start to finish. Therefore, Choice A is the correct answer.

2. Choices B and D should be eliminated from further consideration due to the context in which the word *judiciously* was used in the reading passage. Specifically, concern was expressed that funds be spent judiciously. Nothing in the paragraph suggests a need for concern if the funds were not spent immediately or uniformly. Choice A must be considered, because public funds should be spent legally. However, the word *judiciously* is related to the word *judgment* rather than to the word *judiciary.* It is the latter word that has to do with courts of law and is related to legality, so Choice A is incorrect. On the other hand, *judiciously* and *prudently* both mean *wisely* and *with direction.* Therefore, Choice C is correct.

3. Choice B is the correct choice. No matter what numbers you apply, Choice B still will be correct. This is because when you multiply any number by two and then divide the result in half, you end up with the same number that you began with. For example, suppose that 20 citizens wanted more social activities. Twice that number (40 citizens) wanted more educational activities. But of those 40 citizens, one-half (20 citizens) wanted mainly special job training.

Choice A is incorrect because, first of all, the organization did not have any suggestion boxes; although suggestion boxes were discussed, questionnaires ultimately were used instead. In addition, Choice A is incorrect because it was input about the planning of activities that the leaders of the community organization wanted rather than feedback concerning suggestion boxes.

Choice C also is not correct. Instead of promising the matching funds, the State department representatives promised to investigate (or look into) the possibility of obtaining the matching funds.

Choice D is incorrect because the reading passage does not tell whether telephone surveys or mailed questionnaires provide more accurate information. Remember, the instructions for this question state that the question is to be answered based ONLY on the information in the applicable reading passage.

4. The correct answer is Choice C. Choice A and Choice C both begin with Sentence III, which certainly could be the logical first sentence of a paragraph. However, the next sentence (Sentence I) in Choice A leaves the initial topic of obtaining information from citizens. The third sentence in Choice A would be Sentence IV, *No community should formulate these goals without attempting to obtain the views of its citizenry.* The words *these goals* do not logically refer to anything in the previous two sentences, so Choice A is incorrect.

Choice B also is incorrect because the word *also* in its first sentence (Sentence I) has nothing to logically refer to. *Also* would have to be used in a sentence that comes later in the paragraph.

Choice D has the same problem as Choice A. Choice D begins with Sentence IV, which starts off, *No community should formulate these goals....* Again, the words *these goals* need to refer to something in a previous sentence about goals in order to be logically correct.

5. Choice B is correct. Here are the mathematical computations you might use to arrive at the correct answer of 81%:

   1. The reading passage states that the Smith Paint Company currently employs 2,000 persons. The first part of this question states that 75% of those current employees were hired during the first ten years that the company was in operation. By multiplying 75% by 2,000, you would find that 1,500 of the current employees were hired during the company's first ten years.

   2. The question asks about the first 13 years of the company's operation rather than just the first ten years. Therefore, you need the arithmetical information for the three years that immediately followed the first ten years. You know from the reading passage that the company has been operating for 20 years. You have the information for the first ten years. Twenty minus ten leaves the most recent ten years.

3. You know from the question that 40 persons were hired each year during the five-year period of time between the first ten years and the most recent five years. However, you need information about only the first three years. By multiplying 40 persons per year by three years, you would find that 120 people were hired during the first three years that came immediately after the first ten years of the company's operation.

4. Next, you would need to add 1,500 people (for the first ten years) and 120 people (for the next three years). That would give you a total of 1,620 people hired during the first 13 years.

5. The question asks for the percentage of the Smith Paint Company's total employees hired during its first 13 years. You know that the total number of employees is 2,000. The question then is: 1,620 people is what percentage of 2,000 people? By dividing 2,000 into 1,620, you would find that the correct answer is 81%.

Choice A is incorrect because it deals with only the first ten years that the company was in operation, rather than the first 13 years. If you took 1,500 people (from Step 1 in the explanatory material for the correct answer) and divided that number by 2,000 people, you would arrive at 75%, which is not correct.

Choice C is incorrect. If you correctly arrived at 1,500 people for the first ten years but then incorrectly dealt with the next five years instead of the next three years, you would end up with the wrong answer of 85%. First, you would multiply 40 people by five years and end up with 200 people. Next, you would add 200 to 1,500 and end up with 1,700 people. Finally, you would divide 1,700 by 2,000 and get 85%.

Choice D also is incorrect. If you correctly arrived at 1,500 people for the first ten years but then used the information for the most recent five years instead of the information for the five years that came just before the most recent five years, you would end up with the incorrect answer of 90%. First, you would find from the question that 15% of the total employees were hired in the past five years. Next, you would multiply 15% by 2,000 total employees and end up with 300. Next, you would add 1,500 employees and 300 employees, ending up with a total of 1,800 employees. By dividing 1,800 by 2,000, you would arrive at 90%.

6. Choice A is correct. Here are the mathematical computations you would need to make to arrive at the correct answer of $250,000:

   1. The reading passage states that the amount of Futuron proposed for manufacture each year is 1 million gallons. The question states that the possible profit per gallon would be $1.00. By multiplying $1.00 by 1,000,000, you would find that $1,000,000 would be the total possible profit to be made during the first year.

   2. The question states that the $1,000,000 possible profit would have to be reduced by 50% because of the purchase of new machinery, plus by an additional 25% due to the delay in establishing manufacturing facilities. The possible profit must, therefore, be reduced by 50% plus 25%, or by a total of 75%, leaving only 25% of the $1,000,000 as possible profit.

3. By multiplying 25% by $1,000,000, you would arrive at $250,000 as the actual profit which would be made.

Choice B is incorrect. If the two profit reductions were incorrectly multiplied by one another (50% times 25%) and the product (12 1/2%) added to 50%, there would have been a net reduction of 62 1/2%, yielding $375,000. However, the two profit reductions are independent of each other and should be added together.

Choice C also is incorrect. It would occur if you only took into account the 50% profit reduction. However, as the paragraph states, you must also deduct an additional 25% of the total profit.

Choice D ($750,000) would be made if you incorrectly multiplied the total profit reduction (75%) by $1,000,000. However, the question asks for the profit, not the profit reduction.

7. Both *indeterminate* and *inconclusive* mean *vague* and *indefinite,* so Choice D is correct. Choice A is incorrect, because the word *ineluctable* means inescapable or inevitable. The reading passage does not support the conclusion that the research results are incorrect or unreasonable, so Choice B and Choice C can be eliminated from consideration.

8. Choice D is correct. The reading passage states, *The sales were phenomenal, and there is a great demand for more Futuron to be manufactured. The profits to be made by increasing the manufacturing and sale of Futuron could place the Smith Paint Company in a leading role in the paint industry.* Since the sales of Futuron were phenomenal (remarkable; extraordinary), and there still is a great demand for it, the suggestion of considerable future profit is reasonable.

Choice A is not the most accurate conclusion based on the reading passage. The financial impact of decreasing the production of the traditional paint cannot be ascertained. Therefore, it is not certain that the proposed 50% reduction in the manufacturing of the Smith Paint Company's traditional paint would not financially injure that company. Certainly, Choice D is a more accurate conclusion.

Choice B is incorrect. A greater proportion of the employees being in favor of the proposed increase in Futuron production than not being in favor of it implies that over 50% of the employees are in favor of it. However, the reading passage states that most of the employees (which, logically, means over 50% of the employees) do not want the proposed change to occur.

Choice C also is not the most accurate conclusion. It states that the proposed increase in Futuron production would cause employees considerable health damage. The reading passage is not definite on this issue of health damage. It states, *Initial research indicates that negative physical reactions may result from working closely with the chemicals necessary....* How serious the health damage might be is not stated in the reading passage.

PREPARING WRITTEN MATERIAL

EXAMINATION SECTION
TEST 1

DIRECTIONS: Each of Questions 1 through 5 consists of a sentence which may or may not be an example of good formal English usage.

Examine each sentence, considering grammar, punctuation, spelling, capitalization, and awkwardness. Then choose the correct statement about it from the four options below it.

If the English usage in the sentence given is better than any of the changes suggested in options B, C, or D, pick option A. (Do not pick an option that will change the meaning of the sentence.

1. I don't know who could possibly of broken it. 1.____

   A. This is an example of good formal English usage.
   B. The word "who" should be replaced by the word "whom."
   C. The word "of" should be replaced by the word "have."
   D. The word "broken" should be replaced by the word "broke."

2. Telephoning is easier than to write. 2.____

   A. This is an example of good formal English usage.
   B. The word "telephoning" should be spelled "telephoneing."
   C. The word "than" should be replaced by the word "then."
   D. The words "to write" should be replaced by the word "writing."

3. The two operators who have been assigned to these consoles are on vacation. 3.____

   A. This is an example of good formal English usage.
   B. A comma should be placed after the word "operators."
   C. The word "who" should be replaced by the word "whom."
   D. The word "are" should be replaced by the word "is."

4. You were suppose to teach me how to operate a plugboard. 4.____

   A. This is an example of good formal English usage.
   B. The word "were" should be replaced by the word "was."
   C. The word "suppose" should be replaced by the word "supposed."
   D. The word "teach" should be replaced by the word "learn."

5. If you had taken my advice; you would have spoken with him. 5.____

   A. This is an example of good formal English usage.
   B. The word "advice" should be spelled "advise."
   C. The words "had taken" should be replaced by the word "take."
   D. The semicolon should be changed to a comma.

KEY (CORRECT ANSWERS)

1. C
2. D
3. A
4. C
5. D

TEST 2

DIRECTIONS: Select the correct answer.

1. The *one* of the following sentences which is *MOST* acceptable from the viewpoint of correct grammatical usage is:

    A. I do not know which action will have worser results.
    B. tie should of known better.
    C. Both the officer on the scene, and his immediate supervisor, is charged with the responsibility.
    D. An officer must have initiative because his supervisor will not always be available to answer questions.

    1.____

2. The *one* of the following sentences which is *MOST* acceptable from the viewpoint of correct grammatical usage is:

    A. Of all the officers available, the better one for the job will be picked.
    B. Strict orders were given to all the officers, except he.
    C. Study of the law will enable you to perform your duties more efficiently.
    D. It seems to me that you was wrong in failing to search the two men.

    2.____

3. The *one* of the following sentences which does *NOT* contain a misspelled word is:

    A. The duties you will perform are similiar to the duties of a patrolman.
    B. Officers must be constantly alert to sieze the initiative.
    C. Officers in this organization are not entitled to special privileges.
    D. Any changes in procedure will be announced publically.

    3.____

4. The *one* of the following sentences which does *NOT* contain a misspelled word is:

    A. It will be to your advantage to keep your firearm in good working condition.
    B. There are approximately fourty men on sick leave.
    C. Your first duty will be to pursuade the person to obey the law.
    D. Fires often begin in flameable material kept in lockers.

    4.____

5. The *one* of the following sentences which does *NOT* contain a misspelled word is:

    A. Officers are not required to perform technical maintainance.
    B. He violated the regulations on two occasions.
    C. Every employee will be held responable for errors.
    D. This was his nineth absence in a year.

    5.____

KEY (CORRECT ANSWERS)

1. D
2. C
3. C
4. A
5. B

TEST 3

DIRECTIONS: Select the correct answer.

1. You are answering a letter that was written on the letterhead of the ABC Company jind signed by James H. Wood, Treasurer. What is usually considered to be the correct salutation to use in your reply?

    A. Dear ABC Company:
    B. Dear Sirs:
    C. Dear Mr. Wood:
    D. Dear Mr. Treasurer:

2. Assume that one of your duties is to handle routine letters of inquiry from the public. The one of the following which is usually considered to be MOST desirable in replying to such a letter is a

    A. detailed answer handwritten on the original letter of inquiry
    B. phone call, since you can cover details more easily over the phone than in a letter
    C. short letter giving the specific information requested
    D. long letter discussing all possible aspects of the question raised

3. The CHIEF reason for dividing a letter into paragraphs is to

    A. make the message clear to the reader by starting a new paragraph for each new topic
    B. make a short letter occupy as much of the page as possible
    C. keep the reader's attention by providing a pause from time to time
    D. make the letter look neat and businesslike

4. Your superior has asked you to send an e-mail from your agency to a government agency in another city. He has written out the message and has indicated the name of the government agency.
   When you dictate the message to your secretary, which of the following items that your superior has NOT mentioned must you be sure to include?

    A. Today's date
    B. The full address of the government agency
    C. A polite opening such as "Dear Sirs"
    D. A final sentence such as "We would appreciate hearing from your agency in reply as soon as is convenient for you"

5. The one of the following sentence which is grammatically preferable to the others is:

    A. Our engineers will go over your blueprints so that you may have no problems in construction.
    B. For a long time he had been arguing that we, not he, are to blame for the confusion.
    C. I worked on this automobile for two hours and still cannot find out what is wrong with it.
    D. Accustomed to all kinds of hardships, fatigue seldom bothers veteran policemen.

KEY (CORRECT ANSWERS)

1. C
2. C
3. A
4. B
5. A

TEST 4

DIRECTIONS: Select the correct answer.

1. Suppose that an applicant for a job as snow laborer presents a letter from a former employer stating: "John Smith has a pleasing manner and never got into an argument with his fellow employees. He was never late or absent." This letter

    A. indicates that with some training Smith will make a good snow gang boss
    B. presents no definite evidence of Smith's ability to do snow work
    C. proves definitely that Smith has never done any snow work before
    D. proves definitely that Smith will do better than average work as a snow laborer

2. Suppose you must write a letter to a local organization in your section refusing a request in connection with collection of their refuse.
You should *start* the letter by

    A. explaining in detail the consideration you gave the request
    B. praising the organization for its service to the community
    C. quoting the regulation which forbids granting the request
    D. stating your regret that the request cannot be granted

3. Suppose a citizen writes in for information as to whether or not he may sweep refuse into the gutter. A Sanitation officer answers as follows:
Dear Sir:
    No person is permitted to litter, sweep, throw or cast, or direct, suffer or permit any person under his control to litter, sweep, throw or cast any ashes, garbage, paper, dust, or other rubbish or refuse into any public street or place, vacant lot, air shaft, areaway, backyard or court.

    Very truly yours,
    John Doe

    This letter is *poorly* written CHIEFLY because

    A. the opening is not indented
    B. the thought is not clear
    C. the tone is too formal and cold
    D. there are too many commas used

4. A section of a disciplinary report written by a Sanitation officer states: "It is requested that subject Sanitation man be advised that his future activities be directed towards reducing his recurrent tardiness else disciplinary action will be initiated which may result in summary discharge." This section of the report is *poorly* written MAINLY because

    A. at least one word is misspelled
    B. it is not simply expressed
    C. more than one idea is expressed
    D. the purpose is not stated

5. A section of a disciplinary report written by an officer states: "He comes in late. He takes too much time for lunch. He is lazy. I recommend his services be dispensed with."
This section of the report is *poorly* written MAINLY because

    A. it ends with a preposition
    B. it is not well organized
    C. no supporting facts are stated
    D. the sentences are too simple

5.____

KEY (CORRECT ANSWERS)

1. B
2. D
3. C
4. B
5. C

INTERPRETING STATISTICAL DATA GRAPHS, CHARTS AND TABLES
TEST 1

DIRECTIONS: Each question or incomplete statement is followed by several suggested answers or completions. Select the one that BEST answers the question or completes the statement. *PRINT THE LETTER OF THE CORRECT ANSWER IN THE SPACE AT THE RIGHT.*

Questions 1-8.

DIRECTIONS: Questions 1 through 8 are to be answered SOLELY on the basis of the information and chart given below.

The following chart shows expenses in five selected categories for a one-year period expressed as percentages of these same expenses during the previous year. The chart compares two different offices. In Office T (represented by ▭) a cost reduction program has been tested for the past year. The other office, Office Q (represented by ▰) served as a control, in that no special effort was made to reduce costs during the past year.

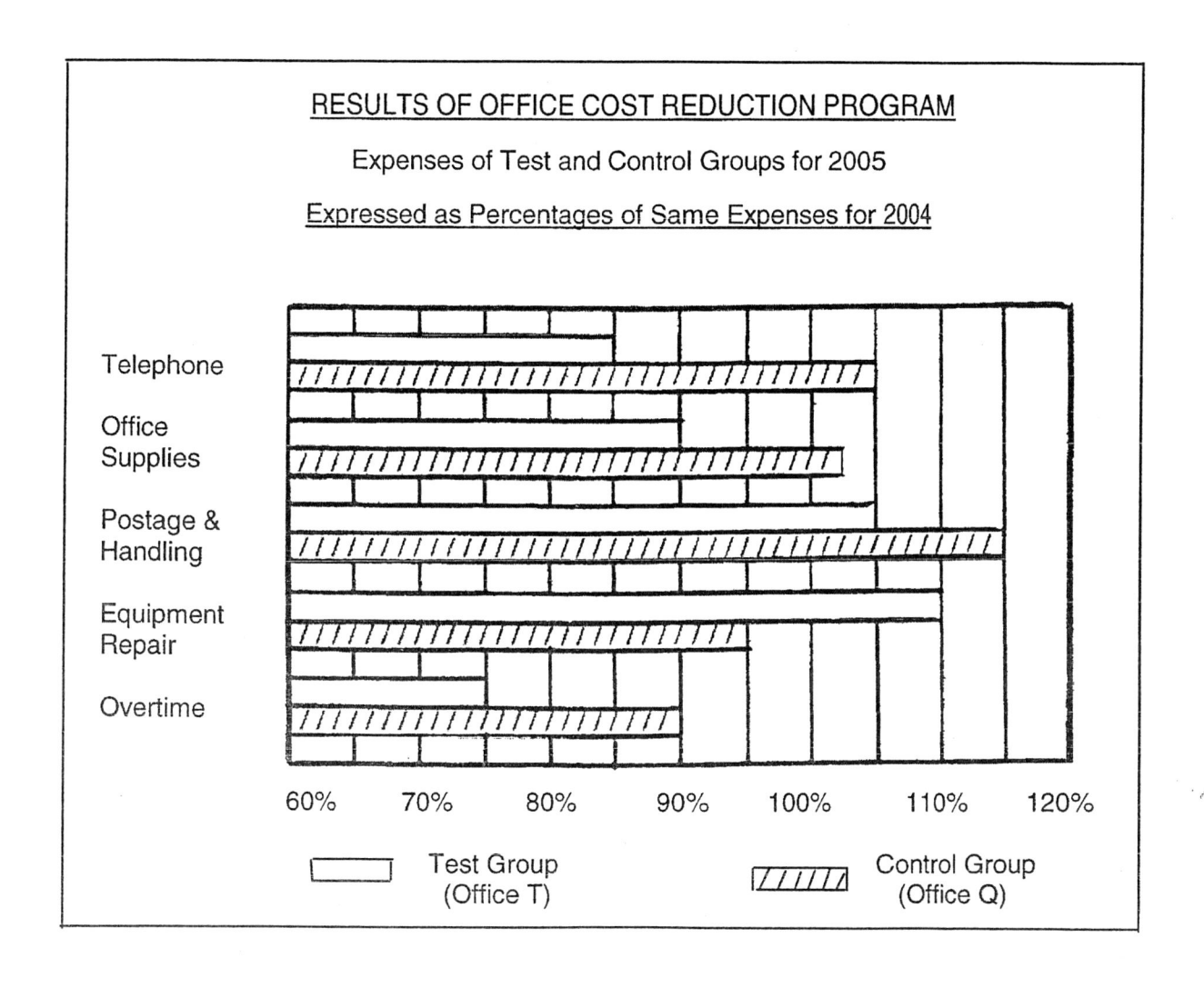

RESULTS OF OFFICE COST REDUCTION PROGRAM

Expenses of Test and Control Groups for 2005
Expressed as Percentages of Same Expenses for 2004

Category	Test Group (Office T)	Control Group (Office Q)
Telephone	85%	105%
Office Supplies	105%	107%
Postage & Handling	100%	117%
Equipment Repair	95%	95%
Overtime	75%	90%

1. In Office T, which category of expense showed the GREATEST percentage reduction from 2004 to 2005?

    A. Telephone
    B. Office supplies
    C. Postage and mailing
    D. Overtime

2. In which expense category did Office T show the BEST results in percentage terms when compared to Office Q?

    A. Telephone
    B. Office supplies
    C. Postage and mailing
    D. Overtime

3. According to the above chart, the cost reduction program was LEAST effective for the expense category of

    A. Office supplies
    B. Postage and mailing
    C. Equipment repair
    D. Overtime

4. Office T's telephone costs went down during 2005 by APPROXIMATELY how many percentage points?

    A. 15
    B. 20
    C. 85
    D. 105

5. Which of the following changes occurred in expenses for Office Supplies in Office Q in the year 2005 as compared with the year 2004?
   They

    A. *increased* by more than 100%
    B. *remained* the same
    C. *decreased* by a few percentage points
    D. *increased* by a few percentage points

6. For which of the following expense categories do the results in Office T and the results in Office Q differ MOST NEARLY by 10 percentage points?

    A. Telephone
    B. Postage and mailing
    C. Equipment repair
    D. Overtime

7. In which expense category did Office Q's costs show the GREATEST percentage increase in 2005?

    A. Telephone
    B. Office supplies
    C. Postage and mailing
    D. Equipment repair

8. In Office T, by APPROXIMATELY what percentage did overtime expense change during the past year?
   It

    A. *increased* by 15%
    B. *increased* by 75%
    C. *decreased* by 10%
    D. *decreased* by 25%

KEY (CORRECT ANSWERS)

1. D
2. A
3. C
4. A

5. D
6. B
7. C
8. D

TEST 2

Questions 1-7.

DIRECTIONS: Questions 1 through 7 are to be answered SOLELY on the basis of the information contained in the graph below which relates to the work of a public agency.

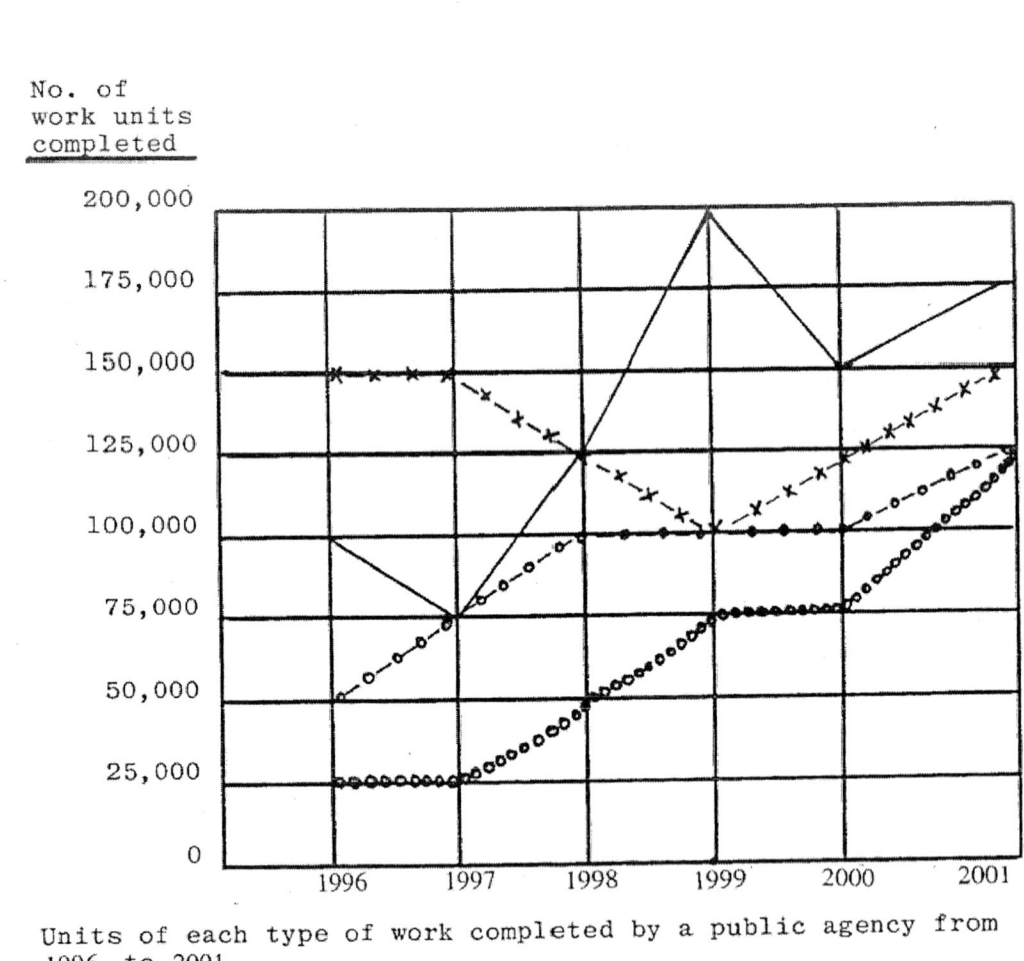

```
No. of
work units
completed

200,000
175,000
150,000
125,000
100,000
 75,000
 50,000
 25,000
      0
       1996  1997  1998  1999  2000  2001
```

Units of each type of work completed by a public agency from 1996 to 2001

Letters Written ———————— Applications Processed O—O—O—O

Documents Filed —x—x—x—x—x Inspections Made OOOOOOOOOOOOOOOO

1. The year for which the number of units of one type of work completed was less than it was for the previous year while the number of each of the other types of work completed was more than it was for the previous year was

   A. 1997   B. 1998   C. 1999   D. 2000

2. The number of letters written exceeded the number of applications processed by the same amount in _____ of the years.

   A. two   B. three   C. four   D. five

3. The year in which the number of each type of work completed was GREATER than in the preceding year was

   A. 1998   B. 1999   C. 2000   D. 2001

4. The number of applications processed and the number of documents filed were the SAME in

   A. 1997   B. 1998   C. 1999   D. 2000

5. The TOTAL number of units of work completed by the agency

   A. increased in each year after 1996
   B. decreased from the prior year in two of the years after 1996
   C. was the same in two successive years from 1996 to 2001
   D. was less in 1996 than in any of the following years

6. For the year in which the number of letters written was twice as high as it was in 1996, the number of documents filed was _____ it was in 1996.

   A. the same as
   B. two-thirds of what
   C. five-sixths of what
   D. one and one-half times what

7. The variable which was the MOST stable during the period 1996 through 2001 was

   A. Inspections Made   B. Letters Written
   C. Documents Filed   D. Applications Processed

KEY (CORRECT ANSWERS)

1. B   5. C
2. B   6. B
3. D   7. D
4. C

TEST 3

Questions 1-10.

DIRECTIONS: Questions 1 through 10 are to be answered SOLELY on the basis of the REPORT OF TELEPHONE CALLS table given below.

TABLE – REPORT OF TELEPHONE CALLS

Dept.	No. of Stations	No. of Employees	No. of Incoming Calls In 1999	No. of Incoming Calls In 2000	No. of Long Distance Calls In 1999	No. of Long Distance Calls In 2000	No. of Divisions
I	11	40	3421	4292	72	54	5
II	36	330	10392	10191	75	78	18
III	53	250	85243	85084	103	98	8
IV	24	60	9675	10123	82	85	6
V	13	30	5208	5492	54	48	6
VI	25	35	7472	8109	86	90	5
VII	37	195	11412	11299	68	72	11
VIII	36	54	8467	8674	59	68	4
IX	163	306	294321	289968	289	321	13
X	40	83	9588	8266	93	89	5
XI	24	68	7867	7433	86	87	13
XII	50	248	10039	10208	101	95	30
XIII	10	230	7550	6941	28	21	10
XIV	25	103	14281	14392	48	40	5
XV	19	230	8475	9206	38	43	8
XVI	22	45	4684	5584	39	48	10
XVII	41	58	10102	9677	49	52	6
XVIII	82	106	106242	105899	128	132	10
XIX	6	13	2649	2498	35	29	2
XX	16	30	1395	1468	78	90	2

1. The department which had more than 106,000 incoming calls in 1999 but fewer than 250,000 is   1.___

   A. II B. IX C. XVIII D. III

2. The department which has fewer than 8 divisions and more than 100 but fewer than 300 employees is   2.___

   A. VII B. XIV C. XV D. XVIII

3. The department which had an increase in 2000 over 1999 in the number of both incoming and long distance calls but had an increase in long distance calls of not more than 3   3.___

   A. IV B. VI C. XVII D. XVIII

4. The department which had a decrease in the number of incoming calls in 2000 as compared to 1999 and has not less than 6 nor more than 7 divisions is   4.___

   A. IV B. V C. XVII D. III

5. The department which has more than 7 divisions and more than 200 employees but fewer than 19 stations is   5.___

   A. XV B. III C. XX D. XIII

6. The department having more than 10 divisions and fewer than 36 stations, which had an increase in long distance calls in 2000 over 1999, is   6.___

   A. XI B. VII C. XVI D. XVIII

7. The department which in 2000 had at least 7,250 incoming calls and a decrease in long distance calls from 1999 and has more than 50 stations is

   A. IX	B. XII	C. XVIII	D. III

8. The department which has fewer than 25 stations, fewer than 100 employees, 10 or more divisions, and showed an increase of at least 9 long distance calls in 2000 over 1999 is

   A. IX	B. XVI	C. XX	D. XIII

9. The department which has more than 50 but fewer than 125 employees and had more than 5,000 incoming calls in 1999 but not more than 10,000, and more than 60 long distance calls in 2000 but not more than 85, and has more than 24 stations is

   A. VIII	B. XIV	C. IV	D. XI

10. If the number of departments showing an increase in long distance calls in 2000 over 1999 exceeds the number showing a decrease in long distance calls in the same period, select the Roman numeral indicating the department having less than one station for each 10 employees, provided not more than 8 divisions are served by that department. If the number of departments showing an increase in long distance calls in 2000 over 1999 does not exceed the number showing a decrease in long distance calls in the same period, select the Roman numeral indicating the department having the SMALLEST number of incoming calls in 2000.

    A. III	B. XIII	C. XV	D. XX

KEY (CORRECT ANSWERS)

1.	C	6.	A
2.	B	7.	D
3.	A	8.	B
4.	C	9.	A
5.	D	10.	C

TEST 4

Questions 1-6.

DIRECTIONS: Questions 1 through 6 are to be answered SOLELY on the basis of the information given in the chart below. This chart shows the results of a study made of the tasks performed by a stenographer during one day. Included in the chart are the time at which she started a certain task and, under the particular heading, the amount of time, in minutes, she took to complete the task, and explanations of telephone calls and miscellaneous activities. NOTE: The time spent at lunch should not be included in any of your calculations.

PAMELA JOB STUDY

NAME: Pamela Donald   DATE: 9/26
JOB TITLE: Stenographer
DIVISION: Stenographic Pool

Time of Start of Task	Taking Dicta-tion	Typ-ing	Fil-ing	Tele-phone Work	Hand-ling Mail	Misc. Acti-vities	Explanations of Telephone Calls and Miscellaneous Activities
9:00					22		
9:22						13	Picking up supplies
9:35						15	Cleaning typewriter
9:50	11						
10:01		30					
10:31				8			Call to Agency A
10:39	12						
10:51			10				
11:01				7			Call from Agency B
11:08		30					
11:38	10						
11:48				12			Call from Agency C
12:00	L	U	N	C	H		
1:00					28		
1:28	13						
1:41 2:13		32		12			Call to Agency B
X			15				
Y		50					
3:30	10						
3:40			21				
4:01				9			Call from Agency A
4:10	35						
4:45			9				
4:54						6	Cleaning up desk

SAMPLE QUESTION:

The total amount of time spent on miscellaneous activities in the morning is exactly equal to the total amount of time spent

  A. filing in the morning
  B. handling mail in the afternoon
  C. miscellaneous activities in the afternoon
  D. handling mail in the morning

Explanation of answer to sample question:

2 (#4)

The total amount of time spent on miscellaneous activities in the morning equals 28 minutes (13 minutes for picking up supplies plus 15 minutes for cleaning the typewriter); and since it takes 28 minutes to handle mail in the afternoon, the answer is B.

1. The time labeled Y at which the stenographer started a typing assignment was

   A. 2:15   B. 2:25   C. 2:40   D. 2:50

2. The ratio of time spent on all incoming calls to time spent on all outgoing calls for the day was

   A. 5:7   B. 5:12   C. 7:5   D. 7:12

3. Of the following combinations of tasks, which ones take up exactly 80% of the total time spent on Tasks Performed during the day?

   A. Typing, filing, telephone work, and handling mail
   B. Taking dictation, filing, and miscellaneous activities
   C. Taking dictation, typing, handling mail, and miscellaneous activities
   D. Taking dictation, typing, filing, and telephone work

4. The total amount of time spent transcribing or typing work is how much MORE than the total amount of time spent in taking dictation?

   A. 55 minutes   B. 1 hour
   C. 1 hour 10 minutes   D. 1 hour 25 minutes

5. The GREATEST number of shifts in activities occurred between the times of

   A. 9:00 A.M. and 10:31 A.M.
   B. 9:35 A.M. and 11:01 A.M.
   C. 10:31 A.M. and 12:00 Noon
   D. 3:30 P.M. and 5:00 P.M.

6. The total amount of time spent on taking dictation in the morning plus the total amount of time spent on filing in the afternoon is exactly EQUAL to the total amount of time spent on

   A. typing in the afternoon minus the total amount of time spent on telephone work in the afternoon
   B. typing in the morning plus the total amount of time spent on miscellaneous activities in the afternoon
   C. dictation in the afternoon plus the total amount of time spent on filing in the morning
   D. typing in the afternoon minus the total amount of time spent on handling mail in the morning

KEY (CORRECT ANSWERS)

1. C   4. B
2. C   5. C
3. D   6. D

TEST 5

Questions 1-8.

DIRECTIONS: Questions 1 through 8 are to be answered SOLELY on the basis of the information given in the table below.

	Bronx		Brooklyn		Manhattan		Queens		Richmond	
	May	June	May	June	May	June	May	June	May	June
Number of Clerks in Office Assigned To Issue Applications for Licenses	3	4	6	8	6	8	3	5	3	4
Number of Licenses Issued	950	1010	1620	1940	1705	2025	895	1250	685	975
Amount Collected in License Fees	$42,400	$52,100	$77,600	$94,500	$83,700	$98,800	$39,300	$65,500	$30,600	$48,200
Number of Inspectors	4	5	6	7	7	8	4	5	2	4
Number of Inspections Made	420	450	630	710	690	740	400	580	320	440
Number of Violations Found as a Result of Inspections	211	153	352	378	320	385	256	304	105	247

1. Of the following statements, the one which is NOT accurate on the basis of an inspection of the information contained in the table is that, for each office, the increase from May to June in the number of

   A. inspectors was accompanied by an increase in the number of inspections made
   B. licenses issued was accompanied by an increase in the amount collected in license fees
   C. inspections made was accompanied by an increase in the number of violations found
   D. licenses issued was accompanied by an increase in the number of clerks assigned to issue applications for licenses

2. The TOTAL number of licenses issued by all five offices in the Division in May was

   A. 4800   B. 5855   C. 6865   D. 7200

2 (#5)

3. The total number of inspectors in all five borough offices in June exceeded the number in May by MOST NEARLY

   A. 21%   B. 26%   C. 55%   D. 70%

3.____

4. In the month of June, the number of violations found per inspection made was the HIGHEST in

   A. Brooklyn   B. Manhattan   C. Queens   D. Richmond

4.____

5. In the month of May, the average number of inspections made by an inspector in the Bronx was the same as the average number of inspections made by an inspector in

   A. Brooklyn   B. Manhattan   C. Queens   D. Richmond

5.____

6. Assume that in June all of the inspectors in the Division spent 7 hours a day making inspections on each of the 21 working days in the month.
   Then the average amount of time that an inspector in the Manhattan office spent on an inspection that month was MOST NEARLY

   A. 2 hours   B. 1 hour and 35 minutes
   C. 1 hour and 3 minutes   D. 38 minutes

6.____

7. If an average fine of $100 was imposed for a violation found by the Division, what was the TOTAL amount in fines imposed for all the violations found by the Division in May?

   A. $124,400   B. $133,500   C. $146,700   D. $267,000

7.____

8. Assume that the amount collected in license fees by the entire Division in May was 80 percent of the amount collected by the entire Division in April.
   How much was collected by the entire Division in April?

   A. $218,880   B. $328,320   C. $342,000   D. $410,400

8.____

KEY (CORRECT ANSWERS)

1. C   5. A
2. B   6. B
3. B   7. A
4. D   8. C

TEST 6

Questions 1-8.

DIRECTIONS: Questions 1 through 8 are to be answered SOLELY on the basis of the information contained in the chart and table shown below, which relate to Bureau X in a certain public agency. The chart shows the percentage of the bureau's annual expenditures spent on equipment, supplies, and salaries for each of the years 1997-2001. The table shows the bureau's annual expenditures for each of the years 1997-2001.

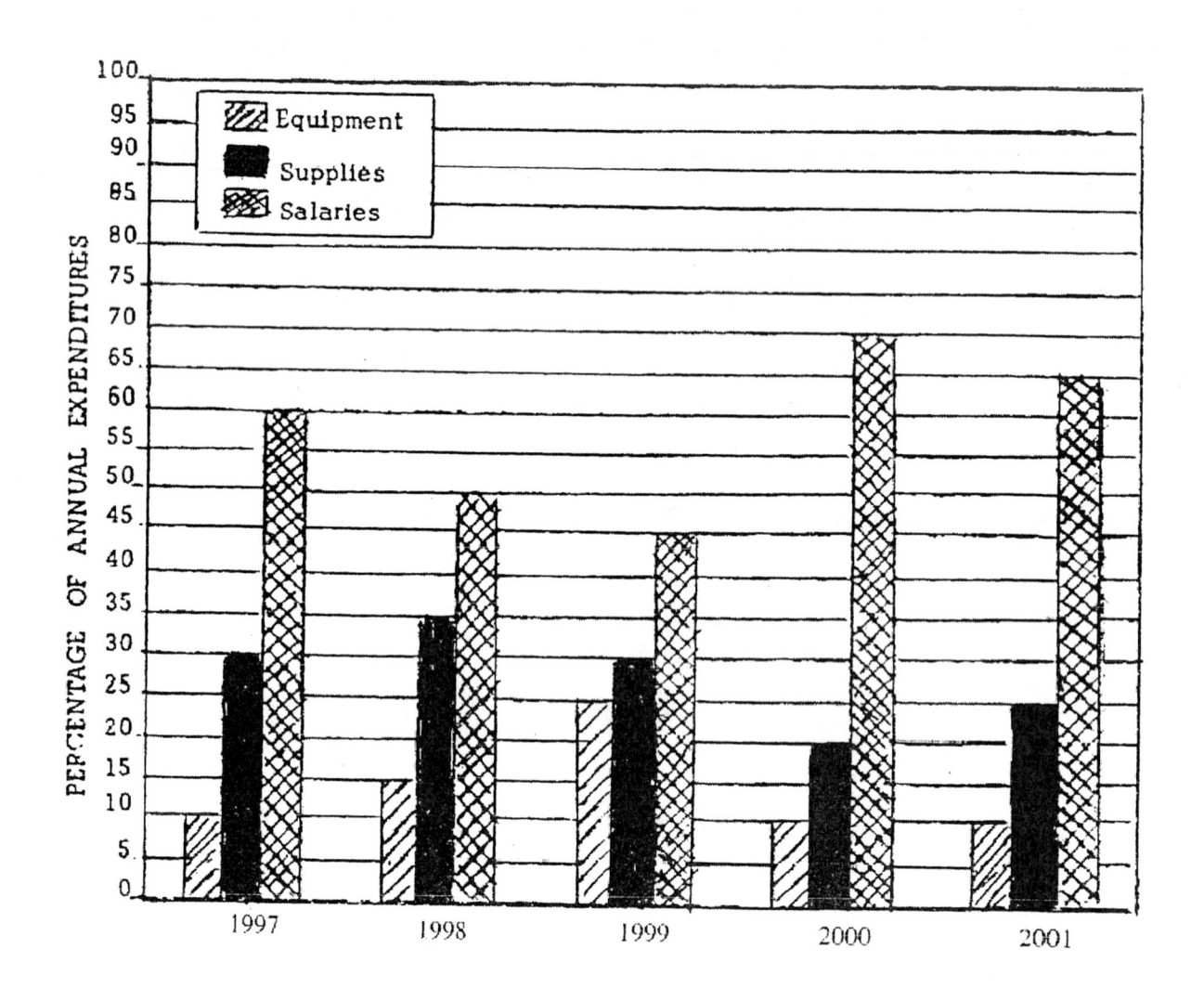

The bureau's annual expenditures for the years 1997-2001 are shown in the following table:

YEAR	EXPENDITURES
1997	$ 8,000,000
1998	$12,000,000
1999	$15,000,000
2000	$10,000,000
2001	$12,000,000

Equipment, supplies, and salaries were the only three categories for which the bureau spent money.

Candidates may find it useful to arrange their computations on their scratch paper in an orderly manner since the correct computations for one question may also be helpful in answering another question.

1. The information contained in the chart and table is sufficient to determine the

   A. average annual salary of an employee in the bureau in 1998
   B. decrease in the amount of money spent on supplies in the bureau in 1997 from the amount spent in the preceding year
   C. changes between 1999 and 2000 in the prices of supplies bought by the bureau
   D. increase in the amount of money spent on salaries in the bureau in 2001 over the amount spent in the preceding year

1._____

2. If the percentage of expenditures for salaries in one year is added to the percentage of expenditures for equipment in that year, a total of two percentages for that year is obtained.
   The two years for which this total is the SAME are

   A. 1997 and 1999
   B. 1998 and 2000
   C. 1997 and 2000
   D. 1998 and 2001

2._____

3. Of the following, the year in which the bureau spent the GREATEST amount of money on supplies was

   A. 2001
   B. 1999
   C. 1993
   D. 1997

3._____

4. Of the following years, the one in which there was the GREATEST increase over the preceding year in the amount of money spent on salaries is

   A. 2000
   B. 2001
   C. 1998
   D. 1999

4._____

5. Of the bureau's expenditures for equipment in 2001, one-third was used for the purchase of mailroom equipment and the remainder was spent on miscellaneous office equipment. How much did the bureau spend on miscellaneous office equipment in 2001?

   A. $4,000,000
   B. $400,000
   C. $8,000,000
   D. $800,000

5._____

6. If there were 120 employees in the bureau in 2000, then the average annual salary paid to the employees in that year was MOST NEARLY

   A. $43,450
   B. $49,600
   C. $58,350
   D. $80,800

6._____

7. In 1999, the bureau had 125 employees.
   If 20 of the employees earned an average annual salary of $80,000, then the average salary of the other 105 employees was MOST NEARLY

   A. $49,000
   B. $64,000
   C. $41,000
   D. $54,000

7._____

8. Assume that the bureau estimated that the amount of money it would spend on supplies in 2002 would be the same as the amount it spent on that category in 2001. Similarly, the bureau estimated that the amount of money it would spend on equipment in 2002 would be the same as the amount it spent on that category in 2001. However, the bureau estimated that in 2002 the amount it would spend on salaries would be 10 percent higher than the amount it spent on that category in 2001.
The percentage of its annual expenditures that the bureau estimated it would spend on supplies in 2002 is MOST NEARLY

   A. 27.5%   B. 23.5%   C. 22.5%   D. 25%

8.____

KEY (CORRECT ANSWERS)

1. D
2. A
3. B
4. C

5. D
6. C
7. A
8. B

ARITHMETICAL REASONING
EXAMINATION SECTION
TEST 1

DIRECTIONS: Each question or incomplete statement is followed by several suggested answers or completions. Select the one that BEST answers the question or completes the statement. *PRINT THE LETTER OF THE CORRECT ANSWER IN THE SPACE AT THE RIGHT.*

1. You have conducted a traffic survey at 10 two-lane bridges and find the traffic between 4:30 and 5:30 P.M. averages 665 cars per bridge that hour. You can't find the tabulation sheet for bridge #7, but you know that 6,066 cars were counted at the other 9 bridges. Determine from this how many must have been counted at bridge #7.

    A. 584 B. 674 C. 665 D. 607

2. You pay temporary help $8.40 per hour and regular employees $9.00 per hour. Your workload is temporarily heavy, so you need 20 hours of extra regular employees' time to catch up. If you do this on overtime, you must pay time and a half. If you use temporary help, it takes 25% more time to do the job.
   What is the DIFFERENCE in cost between the two alternatives? _____ more for _____.

    A. $15; temporary   B. $30; temporary
    C. $60; regular   D. $102; regular

3. An experienced clerk can process the mailing of annual forms in 9 days. A new clerk takes 14 days to process them.
   If they work together, how many days MOST NEARLY will it take to do the processing?

    A. 4 1/2 B. 5 1/2 C. 6 1/2 D. 7

4. A certain administrative aide is usually able to successfully handle 27% of all telephone inquiries without assistance. In a particular month, he receives 1,200 inquiries and handles 340 of them successfully on his own. How many more inquiries has he handled successfully in that month than would have been expected of him based on his usual rate?

    A. 10 B. 16 C. 24 D. 44

5. A basketball team purchased uniforms from a sports shop for $1,072, less discounts of 15% and 10%.
   The check should be made out in the sum of

    A. $804.56   B. $820.08
    C. $837.72   D. none of the above

6. A secretary is entitled to 1 1/3 days of sick leave for every 32 days of work.
   How many days of work must the secretary have to her credit in order to be entitled to 12 days of sick leave?

    A. 272 B. 288 C. 290 D. 512

2 (#1)

7. A school secretary, whose annual salary is $54,850, contributes 9.8% to the retirement fund. Other monthly deductions from her salary are: federal income tax, $700; state income tax, $150; social security tax, $100.
The amount of her monthly check is

   A. $3,272.90   B. $3,172.90   C. $3,174.00   D. $3,164.00

7.___

8. Suppose a review of the completed work of three operators for a certain period shows that operator A processed 250 files and that operator B processed 285, 60 more than operator C completed.
To find the average number of files processed by the three operators, one would need to

   A. subtract, then add, then divide
   B. subtract, then divide
   C. add, then divide
   D. add, then divide, then subtract

8.___

9. If there are 875 files to be processed and an operator completes 320 files by herself, what percentage of the total did she MOST NEARLY complete?

   A. 21%   B. 27%   C. 36%   D. 43%

9.___

10. An operator processed 907 files in one day. To speed the work, two other workers are assigned, and together the three operators process 2,407 files.
The percentage of increase in the number of files processed is MOST NEARLY

    A. 155%   B. 165%   C. 175%   D. 185%

10.___

11. Two operators have processed 368 files and 175 files, respectively.
To find the difference between the number processed by each operator and to check the accuracy of the calculations, it would be BEST to do which of the following?

    A. Add 368 to 175 to find the answer; then subtract 175 from the answer to check.
    B. Add 368 and 175, and divide the sum by two to find the answer; then add 175 and 368, and divide by two to check.
    C. Subtract 175 from 368 to find the answer; then add the answer to 175 to see if it equals 368.
    D. Divide 368 by 175 to find the answer; then multiply the answer by 175 to see if it equals 368.

11.___

12. Four operators were assigned to complete a project. Operator A did 2/5 of the work, Operator B did 1/6 of the work, and Operator C did 1/3 of the work.
How much work must Operator D do to complete the project?

    A. 1/5   B. 1/6   C. 2/3   D. 1/10

12.___

13. A certain job requires that 40% of the 80 pages of a file be scanned automatically, and the rest be copied manually by the operator.
If there are 1,250 files in the entire job, what is the TOTAL number of pages the operator must copy manually?

    A. 40,000   B. 60,000   C. 80,000   D. 100,000

13.___

14. Computer X can upload 120 processed files in an hour, while Computer Z can upload 150 processed files in the same amount of time.
The production per hour of the slower machine is what fraction of the production per hour of the faster machine?

    A. 1/5   B. 2/3   C. 4/5   D. 5/6

14.____

15. Suppose that an operator was given the responsibility for reorganizing the files in her office. She had 3,000 cards to file in drawers 18" long. These drawers hold 100 cards for each 1 1/2 inches of length. In each drawer, 2" of space had to be left empty for ease of card searching.
Of the following, the PROPER order of mathematical procedures to find the fewest number of drawers she will need would be

    A. multiply, divide, subtract, multiply
    B. subtract, divide, multiply, divide
    C. subtract, multiply, divide, divide
    D. divide, divide, subtract, multiply

15.____

16. In arithmetic, there are frequently several ways to arrive at an answer.
Which one of the following can NOT be used to find the value of 20% of 7,372?

    A. 7,372 ÷ .2   B. 7,372 x .2
    C. 7,372 x .20   D. 1/5 of 7,372

16.____

17. A certain department submitted a payroll request for separate checks for each of 115 clerks, 52 typists, 107 technicians, 23 administrators, 12 messengers, 8 drivers, and 35 others. The average amount of each check was $327.53.
The TOTAL payroll was

    A. $113,290.46   B. $114,180.56
    C. $114,280.46   D. $115,290.56

17.____

18. A certain city administration is composed of four departments: Departments W, X, Y, and Z. Of the personnel in this administration, 1/3 work for Department W; 1/4, for Department X; and 1/6, for Department Y.
What part of the administration's personnel is working for Department Z?

    A. 1/4   B. 1/5   C. 1/6   D. 1/7

18.____

19. Suppose an operator finds that the first job he did one day took 35 minutes, the second took 1/4 hour, the third 11 minutes, and the fourth took 17 minutes. Between each job, there was a ten-minute period for record keeping.
If he began the first job at 9:15 A.M., at what time did he FINISH the fourth job?

    A. 10:33 A.M.   B. 10:53 A.M.
    C. 11:03 A.M.   D. 11:13 A.M.

19.____

20. A certain program can process a maximum of 1,000 files per minute. However, this program is not run all the time, and not every batch of files is as large as 1,000. In the first five minutes of an hour, 3,000 files were processed; in the next five minutes, 200 were processed; and in the third five minutes, 600 were processed.
What is the RATIO of actual output of files to maximum possible output of files during this period?

    A. 1:4   B. 3:10   C. 35:100   D. 4:10

20.____

21. A check of the time records of a certain employee reveals that he spent 9 days on sick leave last year. This employee works a 7-hour day.
The average number of hours he was on sick leave each month last year was MOST NEARLY

    A. 1 1/3   B. 5 1/4   C. 9 3/4   D. 12 1/2

22. In the same amount of time, Machine B can process only 2/3 as many files as Machine A, but 1 1/4 times as many cards as Machine C.
If Machine A can process 1,500 files per minute, how many files per minute can Machine C process?

    A. 600   B. 800   C. 1,000   D. 1,200

23. Look at the incomplete balance sheet below.

    Balance Sheet

	Assets		Liabilities
A	$195,679.42	D	$378,429.58
B	$241,382.15	E	_____
C	$486,723.69		
Total		Total	

    If total assets equaled total liabilities, what amount should be shown next to entry E?

    A. $545,355.68   B. $555,355.68
    C. $545,455.68   D. $555,455.68

24. Computer A can process 900 files a minute while Computer B can process 800 files a minute.
At this rate, how much LONGER would it take Computer B to process 36,000 files than it would take Computer A to process them? _____ minutes.

    A. 3   B. 5   C. 7   D. 9

25. An operator wants to find out what 47% of a certain payroll is, and then check his answer. Of the following, the steps he should take are:

    A. Divide the amount of the payroll by .47 and multiply the answer by .47
    B. Divide .47 by the amount of the payroll and multiply the answer by the amount of the payroll
    C. Multiply the amount of the payroll by .47 and multiply the answer by .47
    D. Multiply the amount of the payroll by .47 and divide the answer by the amount of the payroll

KEY (CORRECT ANSWERS)

1.	A		11.	C
2.	C		12.	D
3.	B		13.	B
4.	B		14.	C
5.	B		15.	B
6.	B		16.	A
7.	B		17.	D
8.	A		18.	A
9.	C		19.	C
10.	B		20.	A

21. B
22. B
23. A
24. B
25. D

SOLUTIONS TO PROBLEMS

1. (665)(10) - 6066 = 584 cases

2. Using regular employees, the cost = (20)($9.00)(1.5) = $270 Using temporary help, the cost = (20)(1.25)($8.40) = $210 So, regular employees will cost $60 more than temporary help

3. Let x = number of days. Then, (1/9)(x) + (1/14)(x) = 1. Thus, 14x + 9x = 126. Solving, x = 126/23 = 5 1/2 days

4. 340 - (.27)(1200) = 16 inquiries

5. ($1072)(.85)(.90) = $820.08

6. 12 ÷ 1 1/3 = 9. Then, (9)(32) = 288 days of work

7. Her monthly check = $4570.83 - (.098)($4570.83) - $700 - $150 - $100 ≈ $3172.90

8. First, subtract 60 from 285 to get 225. Then, add: 250, 285, and 225 to get 760. Finally, divide 760 by 3 to get 253 1/3

9. 320/875 ≈ 37% (Selection C is closest with 36%)

10. (2407-907) ÷ 907 ≈ 165%

11. First subtract 175 from 368 to get 193. Second, to check this answer, add 193 to 175.

12. Operator D did $1 - \frac{2}{5} - \frac{1}{6} - \frac{1}{3} = \frac{1}{10}$

13. (.60)(80)(1250) = 60,000 pages

14. 120/150 = 4/5

15. Subtract: 18" - 2" = 16"; divide: 16" 1 1/2" = $10.\overline{6}$, rounded down to 10; multiply: (10)(100) = 1000 cards per drawer.
Finally, divide: 3000 ÷ 1000 = 3 drawers

16. 20% of 7372 = 1474.4 ≠ 7372 ÷ .2, which is 36,860

17. Total payroll = ($327.53)(115+52+107+23+12+8+35) = $115,290.56

18. $1 - \frac{1}{3} - \frac{1}{4} - \frac{1}{6} = \frac{1}{4}$ working for Department Z

19. Time between beginning of 1st job to end of 4th job = 35 + 10 + 15 + 10 + 11 + 10 + 17 = 108 min. = 1 hr. 48 min. Then, 9:15 AM + 1 hr. 48 min. = 11:03 AM

20. Maximum output in 15 min. = (1000)(15) = 15,000 files. Actual output in 15 min. = 3000 + 200 + 600 = 3800 files Then, 3800 ÷ 15,000 = 19:75, which is closest to 1:4

21. (9)(7) = 63 hours per year = 5 1/4 hours per month

22. Machine B can process (2/3) (1500) = 1000 cards per min., so Machine C can process 1000 ÷ 1 1/4 = 800 cards per min.

23. Entry E = Entry A + Entry B + Entry C - Entry D = $545,355.68

24. 36,000/800 - 36,000/900 = 5 min.

25. Multiply the payroll by .47. To check, take answer obtained and divide by payroll amount. (Should get .47)

TEST 2

DIRECTIONS: Each question or incomplete statement is followed by several suggested answers or completions. Select the one that BEST answers the question or completes the statement. *PRINT THE LETTER OF THE CORRECT ANSWER IN THE SPACE AT THE RIGHT.*

1. 3/4 of 1 percent expressed as a decimal is

    A. 7.5   B. .75   C. .075   D. .0075

2. If one telephone operator can handle 50 calls in 6 minutes and another can take care of the same number in 3 minutes, then both working together can dispose of the 50 calls in _____ minute(s).

    A. 1/2   B. 1   C. 1 1/2   D. 2

3. If an operator sells two cars at $6,000 each, making a profit of 20 percent on one and taking a loss of 20 percent on the other, then, on the whole transaction involving the purchase and sale of the two cars, she will

    A. break even   B. gain $500
    C. lose $500   D. do none of the above

4. If X percent of the length of telephone wire A is equal to Y percent of the length of telephone wire B, and telephone wire B measures Z feet, then the length of telephone wire A, expressed in feet, is

    A. YZ/X   B. 100XY   C. 100Z/XY   D. 100YZ/X

5. If there were 107,147 employees in all classes of the city service, and 629 of these were in the exempt class, then the percentage of city employees in the exempt class was MOST NEARLY _____ percent.

    A. 1/4 of 1   B. 1/2 of 1   C. 3/4 of 1   D. 1

6. The sum of 90.79, 79.09, 97.90, and 9.97 is

    A. 277.75   B. 278.56   C. 276.94   D. 277.93

7. A cube-shaped box has a side of S inches. The volume of the box is S^3 cubic inches. If each side of the box were increased by 3 inches, the volume would then be represented by

    A. $(S+3)^3$ B. S^3+3 C. $(3S+9)^3$ D. S^3+3^3

8. In an agency, 7/12 of the employees are engaged in clerical work, 1/3 of the employees are engaged in supervisory work, and 1/4 of the employees are not engaged in either clerical or supervisory work.
    How many employees in this agency are engaged in BOTH clerical and supervisory work?

    A. 1/6   B. 1/12   C. 1/3   D. 1/4

9. A new computer installation has the memory capacity to run 15 jobs simultaneously, whereas the old computer installation has the memory capacity to run 5 jobs simultaneously.
If it took the old computer 2 hours and 36 minutes to run 250 jobs, how long will it take the new computer to run 625 jobs, assuming it takes the same amount of time for both computers to run each single job?

   A. 52 minutes
   B. 1 hour 30 minutes
   C. 1 hour 50 minutes
   D. 2 hours 10 minutes

10. In a right triangle, the area is equal to 1/2 the product of two legs. Assume you have the following five right triangles with legs as indicated:
    Triangle I   legs 9 inches and 7 inches long
    Triangle II   legs 8 inches and 8 inches long
    Triangle III   legs 3 inches and 13 inches long
    Triangle IV   legs 5 inches and 12 inches long
    Triangle V   legs 4 inches and 16 inches long
    Which of the above triangles have the SAME area?

    A. I and II
    B. III and IV
    C. I and V
    D. II and V

11. Due to a nationwide fuel shortage, the speed limit on a major highway was lowered 5 miles per hour. Assume that a certain motorist always drives at the legal speed limit. If he were able to drive 99 miles in 2 1/5 hours at the original speed limit, how long will it take him to drive 100 miles at the new speed limit?
    2 hours _____ minutes.

    A. 12
    B. 20
    C. 30
    D. 50

12. If the pressure (P) of a gas in a closed container varies directly with the temperature (T) and inversely with the volume (V) of the container, which of the following is TRUE?
    If the

    A. temperature is increased, the volume is increased
    B. pressure is decreased, the temperature is increased
    C. volume is increased, the pressure is increased
    D. temperature is increased, the pressure is increased

13. An operator processes an average of 75 files an hour for a normal work day of 7 hours. If 20% of the files must be verified, how many of the operator's files must be verified in a normal 5-day work week?

    A. 115
    B. 263
    C. 525
    D. 2,625

14. If the Law of Division applying to exponents states that $X^m \div X^n = X^{m-n}$, what does $2^6 \div 2^4$ equal?

    A. 1
    B. 4
    C. 8
    D. 16

15. In one state, the tax rate on the purchase price of an automobile is 3% higher than the tax rate in a neighboring state. The base price of the automobile is $3,000 in both states. If the automobile costs $3,120 in the state with the lower tax rate, what does it cost in the state with the higher tax rate?

    A. $3,120
    B. $3,210
    C. $3,300
    D. $3,936

16. An employee earns $120 a day and works 5 days a week. He will earn $5,400 in _____ weeks.

    A. 5   B. 7   C. 8   D. 9

17. In a certain bureau, the entire staff consists of 1 senior supervisor, 2 supervisors, 6 assistant supervisors, and 54 associate workers.
    The percent of the staff who are NOT associate workers is MOST NEARLY

    A. 14%   B. 21%   C. 27%   D. 32%

18. In a certain bureau, five employees each earn $2,500 a month, another 3 employees each earn $3,000 a month, and another two employees each earn $3,500 a month. The monthly payroll for these employees is

    A. $9,000   B. $22,000   C. $28,500   D. $30,000

19. An employee contributes 5% of his salary to the pension fund.
    If his salary is $3,000 a month, the amount of his contribution to the pension fund in a year is

    A. $1,200   B. $1,800   C. $2,400   D. $3,000

20. The number of square feet in an area that is 50 feet long and 30 feet wide is

    A. 80   B. 150   C. 800   D. 1,500

21. The sum of 5 1/2, 4, 3 1/4, and 2 is

    A. 14 3/4   B. 13 1/2   C. 12   D. 10 1/4

22. The sum of 2.6", 1.2", and 4.1" is

    A. 6.6"   B. 7.3"   C. 7.9"   D. 8.2"

23. The fraction 3/8 expressed as a decimal is

    A. 0.250   B. 0.281   C. 0.375   D. 0.406

24. The sum of 2' 6", 0' 3", and 3' 1" is

    A. 2' 9"   B. 5' 7"   C. 5' 10"   D. 15' 0"

25. A man and boy working together complete a job in 8 hours. If a boy does half as much work as a man, two men working together can complete the job in _____ hours.

    A. 7 1/2   B. 7   C. 6 1/2   D. 6

KEY (CORRECT ANSWERS)

1.	D		11.	C
2.	D		12.	D
3.	C		13.	C
4.	A		14.	B
5.	B		15.	B
6.	A		16.	D
7.	A		17.	A
8.	A		18.	C
9.	D		19.	B
10.	D		20.	D

21. A
22. C
23. C
24. C
25. D

SOLUTIONS TO PROBLEMS

1. 3/4 of 1% = (.75)(.01) = .0075

2. Let x = required min. Then, $(\frac{1}{6})(x) + (\frac{1}{3})(x) = 1$. Simplifying, Solving, x = 2

3. Her cost for the 2 vehicles = ($6000 ÷ 1.20) + ($6000 ÷ .80) = $5000 + $7500 = $12,500. Since she sold the 2 vehicles for $12,000, she lost $500.

4. Let L = length of wire A. Then, $(\frac{X}{100})(L) = (\frac{Y}{100})(Z)$.

   Solving, $L = (\frac{Y}{100})(Z)(\frac{100}{X}) = YZ/X$

5. 629 ÷ 107,147 .006, which is closest to 1/2 of 1 percent

6. 90.79 + 79.09 + 97.90 + 9.97 = 277.75

7. Each new side is s+3 inches. New volume = $(s+3)^3$ cubic inches

8. Let x = fraction of employees required in both categories.
   Then, $\frac{7}{12} + \frac{1}{3} + \frac{1}{4} - x = 1$. Solving, $x = \frac{1}{6}$

9. To run 250 jobs, the new computer needs (1/3)(156) = 52 min. So, to run 625 jobs, the new computer would need (625/250)(52) = 130 min. = 2 hrs. 10 min.

10. The areas of triangles I, II, III, IV, V are (in square inches) 31 1/2, 32, 19 1/2, 30, and 32, respectively. Thus, triangles II and V have the same area.

11. $99 \div 2\frac{1}{5} = 45$ mph. The new speed limit is 40 mph, so 100 miles takes 100/40 = 2.5 hrs. = 2 hrs. 30 min.

12. We can write P = KT/V, where K is a constant. If the volume remains constant, then as temperature is increased, the pressure is increased.

13. (75)(7)(5)(.20) = 525 cards to be verified

14. $2^6 \div 2^4 = 2^2 = 4$

15. ($3120-$3000) ÷ $3000 = 4%. So, the tax rate in the other state is 7%. Auto cost = ($3000)(1.07) = $3210

16. ($120)(5) = $600 per week. Then, $5400 ÷ $600 = 9 weeks

17. $(1+2+6)/63 \approx 14\%$

18. $(5)(\$2500) + (3)(\$3000) + (2)(\$3500) = \$28,500$

19. $(\$3000)(12)(.05) = \$1800$ pension contribution in a year.

20. $(50')(30') = 1500$ sq.ft.

21. $5\ 1/2 + 4 + 3\ 1/4 + 2 = 14\ 3/4$

22. $2.6" + 1.2" + 4.1" = 7.9"$

23. $3/8 = .375$

24. $2'\ 6" + 0'\ 3" + 3'\ 1" = 5'\ 10"$

25. A man and a boy = 1 1/2 men working 8 hrs. = 12 man-hours
    Then, $12 \div 2 = 6$ hours

PHILOSOPHY, PRINCIPLES, PRACTICES AND TECHNICS OF SUPERVISION, ADMINISTRATION, MANAGEMENT AND ORGANIZATION

TABLE OF CONTENTS

		Page
I.	MEANING OF SUPERVISION	1
II.	THE OLD AND THE NEW SUPERVISION	1
III.	THE EIGHT (8) BASIC PRINCIPLES OF THE NEW SUPERVISION	1
	1. Principle of Responsibility	1
	2. Principle of Authority	2
	3. Principle of Self-Growth	2
	4. Principle of Individual Worth	2
	5. Principle of Creative Leadership	2
	6. Principle of Success and Failure	2
	7. Principle of Science	3
	8. Principle of Cooperation	3
IV.	WHAT IS ADMINISTRATION?	3
	1. Practices commonly classed as "Supervisory"	3
	2. Practices commonly classed as "Administrative"	3
	3. Practices classified as both "Supervisory" and "Administrative"	4
V.	RESPONSIBILITIES OF THE SUPERVISOR	4
VI.	COMPETENCIES OF THE SUPERVISOR	4
VII.	THE PROFESSIONAL SUPERVISOR—EMPLOYEE RELATIONSHIP	4
VIII.	MINI-TEXT IN SUPERVISION, ADMINISTRATION, MANAGEMENT AND ORGANIZATION	5
	A. Brief Highlights	5
	1. Levels of Management	5
	2. What the Supervisor Must Learn	6
	3. A Definition of Supervision	6
	4. Elements of the Team Concept	6
	5. Principles of Organization	6
	6. The Four Important Parts of Every Job	6
	7. Principles of Delegation	6
	8. Principles of Effective Communications	7
	9. Principles of Work Improvement	7

TABLE OF CONTENTS (CONTINUED)

  10. Areas of Job Improvement   7
  11. Seven Key Points in Making Improvements   7
  12. Corrective Techniques for Job Improvement   7
  13. A Planning Checklist   8
  14. Five Characteristics of Good Directions   8
  15. Types of Directions   8
  16. Controls   8
  17. Orienting the New Employee   8
  18. Checklist for Orienting New Employees   8
  19. Principles of Learning   9
  20. Causes of Poor Performance   9
  21. Four Major Steps in On-The-Job Instructions   9
  22. Employees Want Five Things   9
  23. Some Don'ts in Regard to Praise   9
  24. How to Gain Your Workers' Confidence   9
  25. Sources of Employee Problems   9
  26. The Supervisor's Key to Discipline   10
  27. Five Important Processes of Management   10
  28. When the Supervisor Fails to Plan   10
  29. Fourteen General Principles of Management   10
  30. Change   10

B. Brief Topical Summaries   11
  I. Who/What is the Supervisor?   11
  II. The Sociology of Work   11
  III. Principles and Practices of Supervision   12
  IV. Dynamic Leadership   12
  V. Processes for Solving Problems   12
  VI. Training for Results   13
  VII. Health, Safety and Accident Prevention   13
  VIII. Equal Employment Opportunity   13
  IX. Improving Communications   14
  X. Self-Development   14
  XI. Teaching and Training   14
   A. The Teaching Process   14
    1. Preparation   14
    2. Presentation   15
    3. Summary   15
    4. Application   15
    5. Evaluation   15
   B. Teaching Methods   15
    1. Lecture   15
    2. Discussion   15
    3. Demonstration   16
    4. Performance   16
    5. Which Method to Use   16

PHILOSOPHY, PRINCIPLES, PRACTICES, AND TECHNICS
OF
SUPERVISION, ADMINISTRATION, MANAGEMENT AND ORGANIZATION

I. MEANING OF SUPERVISION

The extension of the democratic philosophy has been accompanied by an extension in the scope of supervision. Modern leaders and supervisors no longer think of supervision in the narrow sense of being confined chiefly to visiting employees, supplying materials, or rating the staff. They regard supervision as being intimately related to all the concerned agencies of society, they speak of the supervisor's function in terms of "growth", rather than the "improvement," of employees.

This modern concept of supervision may be defined as follows:

Supervision is leadership and the development of leadership within groups which are cooperatively engaged in inspection, research, training, guidance and evaluation.

II. THE OLD AND THE NEW SUPERVISION

TRADITIONAL
1. Inspection
2. Focused on the employee
3. Visitation
4. Random and haphazard
5. Imposed and authoritarian
6. One person usually

MODERN
1. Study and analysis
2. Focused on aims, materials, methods, supervisors, employees, environment
3. Demonstrations, intervisitation, workshops, directed reading, bulletins, etc.
4. Definitely organized and planned (scientific)
5. Cooperative and democratic
6. Many persons involved (creative)

III THE EIGHT (8) BASIC PRINCIPLES OF THE NEW SUPERVISION

1. *PRINCIPLE OF RESPONSIBILITY*
Authority to act and responsibility for acting must be joined.
   a. If you give responsibility, give authority.
   b. Define employee duties clearly.
   c. Protect employees from criticism by others.
   d. Recognize the rights as well as obligations of employees.
   e. Achieve the aims of a democratic society insofar as it is possible within the area of your work.
   f. Establish a situation favorable to training and learning.
   g. Accept ultimate responsibility for everything done in your section, unit, office, division, department.
   h. Good administration and good supervision are inseparable.

2. PRINCIPLE OF AUTHORITY

The success of the supervisor is measured by the extent to which the power of authority is not used.

    a. Exercise simplicity and informality in supervision.
    b. Use the simplest machinery of supervision.
    c. If it is good for the organization as a whole, it is probably justified.
    d. Seldom be arbitrary or authoritative.
    e. Do not base your work on the power of position or of personality.
    f. Permit and encourage the free expression of opinions.

3. PRINCIPLE OF SELF-GROWTH

The success of the supervisor is measured by the extent to which, and the speed with which, he is no longer needed.

    a. Base criticism on principles, not on specifics.
    b. Point out higher activities to employees.
    c. Train for self-thinking by employees, to meet new situations.
    d. Stimulate initiative, self-reliance and individual responsibility.
    e. Concentrate on stimulating the growth of employees rather than on removing defects.

4. PRINCIPLE OF INDIVIDUAL WORTH

Respect for the individual is a paramount consideration in supervision.

    a. Be human and sympathetic in dealing with employees.
    b. Don't nag about things to be done.
    c. Recognize the individual differences among employees and seek opportunities to permit best expression of each personality.

5. PRINCIPLE OF CREATIVE LEADERSHIP

The best supervision is that which is not apparent to the employee.

    a. Stimulate, don't drive employees to creative action.
    b. Emphasize doing good things.
    c. Encourage employees to do what they do best.
    d. Do not be too greatly concerned with details of subject or method.
    e. Do not be concerned exclusively with immediate problems and activities.
    f. Reveal higher activities and make them both desired and maximally possible.
    g. Determine procedures in the light of each situation but see that these are derived from a sound basic philosophy.
    h. Aid, inspire and lead so as to liberate the creative spirit latent in all good employees.

6. PRINCIPLE OF SUCCESS AND FAILURE

There are no unsuccessful employees, only unsuccessful supervisors who have failed to give proper leadership.

    a. Adapt suggestions to the capacities, attitudes, and prejudices of employees.
    b. Be gradual, be progressive, be persistent.
    c. Help the employee find the general principle; have the employee apply his own problem to the general principle.
    d. Give adequate appreciation for good work and honest effort.
    e. Anticipate employee difficulties and help to prevent them.
    f. Encourage employees to do the desirable things they will do anyway.
    g. Judge your supervision by the results it secures.

7. *PRINCIPLE OF SCIENCE*
Successful supervision is scientific, objective, and experimental. It is based on facts, not on prejudices.
      a. Be cumulative in results.
      b. Never divorce your suggestions from the goals of training.
      c. Don't be impatient of results.
      d. Keep all matters on a professional, not a personal level.
      e. Do not be concerned exclusively with immediate problems and activities.
      f. Use objective means of determining achievement and rating where possible.

8. *PRINCIPLE OF COOPERATION*
Supervision is a cooperative enterprise between supervisor and employee.
      a. Begin with conditions as they are.
      b. Ask opinions of all involved when formulating policies.
      c. Organization is as good as its weakest link.
      d. Let employees help to determine policies and department programs.
      e. Be approachable and accessible - physically and mentally.
      f. Develop pleasant social relationships.

IV. WHAT IS ADMINISTRATION?

Administration is concerned with providing the environment, the material facilities, and the operational procedures that will promote the maximum growth and development of supervisors and employees. (Organization is an aspect, and a concomitant, of administration.)

There is no sharp line of demarcation between supervision and administration; these functions are intimately interrelated and, often, overlapping. They are complementary activities.

1. *PRACTICES COMMONLY CLASSED AS "SUPERVISORY"*
      a. Conducting employees conferences
      b. Visiting sections, units, offices, divisions, departments
      c. Arranging for demonstrations
      d. Examining plans
      e. Suggesting professional reading
      f. Interpreting bulletins
      g. Recommending in-service training courses
      h. Encouraging experimentation
      i. Appraising employee morale
      j. Providing for intervisitation

2. *PRACTICES COMMONLY CLASSIFIED AS "ADMINISTRATIVE"*
      a. Management of the office
      b. Arrangement of schedules for extra duties
      c. Assignment of rooms or areas
      d. Distribution of supplies
      e. Keeping records and reports
      f. Care of audio-visual materials
      g. Keeping inventory records
      h. Checking record cards and books
      i. Programming special activities
      j. Checking on the attendance and punctuality of employees

3. *PRACTICES COMMONLY CLASSIFIED AS BOTH "SUPERVISORY" AND "ADMINISTRATIVE"*
    a. Program construction
    b. Testing or evaluating outcomes
    c. Personnel accounting
    d. Ordering instructional materials

V. RESPONSIBILITIES OF THE SUPERVISOR

A person employed in a supervisory capacity must constantly be able to improve his own efficiency and ability. He represents the employer to the employees and only continuous self-examination can make him a capable supervisor.

Leadership and training are the supervisor's responsibility. An efficient working unit is one in which the employees work with the supervisor. It is his job to bring out the best in his employees. He must always be relaxed, courteous and calm in his association with his employees. Their feelings are important, and a harsh attitude does not develop the most efficient employees.

VI. COMPETENCIES OF THE SUPERVISOR

1. Complete knowledge of the duties and responsibilities of his position.
2. To be able to organize a job, plan ahead and carry through.
3. To have self-confidence and initiative.
4. To be able to handle the unexpected situation and make quick decisions.
5. To be able to properly train subordinates in the positions they are best suited for.
6. To be able to keep good human relations among his subordinates.
7. To be able to keep good human relations between his subordinates and himself and to earn their respect and trust.

VII. THE PROFESSIONAL SUPERVISOR-EMPLOYEE RELATIONSHIP

There are two kinds of efficiency: one kind is only apparent and is produced in organizations through the exercise of mere discipline; this is but a simulation of the second, or true, efficiency which springs from spontaneous cooperation. If you are a manager, no matter how great or small your responsibility, it is your job, in the final analysis, to create and develop this involuntary cooperation among the people whom you supervise. For, no matter how powerful a combination of money, machines, and materials a company may have, this is a dead and sterile thing without a team of willing, thinking and articulate people to guide it.

The following 21 points are presented as indicative of the exemplary basic relationship that should exist between supervisor and employee:

1. Each person wants to be liked and respected by his fellow employee and wants to be treated with consideration and respect by his superior.
2. The most competent employee will make an error. However, in a unit where good relations exist between the supervisor and his employees, tenseness and fear do not exist. Thus, errors are not hidden or covered up and the efficiency of a unit is not impaired.
3. Subordinates resent rules, regulations, or orders that are unreasonable or unexplained.
4. Subordinates are quick to resent unfairness, harshness, injustices and favoritism.
5. An employee will accept responsibility if he knows that he will be complimented for a job well done, and not too harshly chastised for failure; that his supervisor will check the cause of the failure, and, if it was the supervisor's fault, he will assume the blame therefore. If it was the employee's fault, his supervisor will explain the correct method or means of handling the responsibility.

6. An employee wants to receive credit for a suggestion he has made, that is used. If a suggestion cannot be used, the employee is entitled to an explanation. The supervisor should not say "no" and close the subject.
7. Fear and worry slow up a worker's ability. Poor working environment can impair his physical and mental health. A good supervisor avoids forceful methods, threats and arguments to get a job done.
8. A forceful supervisor is able to train his employees individually and as a team, and is able to motivate them in the proper channels.
9. A mature supervisor is able to properly evaluate his subordinates and to keep them happy and satisfied.
10. A sensitive supervisor will never patronize his subordinates.
11. A worthy supervisor will respect his employees' confidences.
12. Definite and clear-cut responsibilities should be assigned to each executive.
13. Responsibility should always be coupled with corresponding authority.
14. No change should be made in the scope or responsibilities of a position without a definite understanding to that effect on the part of all persons concerned.
15. No executive or employee, occupying a single position in the organization, should be subject to definite orders from more than one source.
16. Orders should never be given to subordinates over the head of a responsible executive. Rather than do this, the officer in question should be supplanted.
17. Criticisms of subordinates should, whoever possible, be made privately, and in no case should a subordinate be criticized in the presence of executives or employees of equal or lower rank.
18. No dispute or difference between executives or employees as to authority or responsibilities should be considered too trivial for prompt and careful adjudication.
19. Promotions, wage changes, and disciplinary action should always be approved by the executive immediately superior to the one directly responsible.
20. No executive or employee should ever be required, or expected, to be at the same time an assistant to, and critic of, another.
21. Any executive whose work is subject to regular inspection should, whever practicable, be given the assistance and facilities necessary to enable him to maintain an independent check of the quality of his work.

VIII. MINI-TEXT IN SUPERVISION, ADMINISTRATION, MANAGEMENT, AND ORGANIZATION

A. BRIEF HIGHLIGHTS

Listed concisely and sequentially are major headings and important data in the field for quick recall and review.

1. *LEVELS OF MANAGEMENT*

Any organization of some size has several levels of management. In terms of a ladder the levels are:

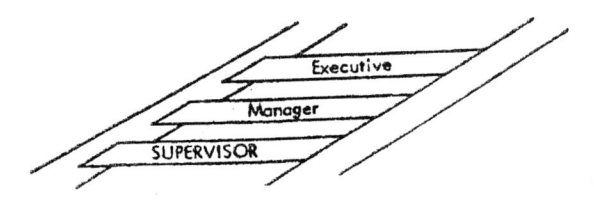

```
        Executive
      Manager
   SUPERVISOR
```

The first level is very important because it is the beginning point of management leadership.

2. WHAT THE SUPERVISOR MUST LEARN
A supervisor must learn to:
(1) Deal with people and their differences
(2) Get the job done through people
(3) Recognize the problems when they exist
(4) Overcome obstacles to good performance
(5) Evaluate the performance of people
(6) Check his own performance in terms of accomplishment

3. A DEFINITION OF SUPERVISOR
The term supervisor means any individual having authority, in the interests of the employer, to hire, transfer, suspend, lay-off, recall, promote, discharge, assign, reward, or discipline other employees or responsibility to direct them, or to adjust their grievances, or effectively to recommend such action, if, in connection with the foregoing, exercise of such authority is not of a merely routine or clerical nature but requires the use of independent judgment.

4. ELEMENTS OF THE TEAM CONCEPT
What is involved in teamwork? The component parts are:

(1) Members   (3) Goals   (5) Cooperation
(2) A leader   (4) Plans   (6) Spirit

5. PRINCIPLES OF ORGANIZATION
(1) A team member must know what his job is.
(2) Be sure that the nature and scope of a job are understood.
(3) Authority and responsibility should be carefully spelled out.
(4) A supervisor should be permitted to make the maximum number of decisions affecting his employees.
(5) Employees should report to only one supervisor.
(6) A supervisor should direct only as many employees as he can handle effectively.
(7) An organization plan should be flexible.
(8) Inspection and performance of work should be separate.
(9) Organizational problems should receive immediate attention.
(10) Assign work in line with ability and experience.

6. THE FOUR IMPORTANT PARTS OF EVERY JOB
(1) Inherent in every job is the *accountability* for results.
(2) A second set of factors in every job is *responsibilities.*
(3) Along with duties and responsibilities one must have the *authority* to act within certain limits without obtaining permission to proceed.
(4) No job exists in a vacuum. The supervisor is surrounded by key *relationships.*

7. PRINCIPLES OF DELEGATION
Where work is delegated for the first time, the supervisor should think in terms of these questions:
(1) Who is best qualified to do this?
(2) Can an employee improve his abilities by doing this?
(3) How long should an employee spend on this?
(4) Are there any special problems for which he will need guidance?
(5) How broad a delegation can I make?

8. PRINCIPLES OF EFFECTIVE COMMUNICATIONS
(1) Determine the media
(2) To whom directed?
(3) Identification and source authority
(4) Is communication understood?

9. PRINCIPLES OF WORK IMPROVEMENT
(1) Most people usually do only the work which is assigned to them
(2) Workers are likely to fit assigned work into the time available to perform it
(3) A good workload usually stimulates output
(4) People usually do their best work when they know that results will be reviewed or inspected
(5) Employees usually feel that someone else is responsible for conditions of work, workplace layout, job methods, type of tools/equipment, and other such factors
(6) Employees are usually defensive about their job security
(7) Employees have natural resistance to change
(8) Employees can support or destroy a supervisor
(9) A supervisor usually earns the respect of his people through his personal example of diligence and efficiency

10. AREAS OF JOB IMPROVEMENT
The areas of job improvement are quite numerous, but the most common ones which a supervisor can identify and utilize are:

(1) Departmental layout
(2) Flow of work
(3) Workplace layout
(4) Utilization of manpower
(5) Work methods
(6) Materials handling
(7) Utilization
(8) Motion economy

11. SEVEN KEY POINTS IN MAKING IMPROVEMENTS
(1) Select the job to be improved
(2) Study how it is being done now
(3) Question the present method
(4) Determine actions to be taken
(5) Chart proposed method
(6) Get approval and apply
(7) Solicit worker participation

12. CORRECTIVE TECHNIQUES OF JOB IMPROVEMENT

Specific Problems	General Improvement	Corrective Techniques
(1) Size of workload	(1) Departmental layout	(1) Study with scale model
(2) Inability to meet schedules	(2) Flow of work	(2) Flow chart study
(3) Strain and fatigue	(3) Work plan layout	(3) Motion analysis
(4) Improper use of men and skills	(4) Utilization of manpower	(4) Comparison of units produced to standard allowance
(5) Waste, poor quality, unsafe conditions	(5) Work methods	(5) Methods analysis
(6) Bottleneck conditions that hinder output	(6) Materials handling	(6) Flow chart & equipment study
(7) Poor utilization of equipment and machine	(7) Utilization of equipment	(7) Down time vs. running time
(8) Efficiency and productivity of labor	(8) Motion economy	(8) Motion analysis

13. A *PLANNING CHECKLIST*
- (1) Objectives
- (2) Controls
- (3) Delegations
- (4) Communications
- (5) Resources
- (6) Resources
- (7) Manpower
- (8) Equipment
- (9) Supplies and materials
- (10) Utilization of time
- (11) Safety
- (12) Money
- (13) Work
- (14) Timing of improvements

14. *FIVE CHARACTERISTICS OF GOOD DIRECTIONS*
In order to get results, directions must be:
- (1) Possible of accomplishment
- (2) Agreeable with worker interests
- (3) Related to mission
- (4) Planned and complete
- (5) Unmistakably clear

15. *TYPES OF DIRECTIONS*
- (1) Demands or direct orders
- (2) Requests
- (3) Suggestion or implication
- (4) Volunteering

16. *CONTROLS*
A typical listing of the overall areas in which the supervisor should establish controls might be:
- (1) Manpower
- (2) Materials
- (3) Quality of work
- (4) Quantity of work
- (5) Time
- (6) Space
- (7) Money
- (8) Methods

17. *ORIENTING THE NEW EMPLOYEE*
- (1) Prepare for him
- (2) Welcome the new employee
- (3) Orientation for the job
- (4) Follow-up

18. *CHECKLIST FOR ORIENTING NEW EMPLOYEES*   Yes   No
- (1) Do your appreciate the feelings of new employees when they first report for work?
- (2) Are you aware of the fact that the new employee must make a big adjustment to his job?
- (3) Have you given him good reasons for liking the job and the organization?
- (4) Have you prepared for his first day on the job?
- (5) Did you welcome him cordially and make him feel needed?
- (6) Did you establish rapport with him so that he feels free to talk and discuss matters with you?
- (7) Did you explain his job to him and his relationship to you?
- (8) Does he know that his work will be evaluated periodically on a basis that is fair and objective?
- (9) Did you introduce him to his fellow workers in such a way that they are likely to accept him?
- (10) Does he know what employee benefits he will receive?
- (11) Does he understand the importance of being on the job and what to do if he must leave his duty station?
- (12) Has he been impressed with the importance of accident prevention and safe practice?
- (13) Does he generally know his way around the department?
- (14) Is he under the guidance of a sponsor who will teach the right ways of doing things?
- (15) Do you plan to follow-up so that he will continue to adjust successfully to his job?

19. *PRINCIPLES OF LEARNING*
    (1) Motivation   (2) Demonstration or explanation   (3) Practice

20. *CAUSES OF POOR PERFORMANCE*
    (1) Improper training for job
    (2) Wrong tools
    (3) Inadequate directions
    (4) Lack of supervisory follow-up
    (5) Poor communications
    (6) Lack of standards of performance
    (7) Wrong work habits
    (8) Low morale
    (9) Other

21. *FOUR MAJOR STEPS IN ON-THE-JOB INSTRUCTION*
    (1) Prepare the worker
    (2) Present the operation
    (3) Tryout performance
    (4) Follow-up

22. *EMPLOYEES WANT FIVE THINGS*
    (1) Security (2) Opportunity (3) Recognition (4) Inclusion (5) Expression

23. *SOME DON'TS IN REGARD TO PRAISE*
    (1) Don't praise a person for something he hasn't done
    (2) Don't praise a person unless you can be sincere
    (3) Don't be sparing in praise just because your superior withholds it from you
    (4) Don't let too much time elapse between good performance and recognition of it

24. *HOW TO GAIN YOUR WORKERS' CONFIDENCE*
    Methods of developing confidence include such things as:
        (1) Knowing the interests, habits, hobbies of employees
        (2) Admitting your own inadequacies
        (3) Sharing and telling of confidence in others
        (4) Supporting people when they are in trouble
        (5) Delegating matters that can be well handled
        (6) Being frank and straightforward about problems and working conditions
        (7) Encouraging others to bring their problems to you
        (8) Taking action on problems which impede worker progress

25. *SOURCES OF EMPLOYEE PROBLEMS*
    On-the-job causes might be such things as:
        (1) A feeling that favoritism is exercised in assignments
        (2) Assignment of overtime
        (3) An undue amount of supervision
        (4) Changing methods or systems
        (5) Stealing of ideas or trade secrets
        (6) Lack of interest in job
        (7) Threat of reduction in force
        (8) Ignorance or lack of communications
        (9) Poor equipment
        (10) Lack of knowing how supervisor feels toward employee
        (11) Shift assignments

    Off-the-job problems might have to do with:
        (1) Health   (2) Finances   (3) Housing   (4) Family

26. THE SUPERVISOR'S KEY TO DISCIPLINE

There are several key points about discipline which the supervisor should keep in mind:
(1) Job discipline is one of the disciplines of life and is directed by the supervisor.
(2) It is more important to correct an employee fault than to fix blame for it.
(3) Employee performance is affected by problems both on the job and off.
(4) Sudden or abrupt changes in behavior can be indications of important employee problems.
(5) Problems should be dealt with as soon as possible after they are identified.
(6) The attitude of the supervisor may have more to do with solving problems than the techniques of problem solving.
(7) Correction of employee behavior should be resorted to only after the supervisor is sure that training or counseling will not be helpful.
(8) Be sure to document your disciplinary actions.
(9) Make sure that you are disciplining on the basis of facts rather than personal feelings.
(10) Take each disciplinary step in order, being careful not to make snap judgments, or decisions based on impatience.

27. FIVE IMPORTANT PROCESSES OF MANAGEMENT

(1) Planning   (2) Organizing   (3) Scheduling
(4) Controlling   (5) Motivating

28. WHEN THE SUPERVISOR FAILS TO PLAN

(1) Supervisor creates impression of not knowing his job
(2) May lead to excessive overtime
(3) Job runs itself -- supervisor lacks control
(4) Deadlines and appointments missed
(5) Parts of the work go undone
(6) Work interrupted by emergencies
(7) Sets a bad example
(8) Uneven workload creates peaks and valleys
(9) Too much time on minor details at expense of more important tasks

29. FOURTEEN GENERAL PRINCIPLES OF MANAGEMENT

(1) Division of work
(2) Authority and responsibility
(3) Discipline
(4) Unity of command
(5) Unity of direction
(6) Subordination of individual interest to general interest
(7) Remuneration of personnel
(8) Centralization
(9) Scalar chain
(10) Order
(11) Equity
(12) Stability of tenure of personnel
(13) Initiative
(14) Esprit de corps

30. CHANGE

Bringing about change is perhaps attempted more often, and yet less well understood, than anything else the supervisor does. How do people generally react to change? (People tend to resist change that is imposed upon them by other individuals or circumstances.

Change is characteristic of every situation. It is a part of every real endeavor where the efforts of people are concerned.

A. Why do people resist change?
   People may resist change because of:
   (1) Fear of the unknown
   (2) Implied criticism
   (3) Unpleasant experiences in the past
   (4) Fear of loss of status
   (5) Threat to the ego
   (6) Fear of loss of economic stability

B. How can we best overcome the resistance to change?
   In initiating change, take these steps:
   (1) Get ready to sell
   (2) Identify sources of help
   (3) Anticipate objections
   (4) Sell benefits
   (5) Listen in depth
   (6) Follow up

B. BRIEF TOPICAL SUMMARIES

I. WHO/WHAT IS THE SUPERVISOR?
1. The supervisor is often called the "highest level employee and the lowest level manager."
2. A supervisor is a member of both management and the work group. He acts as a bridge between the two.
3. Most problems in supervision are in the area of human relations, or people problems.
4. Employees expect: Respect, opportunity to learn and to advance, and a sense of belonging, and so forth.
5. Supervisors are responsible for directing people and organizing work. Planning is of paramount importance.
6. A position description is a set of duties and responsibilities inherent to a given position.
7. It is important to keep the position description up-to-date and to provide each employee with his own copy.

II. THE SOCIOLOGY OF WORK
1. People are alike in many ways; however, each individual is unique.
2. The supervisor is challenged in getting to know employee differences. Acquiring skills in evaluating individuals is an asset.
3. Maintaining meaningful working relationships in the organization is of great importance.
4. The supervisor has an obligation to help individuals to develop to their fullest potential.
5. Job rotation on a planned basis helps to build versatility and to maintain interest and enthusiasm in work groups.
6. Cross training (job rotation) provides backup skills.
7. The supervisor can help reduce tension by maintaining a sense of humor, providing guidance to employees, and by making reasonable and timely decisions. Employees respond favorably to working under reasonably predictable circumstances.
8. Change is characteristic of all managerial behavior. The supervisor must adjust to changes in procedures, new methods, technological changes, and to a number of new and sometimes challenging situations.
9. To overcome the natural tendency for people to resist change, the supervisor should become more skillful in initiating change.

III. PRINCIPLES AND PRACTICES OF SUPERVISION
1. Employees should be required to answer to only one superior.
2. A supervisor can effectively direct only a limited number of employees, depending upon the complexity, variety, and proximity of the jobs involved.
3. The organizational chart presents the organization in graphic form. It reflects lines of authority and responsibility as well as interrelationships of units within the organization.
4. Distribution of work can be improved through an analysis using the "Work Distribution Chart."
5. The "Work Distribution Chart" reflects the division of work within a unit in understandable form.
6. When related tasks are given to an employee, he has a better chance of increasing his skills through training.
7. The individual who is given the responsibility for tasks must also be given the appropriate authority to insure adequate results.
8. The supervisor should delegate repetitive, routine work. Preparation of recurring reports, maintaining leave and attendance records are some examples.
9. Good discipline is essential to good task performance. Discipline is reflected in the actions of employees on the job in the absence of supervision.
10. Disciplinary action may have to be taken when the positive aspects of discipline have failed. Reprimand, warning, and suspension are examples of disciplinary action.
11. If a situation calls for a reprimand, be sure it is deserved and remember it is to be done in private.

IV. DYNAMIC LEADERSHIP
1. A style is a personal method or manner of exerting influence.
2. Authoritarian leaders often see themselves as the source of power and authority.
3. The democratic leader often perceives the group as the source of authority and power.
4. Supervisors tend to do better when using the pattern of leadership that is most natural for them.
5. Social scientists suggest that the effective supervisor use the leadership style that best fits the problem or circumstances involved.
6. All four styles -- telling, selling, consulting, joining -- have their place. Using one does not preclude using the other at another time.
7. The theory X point of view assumes that the average person dislikes work, will avoid it whenever possible, and must be coerced to achieve organizational objectives.
8. The theory Y point of view assumes that the average person considers work to be as natural as play, and, when the individual is committed, he requires little supervision or direction to accomplish desired objectives.
9. The leader's basic assumptions concerning human behavior and human nature affect his actions, decisions, and other managerial practices.
10. Dissatisfaction among employees is often present, but difficult to isolate. The supervisor should seek to weaken dissatisfaction by keeping promises, being sincere and considerate, keeping employees informed, and so forth.
11. Constructive suggestions should be encouraged during the natural progress of the work.

V. PROCESSES FOR SOLVING PROBLEMS
1. People find their daily tasks more meaningful and satisfying when they can improve them.
2. The causes of problems, or the key factors, are often hidden in the background. Ability to solve problems often involves the ability to isolate them from their backgrounds. There is some substance to the cliché that some persons "can't see the forest for the trees."
3. New procedures are often developed from old ones. Problems should be broken down into manageable parts. New ideas can be adapted from old ones.

4. People think differently in problem-solving situations. Using a logical, patterned approach is often useful. One approach found to be useful includes these steps:
   (a) Define the problem   (d) Weigh and decide
   (b) Establish objectives   (e) Take action
   (c) Get the facts   (f) Evaluate action

VI. TRAINING FOR RESULTS

1. Participants respond best when they feel training is important to them.
2. The supervisor has responsibility for the training and development of those who report to him.
3. When training is delegated to others, great care must be exercised to insure the trainer has knowledge, aptitude, and interest for his work as a trainer.
4. Training (learning) of some type goes on continually. The most successful supervisor makes certain the learning contributes in a productive manner to operational goals.
5. New employees are particularly susceptible to training. Older employees facing new job situations require specific training, as well as having need for development and growth opportunities.
6. Training needs require continuous monitoring.
7. The training officer of an agency is a professional with a responsibility to assist supervisors in solving training problems.
8. Many of the self-development steps important to the supervisor's own growth are equally important to the development of peers and subordinates. Knowledge of these is important when the supervisor consults with others on development and growth opportunities.

VII. HEALTH, SAFETY, AND ACCIDENT PREVENTION

1. Management-minded supervisors take appropriate measures to assist employees in maintaining health and in assuring safe practices in the work environment.
2. Effective safety training and practices help to avoid injury and accidents.
3. Safety should be a management goal. All infractions of safety which are observed should be corrected without exception.
4. Employees' safety attitude, training and instruction, provision of safe tools and equipment, supervision, and leadership are considered highly important factors which contribute to safety and which can be influenced directly by supervisors.
5. When accidents do occur they should be investigated promptly for very important reasons, including the fact that information which is gained can be used to prevent accidents in the future.

VIII. EQUAL EMPLOYMENT OPPORTUNITY

1. The supervisor should endeavor to treat all employees fairly, without regard to religion, race, sex, or national origin.
2. Groups tend to reflect the attitude of the leader. Prejudice can be detected even in very subtle form. Supervisors must strive to create a feeling of mutual respect and confidence in every employee.
3. Complete utilization of all human resources is a national goal. Equitable consideration should be accorded women in the work force, minority-group members, the physically and mentally handicapped, and the older employee. The important question is: "Who can do the job?"
4. Training opportunities, recognition for performance, overtime assignments, promotional opportunities, and all other personnel actions are to be handled on an equitable basis.

IX. IMPROVING COMMUNICATIONS

1. Communications is achieving understanding between the sender and the receiver of a message. It also means sharing information -- the creation of understanding.
2. Communication is basic to all human activity. Words are means of conveying meanings; however, real meanings are in people.
3. There are very practical differences in the effectiveness of one-way, impersonal, and two-way communications. Words spoken face-to-face are better understood. Telephone conversations are effective, but lack the rapport of person-to-person exchanges. The whole person communicates.
4. Cooperation and communication in an organization go hand in hand. When there is a mutual respect between people, spelling out rules and procedures for communicating is unnecessary.
5. There are several barriers to effective communications. These include failure to listen with respect and understanding, lack of skill in feedback, and misinterpreting the meanings of words used by the speaker. It is also common practice to listen to what we want to hear, and tune out things we do not want to hear.
6. Communication is management's chief problem. The supervisor should accept the challenge to communicate more effectively and to improve interagency and intra-agency communications.
7. The supervisor may often plan for and conduct meetings. The planning phase is critical and may determine the success or the failure of a meeting.
8. Speaking before groups usually requires extra effort. Stage fright may never disappear completely, but it can be controlled.

X. SELF-DEVELOPMENT

1. Every employee is responsible for his own self-development.
2. Toastmaster and toastmistress clubs offer opportunities to improve skills in oral communications.
3. Planning for one's own self-development is of vital importance. Supervisors know their own strengths and limitations better than anyone else.
4. Many opportunities are open to aid the supervisor in his developmental efforts, including job assignments; training opportunities, both governmental and non-governmental -- to include universities and professional conferences and seminars.
5. Programmed instruction offers a means of studying at one's own rate.
6. Where difficulties may arise from a supervisor's being away from his work for training, he may participate in televised home study or correspondence courses to meet his self-develop- ment needs.

XI. TEACHING AND TRAINING

A. The Teaching Process

Teaching is encouraging and guiding the learning activities of students toward established goals. In most cases this process consists in five steps: preparation, presentation, summarization, evaluation, and application.

1. Preparation

   Preparation is twofold in nature; that of the supervisor and the employee.
   Preparation by the supervisor is absolutely essential to success. He must know what, when, where, how, and whom he will teach. Some of the factors that should be considered are:

   (1) The objectives
   (2) The materials needed
   (3) The methods to be used
   (4) Employee participation
   (5) Employee interest
   (6) Training aids
   (7) Evaluation
   (8) Summarization

Employee preparation consists in preparing the employee to receive the material. Probably the most important single factor in the preparation of the employee is arousing and maintaining his interest. He must know the objectives of the training, why he is there, how the material can be used, and its importance to him.

2. Presentation

In presentation, have a carefully designed plan and follow it.
The plan should be accurate and complete, yet flexible enough to meet situations as they arise. The method of presentation will be determined by the particular situation and objectives.

3. Summary

A summary should be made at the end of every training unit and program. In addition, there may be internal summaries depending on the nature of the material being taught. The important thing is that the trainee must always be able to understand how each part of the new material relates to the whole.

4. Application

The supervisor must arrange work so the employee will be given a chance to apply new knowledge or skills while the material is still clear in his mind and interest is high. The trainee does not really know whether he has learned the material until he has been given a chance to apply it. If the material is not applied, it loses most of its value.

5. Evaluation

The purpose of all training is to promote learning. To determine whether the training has been a success or failure, the supervisor must evaluate this learning.
In the broadest sense evaluation includes all the devices, methods, skills, and techniques used by the supervisor to keep himself and the employees informed as to their progress toward the objectives they are pursuing. The extent to which the employee has mastered the knowledge, skills, and abilities, or changed his attitudes, as determined by the program objectives, is the extent to which instruction has succeeded or failed.
Evaluation should not be confined to the end of the lesson, day, or program but should be used continuously. We shall note later the way this relates to the rest of the teaching process.

B. Teaching Methods

A teaching method is a pattern of identifiable student and instructor activity used in presenting training material.
All supervisors are faced with the problem of deciding which method should be used at a given time.
As with all methods, there are certain advantages and disadvantages to each method.

1. Lecture

The lecture is direct oral presentation of material by the supervisor. The present trend is to place less emphasis on the trainer's activity and more on that of the trainee.

2. Discussion

Teaching by discussion or conference involves using questions and other techniques to arouse interest and focus attention upon certain areas, and by doing so creating a learning situation. This can be one of the most valuable methods because it gives the employees 'an opportunity to express their ideas and pool their knowledge.

3. Demonstration

The demonstration is used to teach how something works or how to do something. It can be used to show a principle or what the results of a series of actions will be. A well-staged demonstration is particularly effective because it shows proper methods of performance in a realistic manner.

4. Performance

Performance is one of the most fundamental of all learning techniques or teaching methods. The trainee may be able to tell how a specific operation should be performed but he cannot be sure he knows how to perform the operation until he has done so.

5. Which Method to Use

Moreover, there are other methods and techniques of teaching. It is difficult to use any method without other methods entering into it. In any learning situation a combination of methods is usually more effective than anyone method alone.

Finally, evaluation must be integrated into the other aspects of the teaching-learning process.

It must be used in the motivation of the trainees; it must be used to assist in developing understanding during the training; and it must be related to employee application of the results of training.

This is distinctly the role of the supervisor.

ANSWER SHEET

ST NO. ____________ PART ______ TITLE OF POSITION ______________________________
(AS GIVEN IN EXAMINATION ANNOUNCEMENT - INCLUDE OPTION, IF ANY)

ACE OF EXAMINATION ______________________________ ______________ DATE ______________
(CITY OR TOWN) (STATE)

RATING

USE THE SPECIAL PENCIL. MAKE GLOSSY BLACK MARKS.

1 A B C D E	26 A B C D E	51 A B C D E	76 A B C D E	101 A B C D E
2 A B C D E	27 A B C D E	52 A B C D E	77 A B C D E	102 A B C D E
3 A B C D E	28 A B C D E	53 A B C D E	78 A B C D E	103 A B C D E
4 A B C D E	29 A B C D E	54 A B C D E	79 A B C D E	104 A B C D E
5 A B C D E	30 A B C D E	55 A B C D E	80 A B C D E	105 A B C D E
6 A B C D E	31 A B C D E	56 A B C D E	81 A B C D E	106 A B C D E
7 A B C D E	32 A B C D E	57 A B C D E	82 A B C D E	107 A B C D E
8 A B C D E	33 A B C D E	58 A B C D E	83 A B C D E	108 A B C D E
9 A B C D E	34 A B C D E	59 A B C D E	84 A B C D E	109 A B C D E
10 A B C D E	35 A B C D E	60 A B C D E	85 A B C D E	110 A B C D E

Make only ONE mark for each answer. Additional and stray marks may be counted as mistakes. In making corrections, erase errors COMPLETELY.

11 A B C D E	36 A B C D E	61 A B C D E	86 A B C D E	111 A B C D E
12 A B C D E	37 A B C D E	62 A B C D E	87 A B C D E	112 A B C D E
13 A B C D E	38 A B C D E	63 A B C D E	88 A B C D E	113 A B C D E
14 A B C D E	39 A B C D E	64 A B C D E	89 A B C D E	114 A B C D E
15 A B C D E	40 A B C D E	65 A B C D E	90 A B C D E	115 A B C D E
16 A B C D E	41 A B C D E	66 A B C D E	91 A B C D E	116 A B C D E
17 A B C D E	42 A B C D E	67 A B C D E	92 A B C D E	117 A B C D E
18 A B C D E	43 A B C D E	68 A B C D E	93 A B C D E	118 A B C D E
19 A B C D E	44 A B C D E	69 A B C D E	94 A B C D E	119 A B C D E
20 A B C D E	45 A B C D E	70 A B C D E	95 A B C D E	120 A B C D E
21 A B C D E	46 A B C D E	71 A B C D E	96 A B C D E	121 A B C D E
22 A B C D E	47 A B C D E	72 A B C D E	97 A B C D E	122 A B C D E
23 A B C D E	48 A B C D E	73 A B C D E	98 A B C D E	123 A B C D E
24 A B C D E	49 A B C D E	74 A B C D E	99 A B C D E	124 A B C D E
25 A B C D E	50 A B C D E	75 A B C D E	100 A B C D E	125 A B C D E

ANSWER SHEET

TEST NO. ____________ PART ______ TITLE OF POSITION ____________________
(AS GIVEN IN EXAMINATION ANNOUNCEMENT - INCLUDE OPTION, IF ANY)

PLACE OF EXAMINATION ____________________ (CITY OR TOWN) ____________ (STATE) DATE ______

RATING

USE THE SPECIAL PENCIL. MAKE GLOSSY BLACK MARKS.

1 A B C D E	26 A B C D E	51 A B C D E	76 A B C D E	101 A B C D E
2 A B C D E	27 A B C D E	52 A B C D E	77 A B C D E	102 A B C D E
3 A B C D E	28 A B C D E	53 A B C D E	78 A B C D E	103 A B C D E
4 A B C D E	29 A B C D E	54 A B C D E	79 A B C D E	104 A B C D E
5 A B C D E	30 A B C D E	55 A B C D E	80 A B C D E	105 A B C D E
6 A B C D E	31 A B C D E	56 A B C D E	81 A B C D E	106 A B C D E
7 A B C D E	32 A B C D E	57 A B C D E	82 A B C D E	107 A B C D E
8 A B C D E	33 A B C D E	58 A B C D E	83 A B C D E	108 A B C D E
9 A B C D E	34 A B C D E	59 A B C D E	84 A B C D E	109 A B C D E
10 A B C D E	35 A B C D E	60 A B C D E	85 A B C D E	110 A B C D E

Make only ONE mark for each answer. Additional and stray marks may be counted as mistakes. In making corrections, erase errors COMPLETELY.

11 A B C D E	36 A B C D E	61 A B C D E	86 A B C D E	111 A B C D E
12 A B C D E	37 A B C D E	62 A B C D E	87 A B C D E	112 A B C D E
13 A B C D E	38 A B C D E	63 A B C D E	88 A B C D E	113 A B C D E
14 A B C D E	39 A B C D E	64 A B C D E	89 A B C D E	114 A B C D E
15 A B C D E	40 A B C D E	65 A B C D E	90 A B C D E	115 A B C D E
16 A B C D E	41 A B C D E	66 A B C D E	91 A B C D E	116 A B C D E
17 A B C D E	42 A B C D E	67 A B C D E	92 A B C D E	117 A B C D E
18 A B C D E	43 A B C D E	68 A B C D E	93 A B C D E	118 A B C D E
19 A B C D E	44 A B C D E	69 A B C D E	94 A B C D E	119 A B C D E
20 A B C D E	45 A B C D E	70 A B C D E	95 A B C D E	120 A B C D E
21 A B C D E	46 A B C D E	71 A B C D E	96 A B C D E	121 A B C D E
22 A B C D E	47 A B C D E	72 A B C D E	97 A B C D E	122 A B C D E
23 A B C D E	48 A B C D E	73 A B C D E	98 A B C D E	123 A B C D E
24 A B C D E	49 A B C D E	74 A B C D E	99 A B C D E	124 A B C D E
25 A B C D E	50 A B C D E	75 A B C D E	100 A B C D E	125 A B C D E